EAT THIS BOOK

A YEAR OF GORGING AND GLORY
ON THE COMPETITIVE EATING CIRCUIT

RYAN NERZ

 ST. MARTIN'S GRIFFIN   NEW YORK

www.stmartins.com

Library of Congress Cataloging-in-Publication Data

Nerz, Ryan.
    Eat this book : a year of gorging and glory on the competitive eating circuit / Ryan Nerz.—1st ed.
        p.   cm.
    ISBN 0-312-33968-2
    EAN 978-0-312-33968-5
    1. Gastronomy.   2. Food habits.   I. Title.

TX631.N47 2006
641.01'3—dc22

2005045645

First Edition: April 2006

10 9 8 7 6 5 4 3 2 1

For Audree and Clifford Perrine
and for
Dale Pontoosh

CONTENTS

ACKNOWLEDGMENTS

I would like to thank Alex Glass and Marc Resnick, who made this book happen. Thanks to the many people who gave sage editorial advice—Tristan Patterson, Ezra Edelman, Lisa Papademetriou, Dale Pontoosh, Melissa Matlins, Nicholas Arons, Javier Guzman, and Kaitlin O'Brien. Heartfelt thanks to Amy Esposito and Loukas Barton for the photos, and to Jeff Kulkarni for the interview. And cheers to my IFOCE people—Dave Baer, the Shea brothers, Nancy Goldstein, Mike Castellano, Mark Faris, Yesenia Ortiz, Alexis Schnieder, and Kate Westfall. Big shout-out to Brian Wilhelm and Stephanie Corn for their help with the Web site (www.eatthisbook.com). And most of all, much love to all the eaters, especially guys like Beautiful Brian Seiken, Kid Cary DeGrossa, Ray the Bison Meduna, and Jalapeno Jed Donahue, whom I didn't get to cover as extensively as I'd hoped. Finally, a sincere rest in peace to Everett Scott Willard and Crawfish Nick Stipelcovich.

EAT THIS BOOK

PROLOGUE
BEDLAM IN PHILLY

It's an important event in American culture. There's probably nothing in America that speaks to the average American guy as much as Wing Bowl. . . . What you have here is an Olympic event for the couch potato.

—Al Morganti, *WIP Morning Show*

JANUARY 30, 2004
PHILADELPHIA, PENNSYLVANIA

It's 4:00 A.M., pitch-black and frigid out. The only people left on the roads are truck drivers, cabbies, and those with suspicious motives. Even the partyers have grabbed their last Philly cheesesteaks and headed home. And yet the parking lot outside the Wachovia Center is jam-packed. Hordes of young men in hooded sweatshirts and stocking caps are raising plastic cups into the air, woo-hoo-ing and cackling like madmen. They gather in clumps around cars and bonfires, chanting and dancing and drinking, always drinking. There's one on top of a truck, ripping off his shirt. There's one tossing a full beer into a fire. Over there, between those cars—there's one pissing on a tire.

A Jeep full of teenage girls drives by and is instantly besieged by rabid, dead-eyed guys on all sides. Most of them are wearing green jerseys, so it looks like the formation of an organized mob. Hard rock music—an anthem for mayhem—blares from someone's car, and one begins to wonder whether there's something more than beer in all those plastic cups.

What the *hell* is going on? Who is running the show, and at what point should the riot police be called in? Why are all these people here? The answer comes in the form of a rebel yell, performed spontaneously by three sloshed revelers. *"Wing Bowl! Wing Bowl! Wing Bowl!"*

Meanwhile, at the arena's back gate, nine workers start unloading nearly seven thousand chicken wings from a fleet of trucks. As 4:30 A.M. approaches, the masses begin to migrate. A line has formed, beginning at the arena's entrance and slithering around the perimeter of the parking lot like a snake. At 5:30, the doors open. People squeeze through the turnstiles and sprint into the arena. With free admission and minimal door security, the entrance vomits forth a steady stream of humanity.

Once inside, the meaning behind the hysteria doesn't immediately reveal itself. The infield is a hockey rink without the ice, Plexiglas boards separating fans from whatever show awaits. Twenty thousand people are hurrying to get the best seats. A row of empty tables faces a host of reporters and bystanders, but nothing is happening. The few dozen young ladies prancing about onstage, half-dressed in outfits that don't much test the imagination, are the only evidence of things to come.

At 7:20 A.M., the show finally starts. A man wearing a vest and some undies, flanked by two curvaceous coeds and holding a caged live chicken, enters the stadium and does a lap around the circular promenade. Then an odd procession begins—what cynics might call a parade of freaks. The central characters have names like Totally Apauling and Wingo Starr. They are surrounded by entourages packed with friends and scantily clad dames called Wingettes—a nice way of saying "strippers." Each character's approach has a concept behind it, the depths of which vary greatly.

Dan the Cop, who qualified for the contest by eating fourteen hundred cheese balls, pushes a wheelbarrow filled with giant cheese balls, two of which hang from his groin. His T-shirt reads EAT THESE. Johnny Huevos makes a grand entrance in his Lord of the Wings outfit. A hole in the suit shows off his hairy paunch, a sight that can only be described as unpleasant. A rubber chicken dangles just out of the reach of Chitlins Chuck, who is held back by a half dozen ropes. The aptly named Dough Boy, a 390-pound ball of pudge, comes out with his hands pressed together in prayer, dressed like Friar Tuck. An emcee explains that this is his last Wing Bowl because afterward he's getting gastric bypass surgery. "So in honor of the fact that this is technically his last meal," she says, "he is coming in as the Last Supper."

The eater known as Coondog enters the arena entourageless, wearing a smug smile, a Mohawk, and a Green Bay Packers jersey. With a jolt, he lifts a pair of signs that show the score of the Philadelphia Eagles' recent loss to the Panthers in the NFC Championship game. The shower of cups and cans is so violent that he's forced to cower next to the Plexiglas in the fetal position. Apparently prepared for the assault, Coondog uses his signs as shields. *Dear Lord.* Whatever happened to the city of brotherly love?

The reception of the "New York eaters," as they're contemptuously called, isn't much warmer. Their approach is decidedly different from that of the other eaters. They seem to be a team, and they don't have concepts. They do, however, wear the same navy blue T-shirts, each one emblazoned with an obscure combination of letters: IFOCE. One of them, an enormous black man with a boyish smile, named Badlands, grabs the microphone and dedicates a rap to the crowd. His lyrics are drowned out by boos. The last and most noteworthy of the IFOCE eaters is a hundred-pound Asian woman named the Black Widow, who's wearing lavender eye shadow and a black boa around her neck. Contradicting her nickname, she smiles and waves at the crowd as if this were a bake sale.

A competitive eater, his cheeks stained by
wing sauce and lipstick, chews while being cheered on by an entourage of
Wingettes.

When the *Rocky* theme starts playing, the mood suddenly shifts.
Before the announcer even utters a word, fans stand up and lift their
cups in homage. "One of the all-time best," says the announcer. "Our
reigning champion, at 314 pounds, from Woodbury Heights, New Jersey, at two-to-one odds, it's El Wingador!" The place goes bananas,
but the entourage is so massive it's hard to see whom all the ruckus is
for. Finally, a man in a white satin boxer's robe emerges from the tunnel. The roar from the crowd is so epic, the emotion so pure, you
would've thought Rocky Balboa himself had just entered the building.
A truck driver by profession, El Wingador is a demigod here, wor-

shiped like a hybrid of Obi-Wan Kenobi and the heavyweight champion of the world.

8:00 A.M. Time for the main event. As Wingettes start setting paper plates stacked high with wings before their assigned contestants, two blond dominatrices pose for pictures with a man in a chicken mascot costume. A stirring rendition of "God Bless America" is sung. Bathing in a shower of confetti, one dominatrix climbs a ladder and tosses an egg to the arena floor. Splat. "Three . . . two . . . one!" And they're off.

At first, the actual eating contest seems somewhat anticlimactic for the wasted crowd. Because the competition takes place between plate and mouth, the masses depend on the JumboTron to see what's going on. The images on the giant screen are arresting—large men eating chicken as fast as they can, surrounded by bare midriffs, hot shorts, and fake breasts. But attention spans being what they are, the crowd soon starts watching itself. A fight breaks out and people swarm toward it, standing on their seats for a better look. Every few minutes some anonymous booze-soaked woman gets up on someone shoulder's and shows off her tits for several thousand leering men. The crowd's attention is briefly recaptured by the halftime show, which consists of two men crushing a twelve-pack of beer cans against their foreheads until they are ribboned with bloody, beer-drenched cuts.

What is this? What's happening here? To call it a wing-eating competition is in no way satisfying. It's a cultural dramedy of some sort, but celebrating what? Its origins shed a little light on the subject. Wing Bowl began in 1991 as a publicity stunt, the brainchild of Al Morganti and Angelo Cataldi, on-air personalities at the *WIP Morning Show*, a popular radio sports show in Philadelphia. In the early nineties, as the Super Bowl approached each January, Philadelphia Eagles fans found themselves left out. To simultaneously lift the community spirit and mock the Buffalo Bills fans who kept cheering their team to annual Super Bowl losses, the *WIP* crew decided to do what they do best—mock them. Stealing Buffalo's signature food-stuff, the buffalo wing, and borrowing heavily from professional wrestling, they created a cultural event that, while undeniably American, defies explanation.

Angelo Cataldi describes it as "Fellini meets Hells Angels at a family picnic." Others call it a frat-party-gone-awry meets pro wrestling event meets *Girls Gone Wild* video. Whatever it is, even the most gifted fortune-teller couldn't have predicted that a stunt with two contestants in a hotel lobby would blossom within a decade into a madcap bacchanal that packs a sports arena.

An even better question is: *Why?* What does it mean that Americans choose *this* as entertainment? Maybe the answer is self-evident: tits and ass, gorging and binge drinking. It sounds superficially like Everyman's dream of the perfect party—paradise through the lens of the average Howard Stern listener. But as the event moves forward and the mob's attention grows more focused on the actual wing-eating competition, it seems that there's something more to it. These people are here, at least in part, to answer that age-old question: *How much can you eat?* Just as part of the appeal of NASCAR is that *everyone drives,* the appeal here is that *everyone eats.* So the competitors are not larger-than-life athletes but regular Joes like themselves, competing at an event that they participate in every day—eating.

It seems significant that four of the final five eaters weigh over three hundred pounds. This is the fat man's revenge, his chance to be lionized by thousands and surrounded by beautiful women. The second fourteen-minute round ends in a tie for first between two IFOCE eaters—Cookie Jarvis, a 410-pound man, and Sonya Thomas, a waif-like woman, both of whom have downed a staggering 153 wings in twenty-eight minutes. At stake is not only a $17,000 Suzuki Verona automobile, but the last dominion of Everyman.

The two-minute overtime eat-off is pure Darwinism. Both eaters shred meat from bones in a carnivorous frenzy. The image seems like a tangible metaphor for America's rampant consumerism, but that's not the point. The speed-eating itself is legitimately entertaining, so much so that thousands of drunken men are no longer focused on all the breasts and midriffs. They appreciate the speed, the rhythm, the technique, even the *talent* involved here. A commentator notes that Sonya is eating mainly drumsticks, wheeling them around in her mouth like corn on the cob, while Cookie is attacking the wings. Could this be the deciding factor? "Cookie Jarvis is eating with abandon, but he is facing a master!" says George Shea, one of the emcees. "This man has his back against the wall and there is only one thing that is standing between him and victory, and that is chicken wings!"

The buzzer sounds. Judges grab the plates and start tallying. The fans seem impatient for the outcome. This is real drama. "We have a winner!" the emcee yells. It's Sonya Thomas, 167 wings to 165. Confetti rains down. Sonya is wrapped in a gold lamé cape like a superhero. Somebody places a crown on her head, but it's too big and keeps falling down. The eater known as Badlands hoists her onto his shoulder with one hand. He sets her down, and she climbs atop her new car and smiles for the flashing cameras.

The crowd cheers heartily, but one senses an undercurrent of disappointment at the crowning of the first female champion. *This is supposed to be for fat guys!* With all the objectification of women going on, the fact that a tiny, pretty woman has won the eating competition throws everything out of whack. Things are not as they're supposed to be. Everyman's hope is dashed. The fat guy has lost at his own game and been replaced by a pretty little princess.

1

A CARNIVAL BARKER
IN TRAINING

Observe the Shea brothers, press agents by trade, carnival barkers in spirit, as they do, in tandem, the most exquisite deadpan in both businesses.

—Joyce Wadler, *The New York Times*

George Shea (right) chuckles at a comment made by his brother, Rich Shea, during the introduction of the September 2003 Cannoli Eating Contest, part of the Feast of San Gennaro in New York's Little Italy. *(Courtesy of Matt Roberts/IFOCE)*

Ever since I was a young boy, I've wanted to be a competitive-eating emcee. Okay, that's a lie, but it's not as far-fetched as it sounds. When I moved to New York after graduating from an Ivy

League college in 1997, I wanted to become a writer. My first job was as an editor of children's books, but I grew tired of editing other people's material and quit. I began writing whatever the world would pay me to write—pseudonymous contributions to the Sweet Valley High series, unauthorized biographies of teen stars, restaurant and music reviews. I used my friends' names for characters in steamy teen-romance novels, which amused them greatly. As the author of a character guide to Digimon, a popular Japanimation TV show on the Fox Kids network, I found myself almost disturbingly excited to sit around watching cartoons each afternoon. The pay wasn't overwhelming, but I was having a blast in New York and my job provided priceless conversation at parties and on dates.

To pay the bills, I took odd jobs. I waited tables, conducted exit polls, edited personal essays for college applicants, and even modeled for the covers of young-adult novels. On the side, I wrote short stories and screenplays, all the while filling notebooks with ideas for my big breakthrough in the glamorous world of media—but it never came. In the fall of 2001, I fled New York for Berlin to improve my German and write a "real" novel.

Upon my return to the Big Apple in 2002, I decided that "entertainer" was a more apt description of what I wanted to be. I took acting classes and got headshots made. While acting in a dreadful off-off-Broadway play, I found myself reading a novel backstage instead of focusing on my lines. For reasons that eluded everyone but me, I charged a $700 wolf mascot costume to my credit card. It arrived in a giant box, and I immediately began planning my debut as a performance artist.

After e-mailing dozens of friends, I showed up in the costume on the corner of Prince and Broadway, in Manhattan's chic SoHo district. I placed my cassette player on the ground and pushed play. The idea was to do a sort of live music video that would turn heads and shake up all those dead-serious downtown fashionistas. Despite a particularly moving flute solo, the Wolf garnered a total of $5 for his efforts.

Sadly, this performance felt more on-point than anything else I'd done to date. It was at the very least original and felt like a step toward one of my major life goals—getting paid to play.

In June of 2003, I met for drinks with an old buddy, Dave Baer, who shares my interest in all things absurd. He was working for a company called the International Federation of Competitive Eating. I was aware of his offbeat job, having accompanied him back in 1997 to a hot-dog-eating contest in the food court of a mall in upstate New York. My only memory was that Dave, in an attempt to recruit competitors, had played a song from the *Boogie Nights* sound track. The song was "You Sexy Thing," by Hot Chocolate, and the chorus began as follows: "I believe in miracles / Where you from? / You sexy thing." When it came around to the chorus, Dave crooned his own falsetto version into the microphone: "I believe in . . . *hot dogs!*" The mallgoers stared up from their food trays, confused, while I doubled over with laughter.

Over drinks, Dave explained that the IFOCE, or the "circuit," as he called it, was growing at an improbably fast rate. He described one of his favorite "gurgitators," Eric "Badlands" Booker, an affable subway conductor on New York's 7 line, who trained by meditating and eating huge portions of cabbage. I was intrigued. The next day, I pitched the idea of chronicling a "training meal" for the Nathan's Famous Fourth of July hot-dog-eating contest to an editor at the *Village Voice*. Within a few hours, they offered to pay me fifty cents a word for the piece.

A few months later, I received an e-mail from Dave that changed my life. Would I be interested in hosting a Meat Pie Eating Competition in Natchitoches, Louisiana? They would pick up my travel expenses and pay me fairly handsomely for a few hours of work. It was a no-brainer. Frankly, I would have considered such an undertaking pro bono. My only questions were, What in the Sam Hill is a meat pie? And how do you pronounce *Natchitoches*?

Of course, I had no conception that this strange gig would turn into hundreds of gigs. I had no clue that "competitive eating emcee" would become my job title, that I would befriend dozens of pro eaters and write a book on the subject. I couldn't have imagined announcing an onion-eating contest in Maui, or witnessing the circuit's first-ever Heimlich maneuver at a jambalaya-eating contest. I couldn't have known that I would emcee the Nathan's Famous contest on the Fourth of July after appearing on the *Today* show, and later compete against the great Kobayashi in a burger-eating contest. At the time, it just seemed like an amusing adventure, some quick cash, and a funny story to tell my friends.

I was told to report to IFOCE headquarters for a brief tutorial. The office is in Chelsea, a trendy section of Manhattan, on the fourth floor. I naïvely expected the International Federation of Competitive Eating's office space to have an odd carnival feel to it. I imagined a training room in the back where one watched through observation windows huge men shove food down their gullets. There would be rows of cubicles with employees' feet kicked up on their desks, laughing hysterically into their phones. Perhaps a few eaters would be in cages, fed on occasion and released only before big contests.

In reality the vibe at IFOCE HQ is serious and diligent. (This is not to say it's normal. On one visit, I found the office filled with giant metal boxes that held corporate mascots like Charlie Tuna, the Michelin Man, Crash Test Dummy, and the California Raisin.) The office looks like your standard Manhattan corporate loft space, with five partially enclosed offices around the perimeter, four desks in an airy middle section, and a conference room with an oval table and a television.

I met with Dave Baer, along with George and Rich Shea, the brother duo who founded the IFOCE, in the conference room. My instructions were straightforward. All eaters had to be over the age of eighteen, the reasoning being that if you're old enough to vote, you're old enough to gorge responsibly. Each contestant had to sign a waiver that I would later return to the office. Under no circumstances would

I allow eaters to compete who were underaged, under the influence of alcohol or drugs, or otherwise mentally or emotionally incapacitated.

I was given a checklist for hosting the contest. It included such details as food prep, quantity, and delivery, table space, sponsor signage, sufficient water for eaters, contest judges, eater relations, and sound system prep. There would be an emergency medical technician (EMT) at the event in case of, well, an emergency. I was not to start the competition until I had confirmed that an EMT was present.

As for the presentation, I was told to "provide maximum pageantry." I would start the show with a broad introduction to the sport of competitive eating. Such background info as speed-eating records and the history of the Nathan's Famous contest would help distinguish the event as a *sport,* as opposed to a local pie-eating contest. Then I would narrow the scope of my monologue to the event of the day, which in this case would be meat pies.

As a host, my job was to let a story unravel before the spectators' eyes. I had to strike a delicate balance between the facts—that we were witnessing history in the form of a first-ever meat-pie-eating record on the professional speed-eating circuit—and the inherent absurdity of the affair. George and Rich stressed that I should capture the depth of the sport, explaining that some eaters were rookies with natural capacity but mediocre jaw strength, while others were sprinters who might not have the endurance to go the distance. I would bring a stopwatch and keep track of the time for the audience and eaters.

To establish drama, I would announce eaters in order of their experience or perceived abilities. Local eaters hungry for victory were introduced first, and then any IFOCE-ranked eaters, whose eating exploits should be memorized and duly embellished. To help get the crowd emotionally invested in the contest, I would stress that the local eaters were going up against professionals—"ringers" brought in from out of town. Using melodramatic background music and straight-faced commentary, I would capture at once a humorous spectacle and a dramatic sporting event.

My uniform would be that of a turn-of-the-century carnival barker. Regardless of weather or inclination, I would wear a blue blazer and a tie. George Shea handed me an Italian-made straw boater laced with a blue-and-red ribbon. I must confess that I experienced a visceral surge of pride upon receiving the hat. It was circular with a stiff brim, a style rarely seen since the 1930s. I got the sense that it could transform me into an almost fictional character, allowing me to say things I normally wouldn't. As I was leaving the office, hat in hand, it occurred to me that this whole IFOCE thing treaded a fine line between fiction and reality, and I was deeply curious to find out how it all—this hat, this sport, and this league—came to be.

JULY 4, 1988.
CONEY ISLAND.

At the corner of Surf and Stillwell Avenues, a crowd has gathered in Schweikerts Alley, on the west side of Nathan's Famous hot dog stand. Center stage behind a couple of hot-dog-covered tables stands publicist Max Rosey on a pedestal, bullhorn in hand, wearing a foam carnival barker's hat and a Nathan's Famous T-shirt. The precontest ceremony is almost nonexistent. Max welcomes the crowd. The eaters shuffle in and take their places at the table. "Get in line," Max yells in a high-pitched voice. "Everybody ready? Get set. Go!" And they're off.

A plucky young employee at Max Rosey's PR firm, George Shea, is a judge at the contest. His memories are fragmented and a bit haunted, almost as if the contest had caused him lasting post-traumatic stress: "There was a gentleman at the area of the table I was given who had a wen, a big wen on his forehead, a genetic disfigurement. I was brutally hungover, and it was 103 degrees, and I almost passed out looking at this guy with a wen on his head. It was not an attractive growth."

When the twelve minutes are up, Max announces the winner, Jay

Green, who has consumed thirteen hot dogs and buns at a just over a dog-a-minute clip. George's memory of the winner, while limited, is consistent with Coney Island's tradition of carnival sideshows. "Jay's eyes were a little askew," he says. "And he was an out-of-work taxi driver, which is interesting because taxi drivers can always find work. But he had a bad back, I think."

Three years later, in January of 1991, Max Rosey lay in a hospital bed at St. Luke's Hospital on the Upper West Side of Manhattan, suffering from the latter stages of metastasized bone cancer. George Shea went to visit him. To distract his mentor from the unbearable pain, George began to speak in hushed tones about the history of the Nathan's Famous contest. Out of nowhere, Max started talking about a yellow belt that lay somewhere in Japan, but whose rightful place was here in America. "He said the belt was created by the descendants of Fabergé, such was its workmanship," George remembers. "But I didn't give much thought to it, because he was on an extraordinary dose of codeine."

When Max passed, Nathan's Famous decided it was only appropriate to relinquish their contract with Rosey's former firm. But George Shea, who had taken over for his mentor, made a suggestion: Instead of maintaining a monthly contract, how about they pay a publicity retainer for the month of July, just for the hot dog contest? Nathan's agreed.

Fast-forward to the summer of 1997, six years later. A Japanese man with a thirty-inch waist named Nakajima had recently supplanted a crew of Americans the size of NFL linebackers as the hot dog champ, and Nathan's was suddenly awash in a deluge of media exposure. "That was the spark when God's finger touched Adam and it created, in my mind, the whole future of competitive eating," says George Shea. The company he had recently formed with his brother Rich, Shea Communications Group, suggested that Nathan's Famous sponsor a circuit of qualifying contests leading up to the grand finale on the Fourth. Nathan's agreed, and the forerunner of the modern American competitive-eating circuit was born.

While conducting a dozen or so Nathan's qualifiers per year, George and Rich Shea were forced to learn the old-school carnival barker's trick of "filling the tent." Because many of the events were held in food courts of anonymous suburban malls, and because competitors had rarely signed up beforehand, the Shea brothers had to recruit them. "In 1997 and '98, you used to go to a mall with no competitors," says George. "None. And you'd get up there on the mic and just start talking. 'You, sir! Don't turn your back on America!' "

Though the exact date of the IFOCE's conception remains a mystery, certain facts are indisputable. There was, for example, a historic meeting in the fall of 1997 at a downtown Manhattan restaurant that included George and Rich Shea, former hot dog champs Mike DeVito and Ed Krachie, and *New York Post* scribe Gersh Kuntzman. The first official minutes were taken, and several rules and regulations were decided upon. Perhaps more notably, the meal itself had elements of competitive consumption. "That was the first time George and I realized who we were dealing with, because we invited two competitive eaters," remembers Rich Shea. "They ate shrimp with reckless abandon, and Ed Krachie drank a lot of wine."

The name International Federation of Competitive Eating was derived from an inscription they'd noticed on the fabled Mustard Yellow Belt. The inscription read: IHF, for the International Hot Dog Federation. According to George Shea, the story of how the Mustard Yellow International Belt returned to America's shores was the founding myth in modern American competitive-eating history. It should be noted, however, that George possesses a rich imagination, so his "oral history" of American competitive eating exists somewhere between reality and make-believe.

In 1993, Mike "the Scholar" DeVito, known for his erudite approach to the sport (he was the first to realize that a two-dog-a-minute pace would result in a then record-breaking total of twenty-four dogs), competed against a diminutive Japanese woman named Orio Ito. It was a thirty-minute, one-on-one hot-dog-eating contest held under the Brooklyn Bridge and filmed by TV Tokyo. Mike won the contest, eighteen dogs to sixteen, and the upset cast a pallor of shame upon the dethroned Japanese champ. Afterward, TV Tokyo filmed Ms. Ito leaning over the railing, donating her half-digested tube steaks to the fish in the East River.

Less than two weeks later, an unmarked package arrived at Shea Communications with postage from Japan. Inside the package was a

Mike "the Scholar" DeVito towers over the diminutive Orio Ito before their 1993 hot dog challenge beneath the Brooklyn Bridge. *(Courtesy of Bill Mitchell)*

bejeweled belt like those worn by boxing champions, but unparalleled in its beauty and craftsmanship. Accompanying the belt was a note written in pidgin English: "Me lost contest. Belt now DeVito." That he failed to save the box and note—both treasured historical artifacts—remains a source of great frustration for George Shea.

The name IFOCE not only honored the legend of the belt, it also expressed the Shea brothers' intentions. The *international* part reflected their desire to cement a global league involving a legitimate sport, and the *competitive eating* part meant that the league would not be limited to hot dogs. Unlike more pedestrian league names like NFL or NBA, the term IFOCE was a cumbersome combination of letters and thus inherently memorable. (The accepted pronunciation is I-F-O-C-E, not "eye-fose.") In addition to the league name, the founding fathers drew up a rough sketch of the league's coat of arms. It featured crossed ketchup and mustard bottles between two winged lions biting either ends of the same hot dog. The league's motto was written in Latin beneath the dragons: IN VORO VERITAS, roughly translated as "In gorging, truth."

In July of 1999 the league's name was introduced to a national TV audience for the first time. After a controversial decision between "Hungry" Charles Hardy and Steve Keiner in the 2000 Nathan's Famous finals (in which Keiner allegedly started eating before the contest officially began), Hardy was invited onto *The Tonight Show with Jay Leno*. After discussing the controversy, Leno asked Hardy, "So who decides these things?" Hardy didn't hesitate. "The International Federation of Competitive Eating," he said.

But it wasn't until July 4, 2001, that competitive eating hit the big time. On that day, Takeru Kobayashi of Japan doubled the hot dog record by eating fifty hot dogs and buns in twelve minutes. The image of a 131-pound man downing so many dogs in such a short time was irresistible to the media. Within twenty-four hours, Kobayashi became the face of competitive eating and the platform for the launch of a new sport.

The moment that changed the sport. Takeru Kobayashi, considered by some to be the greatest athlete alive, raises a triumphant fist after doubling the hot dog record on July 4, 2001.

Dave Baer began aggressively pursuing new clients with the lure of media exposure more eye-catching than a mere advertisement, and the circuit blossomed. Food festivals began to hire the IFOCE. Contests like the ACME Oyster Big Easy Eat-Off in New Orleans and New York–based contests featuring cannoli, matzo balls, pelmeni, and Thanksgiving dinner became annual contests or "majors," as the Sheas billed them.

Documentarians, likely encouraged by the popular mockumentaries of Christopher Guest (*This Is Spinal Tap, Best in Show*) flooded the

IFOCE with calls. Within a few years, documentaries appeared on the Discovery Channel, the Travel Channel, and the Food Network. Articles appeared in *The New York Times Magazine, The Wall Street Journal,* and *Playboy.* Competitive eating segments began airing on *SportsCenter, CNN Headline News,* the *Today* show, *CBS Evening News,* and *Last Call with Carson Daly.* In late September of 2001, Fox television shot the Glutton Bowl, a two-hour multidisciplinary IFOCE championship.

As media coverage burgeoned, the circuit developed a personality. American gurgitators like Ed "Cookie" Jarvis and Don "Moses" Lerman started training and checking the IFOCE Web site for upcoming contests. T-shirts were printed with the IFOCE emblem on the front, and a revamped league motto—"Nothing in moderation"—on the back. George and Rich Shea continued to hone their skills on the mic, developing new rules and one-liners. Competitive eaters became "gurgitators," (the term is a registered trademark of the IFOCE) and the tactic of belching midcontest to free up space became known as "catching a burp." Throwing up during competition became a disqualifiable offense known as a "reversal of fortune."

The Shea brothers became known among reporters for their outlandish quips. "To compare Kobayashi to Michael Jordan is a slight to Kobayashi," Rich would say. "He's a triple threat—jaw strength, capacity, and hand speed," George would add. While Rich developed the style of a silver-tongued sports commentator, George's routine sounded increasingly like that of an evangelical preacher, as he belted out lines like "Competitive eating is the battleground upon which God and Lucifer wage war for men's souls!" Whether in a mall food court, a parking lot, or at the Nathan's Famous contest on the Fourth of July, the Shea brothers started introducing the contest in the most bombastic tones imaginable: "Here we stand at the sanctum sanctorum of eating, the Mount Sinai of mastication, the Coliseum of competitive eating, the Madison Square Garden of gurgitation!"

. . .

While pop culture pundits continue to scratch their heads for a reason behind the competitive-eating craze, Rich Shea recognizes it as the "coming-of-age of what we do"—which is publicity. In an era when Joe Schmoes become stars on well-received reality TV shows and Paris Hilton becomes a megastar for doing nothing in particular, public relations no longer nips at the heels of entertainment. It *is* entertainment. And it's addictive, as proven by the popularity of shameless gossip glossies like *Us Weekly* and *People*. "We are essentially a drug cartel supplying a drug cartel," explains George Shea. "That's what we do. We are a Colombian drug cartel, supplying ourselves and the rest of our cartel with what we need, which is media exposure."

Laypeople often compare the growth of competitive eating to that of a long-running reality show, *Fear Factor*. They feel that audiences are simultaneously disgusted and captivated by the sight of watching people stuff their faces. But competitive eaters would beg to differ. They point out that it's a skill about which people are naturally curious. The populist dynamic of competitive eating—that anyone could potentially do it—leaves the average Joe wondering, "I wonder how many hot dogs *I* could eat in twelve minutes?"

Despite the growth of the IFOCE, the Shea brothers claim the league had, until 2003, been draining money every year since its inception. Shea Communications has always made its bread-and-butter earnings from corporate real estate publicity in Manhattan. The brothers Shea, both of whom are married with children and living in the pricey New York metropolitan area, would leave their families on weekends to emcee eating contests, ignoring other clients and swallowing the losses. "You'd look at the books at the end of the year, and you didn't pull much out," says Rich Shea. "But you'd had a hell of a lot of fun."

The transition from carnival sideshow to sports league/entertainment product has not come without its growing pains. The IFOCE is now beset by virtually all the trappings of modern pro sports leagues. There have been contract disputes, resulting in the secession of a few eaters and the founding of a rival league/eaters' union, the Association of Independent Competitive Eaters. Around the competitive-eating campfire, there have even been faint rumblings of a salary cap in the not-so-distant future.

In the wake of Major League Baseball steroids scandals involving players like Jose Canseco, Mark McGwire, and Barry Bonds, some competitive eaters have started clamoring for drug testing. Eaters have complained of the abuse of mysterious "throat relaxers" by top gurgitators. Kobayashi has been accused of surgically adding a second stomach or an extra row of teeth, or perhaps using an unknown herbal appetite booster. There are even allegations that the "munchies" effect produced by marijuana consumption may be aiding a few fringe eaters on the circuit. But the Shea brothers have concluded that these allegations are the brainchild of sore losers. "You have to read between the whines," Rich says. If a drug exists that would significantly aid gurgitators in competition, the Sheas aren't aware of it. "I'm not saying that no one's ever taken Gas-X to reduce the possibility of getting a burp caught underneath their food," George concedes.

As the popularity of competitive eating has surged, the Sheas claim that other sports have sensed the threat and gone on the attack. George points to repeated attacks at contests by "rogue members of the curling community." At one particular contest, George recalls a verbal barrage from an unknown group of hecklers. Looking out into the crowd, he saw signs that read CURLING ROCKS! EATING IS NOT A SPORT. Rich Shea bears no hard feelings and can even empathize to some extent. "You gotta look at where they're coming from. Global warming is a threat to their sport. They're in a bad place."

Despite repeated attempts to reach out to the middle-aged female demographic, the Shea brothers have found it a tough nut to crack. Dave Baer has pursued companies like Campbell's in hopes of sponsoring a soup contest that might appeal to older women, but to no avail. The Sheas sincerely hope that, as changing social mores continue to reshape the roles of American women, the rise of female eaters like Sonya Thomas and Carlene LeFevre will help bring female competitive-eating fans into the fold.

Though the IFOCE has always had a global focus, outside of Japan the league has struggled to penetrate the international marketplace. Indeed, publicized eating competitions exist in England, Germany, Thailand, Ukraine, and Canada, but they remain the exception that proves the norm. The limiting factors for expansion include capital, manpower, and the assumption that social acceptance in some countries may be an uphill battle, especially considering America's beleaguered reputation abroad. That said, Dave Baer receives frequent e-mail requests from countries like Nigeria, China, and Latvia. In 2004, the IFOCE nearly signed a contract to host a plum dumpling-eating contest in the Czech Republic. Soon thereafter, Dave Baer claims that a contract for a contest in Liberia was quashed in the eleventh hour due to security concerns. "The bulk of the budget was for security," Dave recalls, "because there was a civil war going on there. We sent them a proposal that included a $25,000 security detail."

The IFOCE's repeated attempts to be accepted as an Olympic sport have been coldly snubbed, and the feud with Jacque Rogge, head of the International Olympic Committee, has gotten ugly. When Rich Shea went on record claiming that Rogge was "just in it for the frequent-flier miles," the otherwise stoic Belgian was doubtless ruffled but held his tongue.

On April, 1, 2004, the IFOCE decided to take their dispute with the IOC to the streets. They kicked off a SPAM-torch run from Times Square in New York City, traveling twenty-four hundred miles down to the SPAMARAMA festival in Austin, Texas, where the first ever SPAM-eating contest would be held. "We figured if the Olympics won't have us, we'll create our own country club," says George Shea. Dozens of runners from the Northeast to the Southeast participated in the first ever meat-based torch run, spreading a spirit of goodwill across the American heartland. "This torch run comes at a time of deep division in our nation," an emotional George Shea said at a press conference. "The bipartisan outpouring of support for this effort gives one chills."

The scope of the Shea brothers' ambition for the IFOCE knows no bounds. Besides acceptance into the Olympics, George Shea envisions a six-hundred-event circuit with thousands of eaters ranked regionally, nationally, and internationally. There will be so many events that eaters will become specialists in specific foodstuffs. Sprinters, distance eaters, soup slurpers, roughage specialists—all will have a place on the circuit, and the top twenty-five eaters will all be big earners. Rich Shea likens the future eating circuit to the PGA, in which all eaters will carry an official IFOCE-circuit ID card like the PGA's tour card. "Circuit cardholders will be like Vijay Singh down to John Daly. And Daly or somebody's gonna say I need to make my hundred grand so I'm going out as much as I can, whereas Singh is gonna only go to the majors where he can get some real cash."

If competitive eating really is becoming a globally recognized sport, what does that make the Shea brothers? Do they see themselves as coinventors of a new sport, as James Naismith was with basketball? Or do they liken their role to that of master sports promoters like Vince McMahon or Don King? Are they a modern version of Barnum & Bailey, or savvy league cocommissioners like the NBA's David Stern? "We've been called the Ring Ding brothers," George says. "And the Barnum & Bailey of Barf," adds Rich. But really, despite the meteoric rise of America's fastest-growing sport, the Shea brothers have a rather quaint vision of the competitive-eating circuit and their place in it.

"It is very much like a fraternity in which we are the social chairs," George observes. He then steps away from the analogy, explaining that several women are involved and that fraternities often connote "stupid rah-rah morons." But call it what you will—an outlet for hobbyists, an Elks Club for misfits, a clubhouse for like-minded adults. This last analogy is perhaps most appropriate, because the lure that seems to draw eaters, fans, and journalists alike is the common bond of the circuit, the friends, the travel, the humorous spectacle, and the thrill of competition. The competitive-eating circuit is a haven for grown men and women to toss aside their worldly cares and act like kids again.

Somehow, even as competitive eating grows globally and fiscally, the Shea brothers and Dave Baer continue to see it as a clubhouse they founded. "If money were no object," says Rich Shea. "If I were, say, Paul Allen, then we'd have that old social club down on Mulberry Street. And Cookie Jarvis would be walking around. And there would be rooms where the LeFevres could stay when they were in the city. It would be like Beautiful Brian bringing out the coffee and Hal Schimel running around, serving up espressos. That, to me, is what the circuit is."

2

THE GENTLE
GIGANTIC WARRIOR

Before doing battle, in the temple one calculates and will win, because many calculations were made.

—Sun Tzu, *The Art of War*

Badlands Booker gives love to the crowd as George Shea proclaims him the Pumpkin Pie Eating Champion of the World. His coffee-stained jersey would later be hung from the rafters at IFOCE headquarters. *(Courtesy of Matt Roberts/IFOCE)*

When you meet Eric "Badlands" Booker for the first time, one thing is reasonably certain—you'll spot him first. At six foot six, 440 pounds, he is quite simply an enormous human being. The embodiment of rotundity, his head and abdominal region look almost as if a small sphere has been placed atop a much larger one, snowman-style. The effect of his approaching figure brings to mind the Michelin Man, except that his skin is brown and his walk doesn't fit the profile. He struts with a graceful rhythm that's both athletic and confident, and his girth is not of the soft sort. He could be mistaken for a retired NFL lineman. But beyond the stunning approach of this man-mountain in a New York subway conductor's collared shirt, it's the smile that really gets you. At the moment he recognizes you, Bad-lands' face lights up in the most electrifying way.

It's June 28, 2003, and I'm meeting up with Badlands at Hooters in midtown Manhattan. The assignment, given to me by the sports ed-itor of the *Village Voice,* is to share a training meal with one of Amer-ica's top-ranked gurgitators before the upcoming Nathan's Famous Fourth of July Hot Dog Eating Contest. The plan is to write a short, tongue-in-cheek piece, but my flippant research on the subject does not prepare me for Badlands' dead-serious approach to competitive eating. By the time our waitress (clad in those humiliating orange polyester butt-huggers for which Hooters is renowned) comes by to take our order, I am nodding my head in earnest to Badlands' per-sonal recipe for gurgitory success. He has dubbed his formula the Four Tenets of the Sweet Science of Competitive Eating.

The first prerequisite for competitive-eating success, he says, is stomach capacity. The stomach is just like any other muscle and must be trained accordingly. Just as biceps strength increases with each set of curls, "if you get the stomach muscle used to holding lots of food, it'll adapt to the stress that you put it through during an eating contest." A common misconception, Booker notes, is that the stomach stretches, inflating and deflating like a balloon. Actually, it unfolds like an accor-dion. (My subsequent research on the subject proves him correct.)

Booker says the method of choice for increasing stomach capacity is veggie training—"not hitting the buffet, not eating a whole bunch of fatty, greasy foods." Instead, many pro speed-eaters sit down and gorge on large portions of fruits or vegetables. Each eater has his go-to training foodstuff, Badlands explains. Ed "Cookie" Jarvis, for example, pounds down whole watermelons, seeds and all. Ray "the Bison" Meduna trains with cucumber slices. Badlands, for his part, goes with cabbage.

"I'm like the Bubba Gump of cabbage dishes. I make all kinds. Bald cabbage. Savoy cabbage. Red cabbage. Cabbage with smoked turkey wings. Sometimes I have cabbage with seasons, like garlic and peppers. Sometimes I'll put a whole lot of water in it—you know, saturated water cabbage. Sometimes I just eat it raw."

The other accepted technique for improving stomach capacity and elasticity is drinking copious amounts of water. As far as Booker knows, Cookie Jarvis holds the unofficial water record by downing a gallon in a minute and one second. Badlands has done it in a minute and five. When I suggest the prospect of a water-drinking contest, Badlands reveals just how scientific his approach to training is. "Yeah, I think liquid-centric sport would be a good look. But you gotta be careful with water-drinkin', because you don't want people to get waterlogged. What's that called—hyponatremia?" I shrug, clueless. "Yeah, what happens is, when you drink a lot of water, your sodium levels drop. But, hey . . . we could do Gatorade!"

The second ingredient in Badlands' recipe for competitive-eating success is stamina. "In an eating contest, you can tell if someone's tired when they start leaning. You notice Kobayashi eats with both hands, and he never leans." To improve his stamina, Badlands works out on the elliptical machine three times a week. A brown belt in judo, he also spends several hours a week at the local dojo.

The third factor is strategy. Badlands has read Sun Tzu's *The Art of War,* and among its most memorable lessons is that *a battle is over before it's ever fought.* For this reason, Badlands prepares so thoroughly for contests that he has actually been known to interrogate his competitive foodstuff beforehand. In the weeks leading up to the Fourth of July hot dog contest, for example, he starts by cooking up three Nathan's Famous dogs and buns on his George Foreman grill. He then sits with the dogs and just stares at them, meditating, poring over every nook and cranny of their pink-brown, grease-beaded surfaces. Finally, the interrogation begins. "What's the best way to eat you?" he asks the dog aloud. During one such inquiry, Badlands remembers his son Brendan slinking into the room. "What you talkin' to those dogs for, Dad?" he asked.

But Badlands maintained his focus. Over six years, he developed a hot-dog-eating technique that was uniquely his own. He studied the tapes of past Nathan's Famous contests and tested the myriad eating styles. He tried former American hot dog champ Ed Krachie's Chunk 'n' Dunk method, which is basically to dunk hot dog and bun in water, then eat, then repeat. He tried the traditional Japanese method, perfected by Nakajima in the late nineties. Nakajima's innovation was to separate dog and bun, to eat the dog, then dunk the bun and eat it. He sampled the traditionalist method of just eating the hot dog. And finally, he tried the method of the master himself, Takeru Kobayashi, dubbed the Solomon Method. Kobayashi's method is to break the dog in half and eat it in rapid-fire bites. He then breaks the bun in half, dunks it, and eats it.

"But I'm physically bigger than Kobayashi, so why break it in half?" This leap of logic led to Booker's pioneering method, nicknamed the Double Japanese. He takes *two* dogs and devours them bite by bite. Then he takes two buns, dunks them, and eats them one at a time. At first, he ate them both at once, but soon ran into the formidable obstacle of an overstuffed mouth. "That's one of the biggest problems a competitive eater has. Because once you stuff your mouth, it takes a long time to chew that down."

The final tenet of the Sweet Science of Competitive Eating is the most important one of all, Booker assures me. Before and during a contest, a gurgitator must have a strong, focused mind. "You must have your game face on," he says, serious as a heart attack. "You must be in the Zone. You must be one with the dogs."

To maintain his focus, Badlands often meditates before a competition. He learned to meditate from his judo sensei. At the end of each judo session, the entire class does a cool-down meditation. "You know, inhale the positivity and exhale the negativity . . . oxygenate your body." Before most contests, he employs these same techniques. He puts his arms out to his sides, fills his lungs with oxygen, and focuses his mind on the task at hand—which is, of course, eating massive amounts of food in a short time.

At this point, I'm jolted into reality by the sudden appearance of a pair of hooters. It's the waitress, stopping by to check on our progress with the small trough of buffalo wings that lies between us. She asks why we are tape-recording our conversation, and I explain that the guy sitting opposite me is a world-class competitive eater. On cue, Badlands offers to show her his wing-eating technique. He grabs a wing, or a "paddle" as they're known on the circuit, breaks the joint between thumb and forefinger, puts it in his mouth, and strips it across his teeth. When it resurfaces, the bones are stripped clean. Badlands asks me to try it, and my attempt to duplicate the technique is futile, bordering on sad. Our waitress's reaction hovers somewhere between amusement and disgust. She doesn't seem to recognize the talent involved. I guess some people just don't get it.

June 2, 2004

"There's a challenge here . . . it's the number thirteen, called the Molicious, named after the baseball player Mo Vaughn. The challenge is, they have this sandwich that's as tall as a skyscraper . . ."

It's a year later, and Badlands and I are engaged in yet another training meal for the Fourth of July Nathan's Famous contest, which I have just learned I will be co-emceeing. We are seated in the back room of the fabled Carnegie Deli in midtown Manhattan, chewing on a pair of ginormous sandwiches filled with softball-sized lumps of kosher deli meats. With each bite, Badlands accomplishes the competitive-eating equivalent of lapping me. And somehow, his steady devouring does not prevent him from explaining the Carnegie Deli Challenge, which only six humans have been able to achieve.

The Mo-licious more than lives up to the appetite of its namesake, Mo Vaughn, a 270-pound former first baseman for the Mets. It's a three-and-a-half-pound sandwich, composed of a pound of corned beef, a pound of cheese, and a pound and a half of turkey. Stuffed between four slices of rye bread, the sandwich is slathered with Russian dressing and precariously held together with two-hundred-millimeter skewers. "So the challenge is," Badlands explains, "if you have the stomach to order one, and you eat the whole thing, then you get the second one for free."

The second one? Just as I have begun to imagine myself, after an ascetic Ramadan-style forty-eight-hour fast, coming here to assume my rightful place in the annals of competitive eating, my hopes are dashed. Judging from my slowing pace with a plain old corned beef sandwich, I will never achieve what awaits the rare Carnegie Deli Challenge victor . . . an autographed picture on the wall. "You be up on the wall with slimmies like Alfred E. Neuman, Arnold Schwarzenegger, Liv Tyler, Doc Gooden, the Catwoman Halle Berry," Badlands says. "You be up there with them all, just chillin', for the whole world to see."

Of the other iron-stomach gurgitators who have done the Challenge—including Don "Moses" Lerman, Cookie Jarvis, "Krazy" Kevin Lipsitz, and Leon "Justice" Feingold—the one who did it with the most panache was a svelte Japanese woman, Takako Akasaka. When she did it back in the eighties, she effortlessly knocked down the two sandwiches and about ten cups of tea in a cool forty-five minutes. It took Badlands over an hour.

A lot has changed for Badlands in the past year. He has defended his matzo ball title and his fan Web site is up and running. But most importantly, he has just released his debut competitive-eating-themed hip-hop album: *Badlands Booker: Hungry and Focused.* "The Sweet Science of Competitive Eating," not long ago a mere concept, is now the title of the album's third song. It's a head-nodder with Badlands' lyrical formula for gurgitating greatness laid over a loop from Thomas Dolby's eighties rock hit "She Blinded Me with Science."

No bunson burners, or beakers
Just a competitive eater in sneakers
Keep ya lab coats and ya pocket protectors,
And your shirts and ties while I'll electrify

And gain world records, scientific methods
Journey begins, ask myself questions
Who'll be there, what are we eating
When it's taking place, and why I'm competing

Figure that out, begin the research
Plan out the details to come in first
Educated guesses, hypothesis
Through research, conduct experiments

Like training runs, cabbage by the ton
Twenty-one sticks of bubble gum
To excercise the jaw, the check and jowl
Rip meat off bone. Ya feel it louuud!

When asked about his childhood, the conversation focuses on two of Badlands' obsessions: food and hip-hop. He was born in Queens, on February 20, 1969. "I like to say that when they stepped on the moon, I stepped out the womb . . . first thing I grabbed was a fork and a spoon."

Growing up in a rough neighborhood in southeast Jamaica, Queens, Booker always had an uncanny appetite. "Every refrigerator magnet my parents had, had tooth marks on it," Booker says, laughing. "I tried to devour it." His mother and aunt were both excellent cooks, and he found himself going back for seconds and thirds. On the other hand, his grandmother was woefully mediocre in the kitchen. He now credits her meals for his "strong mental training," which has helped him eat unsavory foods competitively.

Though he was generally a good kid, Badlands admits to having "fractured a law or two." He was heavily into hip-hop culture, which in those days meant tagging his name on the trains, "doin' graffiti in the yards. I guess it's poetic justice, because now I'm a conductor on the 7 train," he says with a laugh, referring to his job of thirteen years.

He wrote rhymes from an early age and credits lunchroom rap battles for his fearlessly competitive attitude. One particular battle sticks out in his mind. To test his verbal mettle, Badlands arranged a lunchroom battle with "one of the nicest cats in school," a kid who went by the name Royal Rich. Word got around the school, and soon enough kids were talking about cutting their classes to check out the battle.

Badlands borrowed two of his dad's Kangol hats—one for himself, and one for his man providing the beat box. The lunchroom was packed. Badlands went first, spitting out one of his go-to battle rhymes. Royal Rich responded with an all-out verbal assault, lines like: "Why'd you even waste yo time and go cut yo class? So I could sit here and just whip yo ass?" The lunchroom exploded in "Ohhhh!" As Royal Rich went on to exploit the standard battle-rhyme topic—yo mama—Badlands felt his head sinking lower and lower. By the time Rich had finished, the cafeteria was filled with taunts. "You just got roasted!" "Yo, it's a wrap for you."

Despite the odds, Badlands persevered. He forced his friend to do one last beat box and went off on Royal Rich, and his mama, and any other weakness he could think of. The tide turned ever so slightly, and the cafeteria started to cheer him on. Ultimately, Badlands lost the battle, but he gained the respect of his peers. He compares his brave yet hopeless stand to that of Rocky Balboa getting pummeled by

Apollo Creed but springing up from the mat and winning the respect of both Apollo and the crowd.

Throughout high school, Booker worked hard to secure a record contract. He made demos and shopped them to hip-hop labels. In return, he received a stream of rejection letters that conceded that he had talent but wasn't what they were looking for. Still, Badlands kept writing rhymes and perfecting his product—"I kept pitchin'," he says—biding his time and waiting for an opportunity.

In 1997, while dining with his son near his home in Long Island, Booker spotted Frankster, the Nathan's Famous mascot, hyping a contest. He had watched the Fourth of July contest results for years, and had always wanted to compete. "And I was like, this must be fate, because things happen for a reason." He was too late to sign up for the contest, but when George Shea got a look at him, he saw potential. "Don't worry. We're gonna find a spot for you," George said. With no style or technique, Badlands put down seventeen and a half dogs and buns. "I was putting mustard on them and everything," Badlands says. "I won. I got a big trophy and sixty pounds of hot dogs to train with."

Over the next few years, Eric Booker developed an alter ego. *New York Post* reporter Gersh Kuntzman contributed the first brushstroke by providing the nickname Badlands in one of his articles. (Booker still isn't sure what led to the name, but he likes to say it's because he comes from the "bad lands of New York.") "I was always pretty shy and reserved," Booker admits. "But then Gersh gave me the name Badlands, and George saw something in me that needed to come out. So all my charisma and everything you see in me today, I gotta give it up to them. They awakened the sleeping giant, and the rest is history."

When Booker is in an eating contest, he becomes Badlands. The transformation, he says, is not unlike that of Bruce Banner becoming the Hulk, carefully pointing out that even when Bruce Banner is the Hulk, he still remains Bruce Banner.

Yeah, superhero with a fork and spoon
Train like X-Men in the danger room
Like a pirate, lower epicurean booms
Quicker than soon, bring masticating doom

The first appearance of Badlands as we now know him was at the taping of the two-hour Fox special *The Glutton Bowl*. After extensive interrogations about his food preferences, he was told that he would be eating hard-boiled eggs in the first round. The producers sent him a ticket, and he boarded a plane for the first time in his life, bound for California. Once there, he asked Takeru Kobayashi for advice on eating eggs, having heard that Kobayashi once downed eighty-seven emu eggs in a contest. Kobayashi graciously offered his technique, which was to bite the egg in half, take a drink, and finish the egg with the next bite. The essential part was to establish a bite-and-drink rhythm, in tune to his favorite hip-hop tune if that helped. Armed with this wisdom, Badlands put down thirty-eight eggs in eight minutes to set the record and take the title.

Afterward, the producers encouraged him to ham it up a bit. Talk some trash, they said, act as if you're going to Disneyland. Booker puffed up, and out came Badlands. "I was like, 'Bring it on! I can eat thirty, forty, fifty more eggs! I'm in the Zone! This is Badlands' contest! What? What?'" When the director said, "Cut!" Badlands exhaled and transformed back into Eric Booker. Holding his turgid, aching belly, he vowed not to touch another hard-boiled egg for years.

Though he is by no means a pushover, Eric Booker is one of the nicest, most positive people I've ever met. George Shea once described him as "blessed with a serotonin-rich brain." Whenever you meet up with him, his first question is almost always "What's good?" He has a bit of a stutter, peppering his conversations with "yi-yi-you know" and "right?" and "you know what I'm sayin'?" This lends his speech a mellifluous singsong quality that almost echoes the rhythm of hip-hop.

But when Badlands raps, there isn't the slightest trace of a stutter. His quiet confidence morphs into something a bit more explosive and cocky, a quality that he likes to call "lightning in a bottle." So if you want to hang out with Eric Booker, you can catch him on the 7 train, or at home playing video games with his kids. If you want to hang with Badlands, go check him out at an eating contest. Or better yet, go to his Web site and order yourself a copy of *Hungry and Focused,* where the Badlands bravado is at its best.

> Put a hurting on a food establishment
> Owner sees me and the man is adamant
> To put up the closed sign in a hurry
> And call his supply trucks kinda early
>
> And I know I'm about to be banned
> When he's like, "Don't come back, understand?
> You eat like a sumo, can't feed ya, man!"
> Around the fifth plate realized who I am
>
> They call me Badlands Booker
> Superfly like Ron O'Neal and Snuka
> Putting the pressure on eaters like cookers
> Put on a show for press and onlookers

3

MEAT PIES IN NATCHITOCHES

It just blew the man's mind the way I did the six-pound burger and a pound of french fries in twenty-two minutes, because nobody had ever done it before. So I decided to blow his mind a little more and I ordered a thirty-piece chicken wings after that, and I ate that, too.

—"Bayou" Boyd Bulot

Bayou Boyd Bulot (foreground) contemplates the essence of the meat pie, mid-competition, while Dave "the Masticator" May (far end, bushy hair) gauges his rival's progress. *(Courtesy of Keri Fidelak)*

SEPTEMBER 19, 2003

I arrived in Natchitoches (pronounced NACK-uh-tish), Louisiana, the night before the competition. The town, which was the setting for the movie *Steel Magnolias*, was dubbed by Oprah Winfrey "the best little town in the whole USA!" I don't know if it's the *best* town, but it is pretty. The thirty-three-block Natchitoches Historic District, a cluster of restored nineteenth-century colonial, late Victorian, and Greek Revival buildings, has been designated a National Historic Landmark. Driving down historic Jefferson Street in my rented OldsmoBuick, I was shrouded by weeping willows from above, flanked by the banks of the Cane River Lake on one side and the verandas of bed-and-breakfasts on the other. If not for the cars, I could almost imagine myself clodhopping in a horse-drawn buggy through the antebellum South.

I needed a beer. It was a long flight, half of it spent on one of those claustrophobic propeller planes, and then a forty-minute ride from the airport. Following the sound of music, I discovered that the meat pie festival was already under way. Lines of cars were cruising Jefferson Street at a sleepy crawl. Locals sauntered along a promenade that ran parallel to the river, lined by trailers filled with meat pies and beer. In the middle of the promenade was the main stage, where a zydeco band was playing.

I bought a Budweiser and a meat pie, seizing the opportunity to size up the competitive foodstuff. The crescent-shaped pastry was tasty, even delicious, but all the elements that provided its flavor could be hindrances in competition. While the crispy outer shell of yellowish dough allowed for a satisfying crunch, I sensed that without sufficient moisture it could cause painful mouth injuries when eaten briskly. The interior was a rich, oily mélange of ground beef, onions, and spices—again, tasty, but perhaps a recipe for indigestion in a ten-minute speed-eating format. Despite my gnawing hunger, I was full after one meat pie.

Keri Fidelak, the festival organizer and proprietor of Maison Louisiane, the bed-and-breakfast where I would stay, wasn't answering her phone. So I drank more beer, watched people, and eavesdropped. As a twenty-nine-year-old loner prowling the festival with no apparent destination, I was regarded with curiosity bordering on suspicion by the locals. It was a sensation with which I would soon become familiar.

Finally, I heard the name "Fidelak" spoken aloud, as if cast down from the heavens. I looked to the stage, where a young woman was giving out thank-yous. When she finished, I introduced myself. Immediately, I went from outsider to insider, thanks to that elegant institution known as Southern hospitality. I met her husband, Ben, and other friendly folks with accents that made mine sound coarse in comparison. As the festival began to wind down for the evening, some friendly couple drove me back to the bed-and-breakfast on their motorboat.

The next morning, I woke up early for a formal catered breakfast in the dining room of Maison Louisiane. The cast of characters included a lawyer and a doctor from "N'awlins," their wives, a young couple with a literary bent, and a New Agey college student. They had all driven up for the Meat Pie Tri, a triathlon that would be held Sunday morning. Though *meat pie* and *triathlon* seemed like a contradiction in terms, I decided after some internal debate not to bring this up at breakfast. The only other lodger was the one I hadn't yet met—Boyd Bulot, a gregarious bear of a man with a boyish smile and a soft Southern twang, who looked every bit the part of world oyster-eating champion. Without hesitation, he regaled the breakfast table with the story that I'd been told he would likely tell. . . .

It was the one about the last time he'd drunk alcohol, back at Southeastern Louisiana University. It goes like this: Boyd's been drinking with his college buddies when one of them challenges him to a tequila shot duel. But Boyd's buddy dupes him by taking shots of water. So Boyd drinks himself into a state where it seems only natural to march down to the train tracks, climb on top of a car, and start throwing stuff at his boys below. The next morning Boyd wakes up on top of a train, half-naked. It's cold out. He wipes the sleep from his eyes and looks out. There are mountains. *This ain't naw L'isiana.* He scuttles off to some local business. The secretary, surprised to see a large, half-naked man stumble in from the cold, tells him he's in Tennessee. Eight hours from home. Boyd calls his boys back at the frat house, and they charter a bus to fetch ole Boyd. The ride home is one tremendous party, but Boyd learns his lesson and hasn't had a drop to drink since.

After breakfast, I asked Boyd how he got into competitive eating. Turned out he had stumbled onto the circuit through one of the more conventional vehicles—a restaurant challenge. One night in the spring of 2003, he drove with a group of six buddies up to the French Quarter in New Orleans. While eating at the ACME Oyster House, Boyd's friends noticed the Wall of Fame, which displayed the oyster-eating record of "Crazy Legs" Conti, a New York native, who had eaten thirty-three dozen oysters in three and a half hours in 2001. "That ain't nothin'," Boyd told his friends. Within minutes, the table was flush with cash, his friends having donated around $300 toward the cause. The bet was on. "All right, start crackin'," Boyd said. His buddies started shucking oysters, the whole time hyping to other diners about what Bulot was about to do to the record. In less than two hours, he siphoned down forty-eight dozen slimy bivalves. Had it not been closing time, he was sure the damage would've been greater. He eventually visited three other ACME restaurants, doubling the record at each venue. In Orange Beach, Alabama, he ate his personal best, fifty-six dozen, or a total of 672 oysters.

His talent recognized, Boyd was encouraged to return for ACME's ten-minute speed-eating competition in April 2003, at the French Quarter Festival. That year, he ate eighteen dozen oysters in ten minutes to take Crazy Legs' crown, and he claims he basically stopped after six minutes. "I was just teasin' people, standin' up, drinkin' bottles of root beer and hot sauce."

Bulot is an interesting combination of shy guy and gifted show-man. Despite his prodigious girth, he claims he's not that big of an eater. His favorite aspect of competitive eating is what he calls "trip-pin' people out." Trippin' people out is simply a matter of shocking bystanders with his superhuman eating abilities. His most common stunt is the postcontest I-ain't-full-yet ploy. At a pregame show for the LSU-Oklahoma Sugar Bowl matchup, Boyd decimated twenty-one dozen oysters in four minutes. After his victory, he grabbed a bottle of Tabasco sauce and downed it. When asked how his stomach could handle such intensity, Boyd scoffed. "I'm used to eatin' jabanero pep-pers right off the bush."

Not unlike most professional gurgitators, it was a matter of time before Hollywood took notice. Impressed by his oyster exploits, the producers of *Ripley's Believe It or Not* invited Boyd out to Los Angeles to do a hot dog stunt. He ate forty-one barely cooked hot dogs in ten minutes on the show. Then he showed up three hours later at the Los Angeles Nathan's Famous qualifier and downed seventeen dogs and buns in twelve minutes for a decisive victory over Krazy Kevin Lipsitz (who had flown from Staten Island for the only kosher hot dog contest in the country). Later that week, Bulot was spotted at the Playboy mansion accompanied by a hot blonde. A day later, while eating at Café Piazza on Rodeo Drive, Boyd struck up a conversation with the actor and comedian Ben Stein, who wrote about the experience on the E! network Web site. Though Mr. Stein's account of the conversation was clearly not fact-checked ("AFOCE"?), it did include one useful insight about Boyd: "This man is such a natural for show business it is insane."

Right before the contest, I found myself caught up in a heavy conver-sation about infidelity with Boyd Bulot and Maison Louisiane's maid,

a young woman named Heather. Boyd had recently cut off his engage-
ment with his fiancée, the love of his life. He had caught her cheating
on him with a nongurgitator and was still suffering from a broken
heart. Heather encouraged him to vent his feelings and provided details of her own boy problems. Feeling eternally petty, I kept checking
my watch. As bad as I felt for the big fella, I was nervous as hell about
my first contest, and this wasn't exactly a psych-up session. When I finally found an opening to slip away, I made Boyd promise to leave
soon. He had meat pies to eat.

I arrived at the festival later than planned and sweating profusely
in my wool suit. To give off the impression of responsibility, I advised
Keri Fidelak to make an announcement for all eaters to come sign up.
I found the festival's EMT and advised him to stand by. I checked on
the meat pies, provided in abundance by the Natchitoches Meat Pie
Company. The local competitors introduced themselves and signed
waivers. Among them were a sturdy woman, a college student, and a
nice farmer with a Cajun accent who apologized for being unable to
sign his name.

No less than ten minutes before the competition, Boyd Bulot finally showed. I exhaled and stepped up to the mic. In my best "Let's
get ready to rrrrrumble!" voice, I said, "Welcome to the 2003 Natchitoches Meat Pie Eating Championship!" The crowd responded with,
well, not quite a roar, but not bad either. I could get used to this.

I introduced myself and gave a few facts about the league, stress-
ing the historic significance of the world record we were about to witness. I discussed the fabled (read: fictional) turkey-eating contest that
Louis Juchereau de St. Denis, the founder of the city, had staged
against the Natchitoches Indians in 1715. Then I did my rendition of
the old street-vendor chant that I'd found online: "Hotta meat pies!
Get your hotta meat pies right here!" I threw out a few of the league's
most impressive statistics, most notably the world mayonnaise-eating
record, eight pounds in eight minutes, by Oleg Zhornitskiy. The
crowd let out a collective groan. When the loudspeakers started play-

ing the theme from *Rocky*, it felt like my cue to call out the contestants.

I did my best to improvise competitive eating nicknames and credentials. There was "Hungry" Shawn Hornsby, who had his picture posted in Pizza Huts around the state and was banned for life from their lunch buffet. There was Kenny "Steel Stomach" Simmons, who had been training daily with boudin, a type of Cajun spicy sausage. The IFOCE is an equal opportunity league, I said, so naturally there was a woman in the contest. "Please welcome, the lovely Ms. Vern "the Gurgitator" Guidroc!" The crowd of about four hundred fans went nuts for the lone female contestant.

"What we are about to witness is a classic David and Goliath affair," I said. In this case, our David was a literal one—David "the Masticator" May, a 185-pound rower on the local Northwestern State University crew team, who would be competing in the Meat Pie Tri tomorrow. The moment I said his name, four college guys in the front row peeled off their shirts and yelled, "Go, Dave!" His name was painted across their chests in big black letters—D-A-V-E. "I assure you that Dave isn't just here for the carbo loading, folks," I said. "He understands that the weight of Natchitoches' hopes and dreams rests squarely on his shoulders."

Our final contestant was a Goliath, a heavyweight on the circuit. The current world oyster-eating champion, his intimate knowledge of both meat and pies would certainly aid him in the meat pie discipline. Just months ago, he won the ACME Oyster Eating Championship in N'awlins. And just weeks ago, in Newport News, Virginia, he had put down a six-pound burger and a pound of fries in under a half hour. Though these eating exploits were impressive, his second-place finish in the recent World Crawfish Eating Championship proved that he was, in fact, mortal. "Please welcome to the competitive-eating table a resident of Hammond, Louisiana, standing six foot five and tipping the scales at a mighty 340 pounds, Blazin' . . . Amazin' . . . Bayou Boyd Buloootttt!"

The cheer was loud but tepid—clearly a regionally patriotic crowd. I explained the rules. Half, whole, and quarter meat pies consumed would count toward the final tally. Dunking was permitted. If an eater suffered a reversal of fortune, or what we call on the circuit "urges contrary to swallowing," he or she would be disqualified. The winner would receive $500 and the coveted title of World Meat Pie Eating Champion. The crowd helped me count down from ten, and they were off.

The contest was a blur. I said "meat pie" as many times as possible, because I liked the sound of it. There were no meat pie reversals, so the metal vomit pails to the left of each eater remained empty. Bayou Boyd Bulot, the only professional in the bunch, got out of the gates at a full sprint, took an early lead, and never looked back. At the six-minute mark, the amateurs started to slump over and chew slowly, staring helplessly at their meat pies like dazed cattle. I explained to the crowd that this phenomenon was known on the circuit as "hitting the wall," which was roughly equivalent to the strain felt by a runner at the twenty-mile point of a marathon. "Help 'em out, folks!" I said. "Help 'em over the wall!" At seven minutes, the nice, illiterate Cajun man stepped away from the table. All the while, Bulot kept inhaling meat pies like a magpie would worms.

When the final whistle blew, Bulot had downed sixteen meat pies, a total of six pounds, to set the world record. Second place went to a local upstart, Hungry Shawn Hornsby, who finished with a respectable seven. After declaring Bulot the victor, I walked over to personally congratulate him. "Those deep-fried pies were kinda tough to get through," he said, admitting that he'd suffered some battle wounds. He had cuts on the roof of his mouth, and I noticed that the trauma of cramming meat pies had left an oversized deposit of snot beneath his right nostril. I handed him a tissue and gave him a congratulatory pat on the back.

After the contest, I absconded to my rental car and changed out of my soaked suit. A woman named Mary Ann Nunley, assistant to the mayor, escorted me to a vague civic building for some sort of reception. There was air-conditioning, food, beer, and an LSU football game on TV. Smiling strangers shook my hand, asked me about New York, the contest, and how I'd gotten this bizarre job. I met Burgundy L. Olivier, the spinach-obsessed author of *I Love Spinach,* who drives a green minivan called the Spinach Mobile. I was tempted to ask if she had Popeye fantasies, but decided against it. Everyone was exceedingly pleasant, but I felt frazzled and needed some alone time.

On the way back to Maison Louisiane, I ran into Boyd, who was walking around the festival with Heather, his friend from the kitchen. They were both smiling, and I thought to myself that all's well that ends well. I asked Boyd how he was feeling. Was he full? "Not at all," Boyd replied. "After the competition, I went to that restaurant up the hill and got me an order of the surf 'n' turf."

4

THE ERUPTION
OF DALE BOONE

Go for gold or explode!

—Dale Boone

Dale "Mouth of the South" Boone, the
man every competitive eating fan loves to
hate, rings his cowbell before a contest.

OCTOBER 3, 2003

There is a spot just below the mouth and directly above the chin, which is known on the competitive-eating circuit as the Blind Spot. At this spot, for a brief nanosecond, a competitive eater cannot see the food before it enters his mouth. Amateurs are severely hampered by the Blind Spot, but professional eaters go right through it without hesitation."

The crowd at the World Pulled Pork Barbecue Eating Championship is not amused by my drivel. After what I considered a rather bland performance in Natchitoches, I've decided to try out new, more experimental material. But judging from the blank stares of a few hundred locals at Crossroads Arena in Corinth, Mississippi, the material isn't striking a cord. But at least my co-emcee, Dave Baer, is laughing.

The main thing we've got going for us is a solid cast of eaters. Thanks to the gracious offer of $2,000 in prize money by a man named Reggie Churchwell (who reminds me of Boss Hogg from the *Dukes of Hazzard*), we've got three topflight competitive eaters. Reggie's the promoter of the Hog Wild Festival, a barbecue-cooking competition that features over thirty cooking teams. As accompanying entertainment, Reggie has also arranged a giant carnival, an ugly-truck contest, a hog-calling contest, and the first-ever sanctioned eating competition involving pulled-pork barbecue sandwiches.

As the crowd trickles—and *trickles* is the right term here—into the arena, our warm-up jokes are met with mild enthusiasm at best. Part of the problem is the size of this place. Crossroads Arena can seat ten thousand. In an attempt to spark up some smiles, I give an impromptu history of the sport, starting at the very beginning. "The origins of competitive eating date back to the earliest days of mankind. If you have thirty Neanderthals in a cave and a rabbit walks in, that's a competitive-eating situation." This gets some laughs. It's a line from my notes that I've stolen almost verbatim from the IFOCE Web site.

Dave takes over, lays down the tale of the tape. Today's matchup will feature not only a handful of Mississippi's most ravenous, but three of the finest gurgitators in the *world* as well, including the 2002 IFOCE Rookie of the Year, Dale Boone, one of the most colorful characters on the circuit, who claims to be a direct descendant of Daniel Boone.

"Yee-hawwwwww!" That's Dale Boone. He grabs my microphone and starts ranting at the crowd and his fellow eaters, in keeping with his reputation as the league's most volatile combatant. A balding, big-bellied country boy wearing a coonskin cap, Dale tugs at the suspenders of his overalls and tells the crowd his opponents don't know nothin' about barbecue. Trying to drum up some Southern patriotism, he promises to keep the barbecue belt in the land of Dixie. He may look and sound like a hick, but Dale, a producer of Southeast Asian–oriented television programming in Atlanta, understands that this is entertainment. The crowd's suddenly engaged and awake, if not a little perplexed.

Dave explains that the contest will be no cakewalk for Boone. In addition to a slew of hungry Corinthians, there's Jammin' Joe LaRue, an underrated Florida hot-dog-eating champ who has just recovered from a career-threatening knee injury. Jammin' Joe walks onstage and waves to the crowd. Jammin' Joe is huge, with a forehead so prominent it makes you think of evolution. For this reason, George Shea often introduces him as "the missing link, not between man and ape . . . but between man and *God.*"

"But the real threat to Boone's chances today is the woman known as the Black Widow," Dave says. A dainty little wisp of an Asian woman bounds up onto the stage, waving and smiling. You can see the faint outline of a rib cage beneath her black DKNY T-shirt. She has long, black hair, a pretty face with a chiseled jaw, and the waifish frame of an undernourished teenage girl—the antithesis of what one would imagine a champion gurgitator to look like. The people of Corinth don't know what to think, so they just clap and look at each other.

Sonya Thomas has recently emerged as the most naturally dominant competitive eater ever to hit the circuit. After watching footage of Kobayashi destroying much larger opponents at the 2002 Nathan's Famous Hot Dog Eating Contest, she had a vision. Aware of her inordinate appetite, she surfed the Internet and discovered a Nathan's qualifying event at the Molly Pitcher rest stop on the New Jersey Turnpike. In late June of 2003, she took a vacation day from her job as assistant manager of the Burger King at Andrews Air Force Base in Camp Springs, Maryland. Racing in just before the contest started, she ate eighteen hot dogs and buns in twelve minutes, handily beating a dozen guys twice her size. A month later, on the Fourth of July in Coney Island, Sonya upped her total to twenty-five dogs, setting a new women's record. In August, she won the Hardee's World Thickburger Eating Contest, knocking down seven twelve-ounce burgers in ten minutes. In September, she beat out top-ranked gurgitators Cookie Jarvis and Badlands Booker in chicken soft tacos, downing 43½ in eleven minutes. Despite her improbable dominance, Sonya claimed to reporters that her skills were all natural—she never trained.

"At a hundred pounds, she is living proof that competitive eating isn't just a big man's sport," Dave explains. "Just weeks ago, in front of thousands of screaming Godsmack fans in Indianapolis, she ate sixty-five hard-boiled eggs in under seven minutes, setting a new world record. She has been described as a cross between Billie Jean King, Anna Kournikova, and a wild jackal loose on the Serengeti. Ladies and gentlemen, say hello to the eater known as the Black Widow, Ms. Sonya Thomas!"

The sound guy cues the theme music—time for formal introductions. The sandwiches are brought out in trays of ten apiece. As we start announcing the local contestants, the crowd warms up immeasurably. The question is, do Jeff "the Stuffer" Stark, John "All Gone" Walker, Tim "the Tornado" Roberson, or Jimmy "Bring the Pain" Spain have what it takes to claim one of the top three spots? It will be an uphill battle, but perhaps the locals' experience with pulled-pork barbecue sandwiches will level the playing field. I announce that, just an hour before the competition, Sonya Thomas sampled a barbecue sandwich for the first time in her life, and this unfamiliarity may be to her disadvantage. After introducing the locals, it's time to call out the big guns.

"As an unknown rookie," Dave said. "This next contestant placed second in the conch-fritter-eating championship, eating forty-one fritters in six minutes. He is the current Florida hot-dog eating champion with nineteen hot dogs and buns in twelve minutes. Please welcome a chef from Hollywood, Florida, who stands six feet eight and weighs 280 pounds . . . Jammin' . . . Joe . . . LaRue!"

It's my turn. I look down at my notes at the list of names that Dale Boone has scribbled on my notepad. "Our next eater needs no introduction, because his mouth and his cowbell precede him. He is the pelmeni-eating champion of the world! He is the reindeer-sausage-eating champion of the world! He is an American icon and a gustatory pioneer who traces his roots back to Daniel Boone. Please welcome . . . the son of Otto Jack, the son of Hudson Daniel, son of James Andrew, son of Robert Nelson, son of James, son of Jeremiah, son of Thomas, son of Jonathan, who is the son of Daniel Boone! Give it up for Dale 'Mouth of the South' Boone!"

Dale makes his grand entrance, complete with bell-ringing, yee-hawing, and smack talk. Dave steps to the front of the stage. He explains the Sonya Thomas saga and rattles off her recent flurry of records. Then he puts his finger to his lips to convey the gravity of the moment. "Good people of Corinth, there is a century-old prophecy on the circuit, dismissed by some, that foretells the rise of the One Eater. Like Joan of Arc before her, this chosen eater would be female and slight of stature, but prodigious of appetite. We at the IFOCE believe that this next eater is the living fulfillment of that prophecy. Please put your hands together for The One . . . Ms. Sonya Thomassss!"

The crowd cheers, but almost hesitantly, as if this might be some sort of prank—a reality show where the joke's on them. We ask them to help us count down from ten, and the eating begins. Sonya, Dale, and Jammin' Joe all go with a dunking method from jump. The local eaters start with the purist approach, but after the first few minutes, they're following the pros' examples. Two minutes in, Boone and Sonya are neck and neck, jowl to jowl, with Jammin' Joe trailing not far behind. Three minutes in, I notice that two local eaters are right behind Jammin' Joe. While Dave calls out Sonya's steadily rising total—"Folks, that's nine sandwiches in just over three minutes!"—I focus on the local battle between Tim the Tornado and Stuffer Stark, both of whom have large fan blocs in the audience.

A little over seven minutes in, the eaters begin to hit the wall. I look over and see that something's happening to Dale. His face is glowing pink, and the beads of sweat dotting his forehead are turning into drips. His eating has slowed almost to a halt, and his eyes are getting wide. It's a disquieting sight to behold.

"Dale Boone seems to be showing signs of distress," I announce. "But there's no cause for concern—he's a professional. Dale suffers from the meat sweats, a lesser-known disorder in which protein enzymes mix with adrenaline to cause both delirium and an extremely malodorous form of sweat." I'm trying to comfort crowd members in the front few rows, who look concerned about the eruption of Mt. Boone. And to be honest, they have ample reason to be concerned. A notoriously reckless eater, Dale informed me before the contest that, for reasons unclear, he had agreed to perform a doughnut-eating exhibition on a Tupelo morning news show just hours before the contest. He ate twenty-five glazed doughnuts in a few minutes, a dubious game-day decision.

"Folks," Dave says, "it appears that Dale Boone has reached a breaking point but heroically chooses to eat on."

"That's right, Dave," I say. "And it is that very spirit of perseverance that carried his distant grandfather Daniel Boone through the hard-fought battles of the French and Indian War."

But Dale's stomach has its own agenda. He has stepped away from the table and is rocking back and forth in a self-comforting, cradlelike motion. Suddenly, he bolts upright and lurches forward.

His cheeks puff out, and he puts his hand over his mouth. The crowd gasps. Dale rushes to the back of the stage, jogs down the stairs, and embraces a huge industrial trashcan.

"Elvis has left the building!" Dave announces with gusto.

"It is known by many names on the competitive-eating circuit," I add. "Some call it the reversal of fortune, and to others it is known as a Roman incident . . . you may use the colloquial term *puking*."

"No matter what you call it," Dave chimes in, "it's against the rules. Dale Boone has been disqualified for an incident deemed contrary to the integrity of the sport."

The crowd whoops and hollers. Just as some hockey fans come for the fights, or NASCAR fans for the crashes, some competitive-eating fans apparently come for the vomit.

"An unfortunate turn of events," I say. "But where tragedy strikes, opportunity knocks. Two of your local eaters, Stuffer Stark and Tim the Tornado, are in a dead heat for the $250 third prize. Come on, folks . . . give it up for your local eaters!"

Now the crowd's totally into it. The drama between the two locals compensates nicely for Dale's absence and Sonya's dominance. To get a better look at her progress, I walk out to the front of the eating table. Less than a minute to go and she's chewing almost viciously, her stuffed cheeks all chipmunked out like Dizzy Gillespie's in mid-solo. The woman is insatiable. When the final whistle blows, she's eaten twenty-three sandwiches in ten minutes, setting a world record and winning $1,250 for her efforts. Dave hands her the ornately decorated barbecue belt, which, unsurprisingly, doesn't fit her tiny waist. When she raises it over her head, giggling like a schoolgirl, the crowd gives her a standing ovation.

Jammin' Joe LaRue is officially off the injured reserve list and will pocket $500 for his second place finish of sixteen sandwiches. A local lone wolf, Tim the Tornado Roberson, ekes out third place with eleven sandwiches, one sandwich ahead of Stuffer Stark.

After the competition, I pose for some photos with Sonya, whom I find legitimately awe-inspiring. Besides the shrapnel left at her spot

Sonya Thomas raises the coveted Barbecue Belt aloft for the crowd while Jammin' Joe LaRue looks on with envy.

at the table, no evidence remains that she just participated in an eating contest. Her makeup isn't smudged, her face and shirt are immac-
ulate, and she claims she's still hungry. In the background, I can hear
Dave speaking to a reporter. "If Sonya Thomas truly is the One," he
says, "then tonight marked yet another chapter in the fulfillment of
the prophecy."

Boone walks up, shaking his head shamefully. He complains that
his "incident" wasn't his fault—it was caused by the doughnut eat-off
he did earlier. When Dave reminds him that his participation in that
eat-off was entirely voluntary, he's indignant but fails to offer a compelling rebuttal.

An hour or so later, as I'm leaving Crossroads Arena, Sonya

Thomas approaches me, looking concerned. She explains that Dale Boone told her he wanted to check out the barbecue belt. She claims she handed Boone the belt and she hasn't seen him since. We call Boone. He's back at the hotel, and he's got the belt. "It was just a joke," he says, cackling like a fiend. "I'll give it back."

A few months after the barbecue contest, I ask Dale about what went down in Corinth. He explains that the morning news show coerced him into eating those doughnuts. They interviewed him briefly and then, before cutting to a commercial, coldcocked him out of nowhere with this on-air announcement: "And when we return, Dale Boone will perform a doughnut-eating exhibition."

As for the regurgitation, Dale says that was the result of his unquenchable desire for victory. Though his stomach capacity had been compromised by the doughnut exhibition, his competitive instincts would not let him settle for second place. "When I threw up there in Mississippi, it was point-blank. I was goin' for gold. There is no second in my name. My mind-set for the day was 'Go for gold or explode' . . . and I exploded."

This reckless strategy proves, time and again, to be Dale Boone's undoing. When it goes his way, he is capable of stunning upsets, such as his consecutive upsets in 2004 of Cookie Jarvis, Badlands Booker, and Sonya Thomas in the 84 Lumber World Baked Bean–Eating Championships. (In fact, one might assert that Dale's legacy on the circuit can be summed up in five words: best baked bean eater ever.) But when it goes the other way for Boone, it quite literally goes the other way.

As for the belt-snatching incident, Dale remembers a different version from Sonya. He claims she left the belt unattended in the stands when she went up to pick up her check. Dale says he grabbed the belt, not to steal it, but to hold it for safekeeping and see how long it would take for Sonya to miss it. "What I did was grabbed it for all of us. You know I'm part of the group. Just imagine had I not've grabbed it!"

5

A NOT-SO-BRIEF HISTORY OF COMPETITIVE EATING

Every investigation which is guided by principles of nature fixes its ultimate aim entirely on gratifying the stomach.

—Athenaeus, circa A.D. 200

Before the crowd in Mississippi, I had claimed that the history of competitive eating had started with cavemen battling over their prey. Afterward, a history buff who'd watched the contest interrogated me about the sport's *real* origins over an ice-cold Bud. I fumbled for words and spewed unconvincing half-truths. As a self-styled expert and amateur historian of competitive eating, I was troubled by my own ignorance. It was time to hit the history books.

Though there's scant record of timed events in early history, the pastime of eating to excess has been around since the ancient Romans. Perhaps the most memorable written description of a feast comes from the first-century Roman satire *Satyricon*. The author, Petronius, describes a banquet held by a former slave turned millionaire named Trimalchio, which featured wave after wave of such dishes as beefsteak, testicles and kidneys, sow's udder, lobster, bulls' eyes, and pastry eggs stuffed with garden warblers. At any point in the meal, stuffed guests were encouraged to use the vomitorium to make room for the next course.

Several hundred years later, a few notable British monarchs stepped up to the plate in a big way. In the late fourteenth century, Richard II threw a banquet for over ten thousand guests. The provisions included 14 oxen, 120 sheep, 12 boars, 3 tons of salted venison, 14 calves, 140 pigs, 50 swans, 210 geese, 1,200 pigeons, 720 hens, 100 gallons of milk, and 11,000 eggs. In Tudor times, the more a man weighed, the richer and more heroic he was perceived to be. By 1547, Henry VIII, a colorful chap with a penchant for beheading his wives, had grown so rich and heroic that he had to be carried from room to room by his servants.

But eating competitions as we now know them started in America. From its inception, America lured settlers with its vast landscape of near endless natural resources. Immigrants escaping poverty, religious oppression, or scourges like a potato famine in the mother country were soon celebrating freedom and plentitude in the brave new world. The new Americans zealously gobbled up land, food, and opportunity, but tried not to forget what they'd escaped. Thanksgiving, that annual day of showing gratitude for America's abundance, is arguably nothing more than a family-oriented, untimed, unsanctioned nationwide eating contest.

For over a hundred years, pie-eating contests have been as American as apple pie. By the beginning of the twentieth century, pie-eating contests had become as commonplace at fairs and carnivals as tugs-of-war, three-legged races, dunking tanks, judging livestock, potato-sack races, and the beloved challenge of climbing a greased pole. During World War I, regiments threw pie-eating contests to maintain morale and revel momentarily in their American-ness. As documented in the newspaper *Stars and Stripes,* these contests were held in bold defiance of the act of June 3, 1916, that said, "Enlisted men, Army bands and members thereof are forbidden from engaging in any competitive civilian employment." The contests resumed during World War II. A captivating photo in the Library of Congress shows a mountainside pie-eating contest held on July 4, 1945, by the Eighty-seventh Regiment of the Tenth Mountain Division in Caporetto, Italy. One of the contestants is a woman in a Red Cross uniform.

Early pie-eating contests emphasized fun over competition. The main point was to laugh at messy faces. Contestants were often required to keep their hands behind their backs to minimize cheating and maximize messiness. The contests were usually composed of kids, such as this description of a contest held during the seventh annual outing for the nine hundred employees of the Broadway Department Store of Los Angeles: "A dozen small boys entered the guzzling match, and when the signal was given, they buried themselves in blackberry pies. As pains began to gnaw at them, the young hopefuls gave up. But one lad, pluckier than his fellows, ate on and on. At last the $5 reward was flung to him."

The culinary spark that would ultimately set the competitive-eating world aflame would not be pies, but hot dogs. In 1874, a German immigrant named Charles Feltman invented the frankfurter-and-bun combo we know today as the hot dog. By the end of 1880, Felt-

An equal opportunity sport. Five Broadway show girls compete in an unsanctioned, no-hands "Spaghetti Swooshing" contest in 1948. *(Courtesy of Bettmann/CORBIS*

man owned the most successful German beer garden in Coney Island, the popularity of which was due largely to his ten-cent hot dogs. In the early 1900s, Jimmy Durante and Eddie Cantor, both entertainers at Feltman's Famous Restaurant, encouraged Nathan Handwerker, a Feltman's employee, to undersell his employer.

Thanks in part to his ability to eat hot dogs for free while on the job, Handwerker saved $300 and invested it into the rental of a building at the corner of Surf and Stillwell Avenues. He opened his own stand, Nathan's Famous, where he sold garlic-tinged sausages for five cents apiece. At first, customers, already dubious about what went into hot dogs, were suspicious of the low price. To counter this, Handwerker invited interns from Coney Island Hospital to eat for free, as long as they came dressed in their hospital whites. Some historians claim Handwerker even paid homeless men to shave, dress up in doctor's uniforms, and hang out around his stand. With the onset of Prohibition (which felled Feltman's) as well as the opening of the Stillwell Avenue subway stop in 1921, Nathan's Famous soon became known as Coney Island's Nickel Empire.

The history of the Nathan's Famous hot-dog-eating contest is stored inside the brain of George Shea, a gifted huckster, so some facts are difficult to verify. It is known, however, that Nathan Handwerker started the contest on July 4, 1916, as a vehicle to drum up publicity for his hot dog stand in the tradition of Coney Island sideshows. The format of the contest—a twelve-minute contest at noon on the Fourth of July—has remained largely unchanged over nearly a century. According to Shea, this format was meant to evoke "the patriotic epicenter of the year, in the patriotic geographical center of the nation, Coney Island, which is the seat of immigration and of course the location where the hot dog was created."

Legend has it that the world's first hot-dog-eating champion was a Brooklyn construction worker named Jim Mullin. On July 4, 1916, he ate ten hot dogs and buns in twelve minutes. Afterward he complained to Handwerker that he would have eaten more had the buns

Murray Handwerker   Nathan Handwerker   Ida Handwerker
Nathan's Famous Inc. of Coney Island circa 1922 with the Handwerker Family

The Handwerker family poses in front of the historic Nathan's Famous hot dog stand at the corner of Surf and Stilwell on Coney Island, circa 1922. Notice the price of a frankfurter in the upper right corner: five cents. *(Courtesy of Nathan's Famous, Inc.)*

not been stale. "Make no mistake, Mullin was a titanic figure," says George Shea. "To do what he did in the so-called Dead Dog Era was amazing. In the 1920s, people would say, 'I swear on the teeth of Jim Mullin,' when they wanted to make a vow."

Just weeks before the 2005 Nathan's Famous Hot Dog Eating Competition, a sideshow promoter named Dick Zigun found Jim Mullin's teeth on a construction site, preserved in an old seltzer bottle. The Shea brothers took the teeth—which were preserved in pickle juice—to forensic dentist Stephen Tympanick for analysis. Tympanick noticed that Mullin's incisor was lost early in his life and that his premolars were rotted to the core. Regardless, the Shea brothers intend to keep the teeth on exhibit at IFOCE headquarters. They hope that future competitive eaters will make pilgrimages and pay homage to the teeth, the competitive-eating equivalent of the Shroud of Turin.

The names of the contest's other early winners have been covered up by the sands of time. But in the 1930s, a prolonged grudge match between America's two most accomplished eaters—Stan Libnitz, from Flushing, Queens, and Andrew Rudman, from Brighton Beach, Brooklyn—began making national headlines. By 1938, sworn enemies Libnitz and Rudman had alternated victories at the Nathan's Famous contest for eight consecutive years. Before the 1938 contest, Rudman told the press it would be his last and would thus settle who was champion once and for all.

At the start of the contest, Libnitz, a sprinter, was characteristically quick out of the gate. Six minutes into the contest, he was two dogs ahead. Two minutes later, he was up three and a half. Then, just as the Coney Island crowd had all but conceded the title to Libnitz, he mysteriously stopped eating. As Rudman rallied to win by half of a dog, Libnitz could only manage to point—repeatedly and cryptically— at Rudman's elbow. After the contest, Libnitz complained that Rudman had elbowed him in the gut. But this being before the days of instant replay, the public discourse over the contest raged on unresolved. Libnitz demanded a rematch. Rudman agreed. But soon thereafter, Libnitz claimed his doctor told him he could not compete again without running the risk of a severe and chronic gastrointestinal disorder.

For years afterward, Libnitz claimed that this event was a turning point in his life. Eventually, he wrote about the fateful day in his autobiography, *Stan Libnitz: My Way* (Farrar, Straus & Giroux, 1949). The opening lines of this now out-of-print memoir convey just how important the Nathan's title was to Libnitz: "It was a black day for Coney Island, friends, and for this country. There are thousands of people in this city who know the truth, who know that on July Fourth, a most sacred day in this country, a horrible black deed was done, a horrible black deed against one countryman and one country's honor." Rudman denied any wrongdoing unto his death.

In the 1950s, a German woman named Gerta Hasselhoff— considered by some genealogists to be a distant relative of David Hasselhoff, the former *Baywatch* star—stunned the world by winning the Nathan's Famous title. Gerta's enemies soon demanded that her training method, which consisted largely of gorging on bratwurst and beer, be deemed illegal. Ultimately, the judges from Nathan's Famous ruled that her bratwurst/beer cross-training method was perfectly legal, and she is still hailed as the sport's first female champion.

For the first forty years of the contest, the thirteen-dog barrier remained unsurpassable. Some even speculated that thirteen Nathan's Famous hot dogs and buns marked the precise limit of the human stomach's storage capacity. But in 1959, a one-armed Brooklyn carnival worker named Peter Washburn ate eighteen and a half hot dogs and buns (or HDBs), shocking the world and silencing proponents of the thirteen-dog capacity theory.

From the mid-1960s into the 1970s, competitive eating, like the country's sociopolitical climate, became tainted by those who refused to play by the rules. Instead of using legitimate training techniques, unethical eaters began experimenting with illegal shortcuts. Cheating became so rampant that some techniques were given names. *Dropping the mule* became the term for placing a hot dog on the plate of either an accomplice or a rival. The *sleeper method* involved adding an extra paper plate to the stack (since the hot dogs are served five to a plate, and total dogs eaten are tallied in terms of empty plates).

Perhaps the most significant breakthrough for the organization of the sport came in 1972, when Nathan's Famous hired Coney Island press agent Max Rosey to represent the hot-dog-eating contest. Max Rosey had made his name in PR by pulling inventive stunts to gain media attention for his clients. He once put an elephant on a giant water ski in the Hudson River to promote an amusement park. Armed only with a dream of what competitive eating could be, he drew up an intricate set of rules and did not hesitate to punish eaters for minor infractions.

The 1990s, under the leadership of Rosey's protégé George Shea, became the watershed decade for competitive eating. In late May of

1990, while commuting from his New Jersey home to his job on Wall Street, a man named Mike DeVito saw an ad "twice the size of a postage stamp" in the *Daily News*. The ad sought out big eaters with an open schedule on July Fourth. It said that the previous year's champ, Jay Green, had eaten fourteen hot dogs, and if any eaters thought they could challenge that, they should call George Shea at the number listed.

DeVito called George. He said that, though he felt his prime eating years were behind him—he had been kicked out of a Ground Round for downing thirty-five chicken breasts during an all-you-can-eat special in college—fourteen hot dogs seemed manageable. On the Fourth, DeVito showed up at Schweikert's Alley in Coney Island and was stunned by the packed crowd and TV cameras. When he won the contest with fifteen HDBs, DeVito found the cameras focused on him. "You're just thrown into the limelight," DeVito remembers. "You're on the news. You're in Letterman's monologue. You're like, 'Oh my God. What did I do?' And then you become, like, obsessed. Now you want to win everything. You want to be in the limelight."

The next year, in 1991, DeVito returned to Coney Island wearing his game face, poised to break Peter Washburn's thirty-two-year-old record of seventeen dogs. But out of nowhere, Frank "Large" Dellarossa, a part-time Hofstra University football coach endowed with the girth typically associated with eating talent, put down twenty-one and a half dogs to shatter the record and rewrite the history books. To this day, "Twenty-one in '91!" is a commonly heard rallying cry by Coney Island diehards in search of a new American champ.

In '92, Dellarossa came back and beat DeVito again, nineteen HDBs to seventeen. DeVito left the contest convinced he would return to the winner's circle the following year. He was right. Dellarossa showed up at the 1993 contest, but only to announce his retirement from competitive eating and his decision to move to Hollywood to become an actor. Though he landed only a smattering of bit parts, the legend of Frank "Hollywood" Dellarossa has lived on.

DeVito won at Coney Island again in 1994. His closest competitor was a gargantuan up-and-comer who'd earned his chops on the White Castle circuit in Queens, Ed Krachie. DeVito "did the deuce"—twenty dogs and buns—while Krachie finished with eighteen. After the contest, DeVito donned the Mustard Yellow International Belt for the first time. The introduction of such a beautiful and exalted trophy gave gurgitators something tangible to set their sights on. Competitive eaters worldwide would soon covet the belt in much the same way that pro hockey players salivate for the Stanley Cup, or professional golfers for the cherished green jacket.

According to DeVito, 1994 also marked the year that dunking first occurred at Coney Island. Dunking started not as a speed-eating technique, but for a much more practical reason. "The hot dogs came out burning hot, and we couldn't eat them," DeVito remembers. After a few frantic seconds of pain, contestants started dunking the dogs to cool them down. But when the footage of the event showed up on the evening news, everyone assumed DeVito and the boys had discovered a new technique.

The next year, the DeVito-Krachie rivalry was built up in the New York press. "It was like the Holyfield-Tyson fight," DeVito remembers. This time, Ed Krachie beat DeVito by the slim margin of nineteen and a half to nineteen. The following year, Ed "the Animal" Krachie, noted for his wolflike style of mauling weenies, broke the American record by downing twenty-two. The new victor drew even more media interest, and TV Tokyo called George Shea again. They wanted to arrange a one-on-one showdown between Krachie and a Japanese eater named Hirofumi Nakajima.

The contest occurred on December 4, 1996, at a Nathan's Famous restaurant in midtown Manhattan. When Krachie, a 360-pound machismo-fueled guy's guy, saw the tiny Nakajima, he got cocky. Krachie berated his opponent to the press, poking fun at Nakajima's floral-pattern shirt and requesting a copy of the *Daily News* to read during the contest. As the contest got under way, a derisive chant of

"Noo-dle boy! Noo-dle boy!" rose up in the restaurant. Krachie pulled ahead early, but at the nine-minute mark, Nakajima blew past him. Though Krachie achieved a personal best and set a new American record of twenty-two and a half dogs, Nakajima took the $2,000 first prize and the belt with twenty-three and a quarter.

The press gobbled up both the story and its symbolism—little guy beats big guy, little Japan beats bloated America in a battle between two ravenously consumerist nations. On the next three Independence Days, Nakajima defended his title, the belt annually slipping off his tiny waist. Krachie protested that Nakajima was taking muscle relaxants to aid his swallowing, but the Shea brothers shrugged off the allegation. In 1997, Nakajima upped the world record to twenty-four and a half.

In early 1998, Krazy Kevin Lipsitz, fed up with losing to the Japanese, began pushing for a cross-species league. Having trained with his two dogs for years, Krazy Kevin thought he had found a way to shatter the Japanese stranglehold. "And in a way you can under-

Hirofumi Nakajima, flanked by then New York mayor Rudy Giuliani, raises the Mustard Yellow Belt at a weigh-in before the 1997 Nathan's Famous competition.

stand," Rich Shea explains. "Because Lipsitz never really had much success in the traditional contest. But his dogs were great eaters." The Shea brothers finally relented to Krazy Kevin's requests and approached the Nathan's Famous brass with his idea. "They wanted to move forward with it," George Shea remembers. "But with a man-cat contest instead. It broke Kevin's heart. He was very disappointed."

Steve Keiner briefly restored American predominance in 1999, dropping twenty and a quarter and beating Nakajima, but his victory sparked controversy. Runner-up "Hungry" Charles Hardy, who tied for second with twenty, complained that Keiner had started eating a fraction of a second before the starting gun was fired. George Shea admitted that video footage showed Keiner had jumped the gun, but ruled that replays weren't allowed.

In 2000, the Japanese swept first, second, and third, led by the hundred-pound Kazutoyo "the Rabbit" Arai, who set a new world record with twenty-five and one-eighth dogs and buns. Second place went to Misao Fujita, a pudgy banana-eating champ, and the legendary female meat-bun-eating champ Takako Akasaka took third. The Japanese Sweep, as it has become known, was such a devastating emasculation of the American eaters that journalists and fans could only cling to the hope that things could only get better.

No such luck. The most pivotal event in modern competitive-eating history occurred on July 4, 2001. On that day, twenty-three-year old Takeru "the Tsunami" Kobayashi of Nagano, Japan, ate fifty hot dogs and buns in twelve minutes, doubling Arai's record and sending shock waves through the American competitive-eating community. It's almost impossible to grasp the magnitude of this athletic feat. It eclipses even the most staggering of pro sports records, from Chamberlain's hundred-point game, Gretzky's ninety-two goals in a season, and Oscar Robertson's average of a triple-double over an entire season. By the eight-minute mark, most of Kobayashi's American rivals had stopped chewing to gawk at eating greatness in action. Never before had they seen such lupine voracity. Never before had they seen the Solomon Method, which involved breaking each dog and bun in half before eating them. *Fifty dogs and buns?* Never before had they imagined the bar could be set so impossibly high.

Kobayashi's triumphant victory in 2001 signaled the dawn of a new era in competitive eating. What had long been considered a publicity-driven sideshow now looked more like a sport. As Kobayashi continued to rack up perennial victories over the next four years, the circuit blossomed. The 2005 season will include over one hundred contests and nearly $200,000 in prize money. Extensive media coverage, including ESPN coverage of the Nathan's contest and the Alka-Seltzer U.S. Open of Competitive Eating (a thirty-two-eater single elimination tournament), will lead to over eight hundred million IFOCE media impressions in 2005. Most significantly, competitive eating has become part of American culture. While ten years ago few people had heard of it, these days, when the term "competitive eating" comes up, even the least tuned-in media consumers often say, "You mean like that little Asian guy that eats the hot dogs?"

That little guy's name is Kobayashi, and no American has ever beaten him. The only glimmer of mortality he has shown, in fact, was on July 4, 2002, when some hot dog slush allegedly spurted through his nose after the buzzer at the Nathan's contest. IFOCE commissioner Mike DeVito, however, ruled that none hit the table, and everyone agreed that it would have been a cheap concession of defeat. So the question still weighs heavily on the minds of the American gurgitators: When will the Mustard Yellow International Belt return to American shores, and who will be the champion to don it?

Many experts place our nation's competitive eating hopes on the narrow shoulders of Sonya Thomas. Rising stars such as Tim "Eater X" Janus and Joey Chestnut, a college student and waffle-eating champ from San Jose, California, also seem poised to carry the torch. But thanks to the egalitarian spirit of competitive eating, the next great American champ could be an anonymous nobody somewhere out there decimating an all-you-can-eat buffet. "There could be a great eater just sleeping out in Milwaukee that we don't even know about," Rich Shea says. His brother George agrees. "There are kids out there with innate talent. They may be sitting down to dinner right now. It's a magic that they don't understand. There is a Mozart of competitive eating who is yet to reveal himself."

6

THE MARDI GRAS
MANEUVER

No one's eaten crawfish jambalaya competitively yet. This is a world premiere at Lulu's, and you don't know what's gonna happen.

—Crazy Legs Conti, talking to a Reuters reporter
before the Jambalaya Eating Championship

FEBRUARY 24, 2004

To maximize press coverage, Al Chadsey, the organizer of the Jambalaya Eating Championship at Lulu's Club Mardi Gras in Washington, D.C, has chosen a unique format for the contest. Instead of staging one timed contest, Al and Dave Baer have decided to hold two one-minute qualifying rounds during the day, to determine the field of eaters for the championship ten-minute event that night. Because of this labor-intensive format, Dave has brought me along to help with the details.

The details, I soon discover, involve orchestrating the preparation of copious amounts of crawfish jambalaya. I spend the hour before the contest in the kitchen, inappropriately dressed in a suit and tie, weighing one-pound bowls of jambalaya and jabbering with a jovial chef from France.

As I bring out the last tray of jambalaya, I'm confronted by none other than Dale Boone. Wearing his trademark overalls over an Atlanta Falcons jersey, but without the coonskin cap to cover his bald pate, Dale has a glimmer in his eyes. He says he wants to meet the chef. I lead him to the kitchen, only to realize Dale's not interested in making friends. Instead, he grabs a serving spoon the size of a garden tool and asks to borrow it.

As we walk from the kitchen, Dale stops me for a powwow. This is his chance to beat Sonya Thomas, he says, shaking the spoon for emphasis. He's a sprinter; he can take Sonya in a one-minute contest. The spoon is integral to this scheme, his means to a glorious upset. For some reason, this plan strikes me as perfectly reasonable. No matter that it's just a one-minute qualifier, or that winning it would result in neither prize money nor much lasting prestige on the circuit. I give Dale the go-ahead. Why sabotage such a simple dream?

One thing I appreciate about Dale is that he is one of the few eaters who has fully embraced the WWF element of character development. The cowbell, the yee-haws, the smack talk—they make the emcee's job easier and add to the overall entertainment product. I like that he's willing to exploit regional loyalties to curry favor with the crowd, and that he's willing, on occasion, to play the villain and taunt the crowd. He might be bit of a loose cannon, but I enjoy the Dale Boone Show. If this show includes the use of an oversized spoon, so be it.

We return to the stage at the front of the bar, where the competitive-eating tables are set up. It's four in the afternoon on a Tuesday in late February, but it's Fat Tuesday of Mardi Gras fame, so already the place is beginning to fill up with office runaways and college kids wearing beaded necklaces. There are a handful of reporters and cameramen, but in general, it's a low-key affair. It is a testament to how polarized events on the circuit are that just three weeks ago, twenty thousand screaming fans were cheering Sonya Thomas to a Wing Bowl victory at Philadelphia's Wachovia Center, and now she's doing a one-minute qualifier in a bar. So goes life on the circuit.

Sonya Thomas displays her preternatural
cheek capacity en route to setting the new
world record of nine pounds of crawfish
jambalaya in ten minutes. *(Courtesy of
Matt Roberts/IFOCE)*

I start setting up the competition—three bowls of jambalaya and
a glass of water per contestant. Dave Baer warms up the audience.
"We are setting up the jambalaya, a food that will require both dexterity and capacity. Tonight, another chapter in the illustrious blos-
soming history of Sonya Thomas will be written."

The eaters mill around, stretching and talking to each other.
Sonya smiles radiantly, her silky black hair back in a ponytail, intense
eyes highlighted by lavender eye shadow, clad in jeans, platform
shoes, and a silkscreen T-shirt that reads SONYA THOMAS—THE BLACK

WIDOW OF THE IFOCE. Stu Birdie, a fringe member and moderately acclaimed fan/eater on the circuit, is still wearing his Southwest Airlines uniform, having just come from work. Crazy Legs Conti is decked out in his standard outfit, a personalized version of the modern dandy: a tall black top hat with red dreadlocks peeking out, a blue, ruffled tuxedo shirt, and the ever-present shorts. A resident of New York City's East Village, Crazy Legs' dashing getup seems an apt representation of his nongurgitating résumé. He has worked as a nude model, a sperm donor, a filmmaker, a line cook, and a window washer.

Dave calls out the locals first, including Eddie DiSabatino, a big-boned government contractor named Laurie Randall, and a small, intense character known as Frank "the Liz" Lizbinski. Then he announces Crazy Legs. "A Johns Hopkins University graduate, a writer, and a competitive eater . . . he is the lumberjack-breakfast-eating champ and the former oyster-eating champion, a title he hopes to regain at the French Quarter Festival in three weeks. He is the reigning sourdough-pancake-eating champion with four pounds of pancakes in eight minutes. Ladies and gentlemen, he is Crazy . . . Legs . . . Conti!" The crowd, now lining the bar's New Orleans–esque staircase and balcony, shout out their approval. One fan, however, shouts a slightly more existential response: "Why? Why?"

"This next eater really needs no introduction," Dave says. "Folks, you've heard the stories, the ups and downs. If there is a John Daly of the competitive-eating circuit, his name is Dale Boone." Dale rings not one but *two* cowbells and mugs directly into the Reuters camera. "I'm comin' at you, Black Widow. I'm comin' atcha!" Dave starts to rattle off Dale's stats, but soon gives up and hands Dale the mic, knowing his penchant for addressing the crowd. Dale grabs it and looks directly at Sonya. "You are about to receive an American butt-whoopin' like you've never seen! Black Widow, your day has come, because the big bear is out of hibernation!"

Sonya just laughs, not unnerved in the slightest.

"Save it for the table, Dale," Dave says, taking back the micro-phone.

"Steroids!" a glassy-eyed fan yells out, pointing at Dale. "That's tampering, right there! Him and Barry Bonds."

"Ladies and gentleman, our final eater, and the one you have come here today to see, making her debut in her adopted hometown of Washington, D.C. . . ." As Dave starts reading off Sonya's accolades, the loud shouts from the increasingly lubricated crowd nearly drown out his voice. With the combination of her impossibly slight stature, beauty, underestimated-gender status, and unshakable friendliness, Sonya is, per usual, the overwhelming crowd favorite.

As she walks to her space at the center of the table, I notice Sonya is carrying her own, slightly oversized spoon. She walks past Dale, and he gestures to her chair in a mock-gentlemanly manner. When she sits down, Dale picks a smaller spoon off the table and offers it to Sonya. "Need this?" "Maybe," Sonya answers, putting it back down on the table. Then, with a dramatic flourish, Dale takes the small spoon provided to him, shows it to the crowd, and drops it contemptuously on the table. They have no idea what this means.

As Dave counts down from ten, Dale pulls out the giant serving spoon from beneath the flap in his overalls and smacks it three times against the table. At this point, a vague dread creeps over me. This spoon issue is taking on a life of its own, as things sometimes will with Dale Boone.

When the countdown ends, Dale starts shoveling mounds of jambalaya into his mouth with aggressive, almost superhuman strokes. "Dale Boone is muscling his way through his first bowl with a mammoth-sized spoon," says Dave. "Sonya Thomas is pacing herself. Clearly the overall championship is more important to her than this one-minute qualifying event. Crazy Legs Conti holding his own, rifling down the jambalaya."

In no time, the crowd is helping Dave count down the final seconds. As Dave calls out, "Stop eating!" Dale pushes the last bit of rice into his mouth and pounds the table. He stands over Sonya, staring down at the back of her head, his hands raised victoriously as if to say, "I own you." Looking composed, Dale chews casually and paces the back of the stage, his stomach puffed with pride. In the rafters, the fans start chanting, "Son-ya! Son-ya! Son-ya!"

But wait. It looks as if maybe Dale *has* beaten Sonya. Of course, it's immaterial in a one-minute qualifier in which the top five make the cut, but still. I sigh, happy to see the contest come to an uneventful close. But my relief is premature. A young woman in the crowd spots it first. She points at Dale and shrieks as if she's witnessed an assassination. "Ahh! He's barfing!" *Oh, no.* I look at Dale. He has his hands over his mouth. Then he spits into his hand and throws it over his shoulder, as if that might conceal it. He makes a few panicky hand gestures, then reaches out to Crazy Legs for help. Crazy Legs tries to half-support him without getting too close to the volcano. "Help!" Dale says, gesturing to the EMT.

"This is no longer fun," someone in the crowd calls out, laughing.

On the circuit, it is understood that if you are about to suffer a reversal, you get away from the table, away from the cameras and the fans. Having lost all presence of mind, Dale forgets this maxim. He regurgitates twice on the table, then asks again for the EMT. The EMT, a frail college student less than half Dale's size who's been off in the corner joking with his buddies, hurries to the stage. Meanwhile, Crazy Legs, always nimble-minded, walks over to block the vision of the Reuters camera. I just stand there, mouth agape, clueless and numb. "Ready?" the EMT asks, his arms barely fitting around the circumference of Dale's belly. "Yeah," Dale says. After the first Heimlich maneuver, which dislodges no visible jambalaya, Dale asks for another.

"Ladies and gentleman," Dave announces, "Dale has requested a second Heimlich, just to fully clear the pipe."

After the second Heimlich, which again has no visible effect, Dale simmers down and Lulu's Club Mardi Gras emits a collective sigh of relief. Without hesitation, Dave tells Dale he's disqualified.

"Why?" Dale asks.

"You know why."

Afterward, Dave tells me we've just witnessed the first-ever Heimlich on the IFOCE circuit—not exactly the kind of competitive-eating history I want to be associated with. "That huge spoon didn't help anything," Dave says. I confess that I had a hand in Dale's procurement of the spoon, and Dave scolds me for my negligence. I deserve it. I feel like a moron and vow to never be nonchalant about matters of safety again.

Yet, I feel slightly indignant because, in my opinion, the Heimlich was unnecessary. Why? Because it's common knowledge that if you can ask for the Heimlich, then you don't need it because your windpipe isn't actually clogged. I know this from experience, having choked on a poorly chewed piece of steak as a kid. (After I frantically pounded on the table, my father saved me with a swift and confidently executed Heimlich maneuver.)

Now, this isn't to say that Dale wasn't feeling gastrointestinal discomfort. Shoveling down two pounds of spicy, rice-filled jambalaya in a minute almost guarantees choking or intense heartburn or something. But what if Dale had *really* choked? Would that skinny EMT have been up to the task? If something serious had happened to Dale, would I have been partially liable? It's a daunting possibility, one I'd rather not focus on. I am forced to recognize that competitive eating is potentially dangerous, that one instance of choking could result not only in tragedy, but in the demise of competitive eating as we know it. It is a fear shared by many in the competitive-eating community, and Dale's mishap has driven the point home in a tangible way. Perhaps it's no longer responsible for me to think of this job as the fulfillment of my long-awaited dream—that of getting paid to play.

7
ED KRACHIE AND THE
BELT OF FAT THEORY

I'm surprised there aren't more fat people in it. My vision of an eat-
ing contest is some Homer Simpson–type guy just plowing through.

—Spectator John Lisi, after witnessing
the 2003 Stagg Chili-Eating Contest

After Sonya Thomas won the final round of the Jambalaya Eating Championship by eating a staggering nine pounds in ten minutes—a 10 percent weight gain—a reporter asked me a question I would soon become very accustomed to answering: How can such a tiny person eat so much?

It's a question that has been plaguing American competitive eaters for nearly a decade, ever since the 135-pound Hirofumi Nakajima beat a man three times his size in hot dogs in December of 1996. With the subsequent appearance of Kazutoyo Arai, Takeru Kobayashi, and Sonya Thomas, the question resonates even louder now, at the dawn of the new millennium. The logic we have always taken for granted—that fat people can eat more than skinny people— can officially be stricken from the scientific record. But why . . . *why?*

In November 2003, *Popular Science* finally addressed the question, in an article that shocked scientists and competitive eaters worldwide. Though it did not fully account for the dominance of smaller eaters in the sport of competitive eating, the theory shed some light on clear physiological advantage. Perhaps most stunning about this revolutionary theory was that it was not posited by some ambitious grad student, or by a doctor from Harvard Med, but by a former American hot-dog-eating champion from Queens.

To grasp the origins of the Belt of Fat Theory, one must examine the life and eating career of its creator, Ed Krachie. In the documentary *Red, White, and Yellow,* Krachie's mother claims that he was an eating prodigy from day one: In kindergarten, he regularly polished off an entire box of cereal and a couple of bananas at breakfast. If ever there was a natural on the American competitive-eating circuit, it was Ed "the Animal" Krachie.

Krachie grew up in Maspeth, Queens, where he attended Grover Cleveland High School. After graduation, he stayed in Maspeth and tried to kick-start a career. He briefly attended college and was considering a life in law enforcement like his dad, but could never quite commit. To make some cash while he got his bearings, Ed took a job repossessing cars in some of New York's shadier neighborhoods. Ed's intimidating physique—he's six feet seven inches and well over three hundred pounds—combined with his boss's "psycho ex-cop" mentality was a recipe for success in the repo business. They ran a minimonopoly casing out neighborhoods where other repo guys feared to tread.

When he wasn't working, Ed was hitting the town with his boys. He ran with a group of twenty to thirty drinking buddies that could be found at one of the regular Queens watering holes on any given night. While barhopping, Krachie's buddies started noticing that, on certain nights, bars held eating contests for cash prizes. Krachie entered a few and won. Because Krachie's insatiable appetite was already the stuff of local legend, his friends took it upon themselves to spread the word. They went on reconnaissance missions and found new contests. "Inevitably, twenty guys would get together and we'd go," Ed remembers. "And I'd win, and then I'd have drinkin' money for the night." Though most of these eating exploits have fallen into the sinkhole of history, one notable record remains—thirty-seven White Castle hamburgers in ten minutes.

Every year, on the Fourth of July, the topic of the Nathan's Famous contest would arise. Ed and his friends would see the results on the local news in some bar, or someone would call him up: "Ed, did you see that, man? That guy only ate thirteen!" Ed wanted to get into the contest, but had no idea whom to contact—there was no IFOCE at that point. John Schneider, one of Ed's closest friends, remained obsessed with getting him into the event. He would call each year in July, only to be told by Nathan's headquarters to call back at the first of year—and each year, he'd forget.

In 1994, John remembered. After a few phone calls, he contacted George Shea. Because there was no qualifying series at that point, George asked for Ed's eating credentials. When John described Ed's size and his myriad victories in unsanctioned Queens eating contests, George gave him the nod.

On July 4, 1994, Krachie made his auspicious debut, narrowly losing to Mike DeVito, with eighteen HDBs to DeVito's twenty. It was the beginning of a long friendship between the two fierce competitors. The older DeVito would serve as a wise mentor to Krachie, a sort of competitive-eating Jedi master.

The first lesson Krachie learned from his defeat was about last-second stuffing. Up to the final seconds, Krachie and DeVito had been neck and neck, but while Krachie continued to exhaustedly nibble at his final dog, DeVito took a few quick bites and then stuffed an entire dog into his mouth. While DeVito spent the next minute or so masticating, Krachie slumped in empty-mouthed defeat.

He had a whole year to marinate on his loss, because the Fourth of July competition was, at that time, the only one around. Fortunately, Ed's friends had caught the competition on video, so he was able to review it and fine-tune his skills. He vowed that he would not lose the Mustard Yellow International Belt again due to sloppy technique.

On Independence Day of 1995, Ed Krachie and his pit crew of supporters didn't leave anything to chance. He rolled in about fifty deep—friends, extended family, and a girlfriend. Two of his best friends stationed themselves just past the media barrier on either side of Ed. As the contest wore on, they'd shout tidbits and updates, like "Mike's got sixteen. You've got seventeen. Speed it up!" When the twelve minutes expired, Krachie had fulfilled his destiny. Final tally: DeVito, nineteen Krachie, nineteen and a half.

His life would never be the same. The next morning, at around 4:00 A.M., the phone rang. "Are you Ed Krachie who won the hot-dog-eating contest?" a woman said in a British accent. "We'd like to interview you for BBC radio." By 6:00 A.M., he began fielding a steady stream of phone calls from wacky morning-zoo radio shows across the country. Ed's buddies brought over breakfast and beer, and the party started up again, with Ed intermittently taking interviews. "It was the beginning of a wonderful thing for me," Ed says. "But then there was also a loss of privacy."

As the 1996 competition approached, Ed began to worry about his prospects for a repeat performance. He had taken a job as an apprentice to a mechanical engineer and had realized the job required increased mobility. By watching his calorie intake and working out like a madman, he had lost eighty-five pounds . . . which was great from a health and vanity standpoint, but would he still be able to put the dogs down?

A week and a half before the big show, Ed conducted an exhibition round to check his capacity. He cooked up twenty dogs and shared them with his five-year-old niece, who was delighted by her uncle's eating display. In the end, he put fifteen down easily, with room for more. His goal, he decided, was not just to win, but to break Frank Dellarossa's five-year-old record of twenty-one and a half dogs.

The competition went much the way it had the year before. As the clock ticked down, with the Coney Island faithful on their tiptoes, Ed pushed ahead of DeVito by a dog and a half, then two. The first one to notice history being made, in fact, was DeVito, who was then three dogs down and willing to concede defeat. With thirty seconds left, he got George Shea's attention and, through a stuffed mouth, said, "Record!" George realized and immediately cried out to the crowd, "Ed Krachie is about to break the world hot-dog-eating record, folks!"

"And that's when all hell broke loose," Krachie says.

For the next few days, reporters besieged Krachie. At 10:00 A.M. the next morning, while taking the same morning-show calls from the year before, a photojournalist from the New York *Daily News* knocked at his door. The idea was to do a piece called "A Day in the Life of the Hot Dog King." The reporter followed Ed and his girlfriend around as they went shopping and did errands. The article included information from a nutritionist, who determined that Ed had eaten three weeks' worth of sodium and fat, and nearly three and a half days' worth of calories. The *Daily News* ran the story the next day on the third page. "Must've been a slow news day," Ed offered humbly.

The publicity kept coming. Ed, a John Goodman look-alike with a physical magnitude that's hard to miss, was frequently stopped by fans in Queens. Many media outlets saw Ed, a self-described "beer-drinkin', hardworkin', blue-collar American kind of guy," as a character the masses would relate to. He started getting booked on the talk show circuit—Ricki Lake, Sally Jessy Raphael, and Howie Mandel. At the enormous Manhattan-based telephone company near where Krachie worked, NYNEX, he became an in-house celebrity. During a welcome party for a new member of the board of directors, the company's CEO proudly paraded in the new hot dog champ for an introduction.

A few months after he broke the hot dog record, Krachie got a call at work from TV Tokyo. A producer from the network proposed a showdown between Krachie and a young Japanese eater, a skinny little guy who had allegedly never eaten hot dogs before. The segment would appear as part of a New Year's Eve special on Japanese TV. The prize would be $2,000 for first place, and $500 for second. Was Krachie interested?

He was. The contest took place on December 4, 1996, at a Nathan's Famous restaurant across from the Empire State Building. When Ed Krachie saw Hirofumi Nakajima, his confidence soared. The kid was tiny, smiley, harmless-looking. Though Krachie was generally considered humble, he had also become known for bouts of crowd-pleasing brashness. (In a Nathan's Famous qualifier the year before, Krachie had sat out the first half of the competition. He started eating at the six-minute mark and, despite the handicap, inhaled sixteen dogs for a decisive win.) Before the showdown with Nakajima, Ed asked a New York *Daily News* photographer for a copy of the newspaper. "This is gonna be boring," he said. "I think I wanna read the newspaper while I'm eating."

He never got the chance. The skinny kid, it turned out, was a ringer. Nakajima ate twenty-three and a quarter, surpassing Krachie by one and a quarter dogs and setting a new world record. While onlookers gaped in amazement, Krachie shook his head in shame. He felt he'd been duped. The producers' claim that Nakajima had never eaten dogs before was not so much true as *not true*. "I mean, I'm not a naïve New Yorker, but I took them at their word . . . ," Krachie says. "Sure enough, this guy shows up and not only had he eaten hot dogs before, but he was the reigning Japanese champion. And I really felt like it was another Pearl Harbor."

The stage was set for a Fourth of July showdown. As the big day approached, Krachie's friends encouraged him to roll up to Coney Island in a limousine to psych up the American fans and psych Nakajima out. But Krachie declined. "That's where I drew the line. I told them, 'Listen, I'm the people's champ, man.' "

The people's champ, known for his uninhibited, almost animalistic style of attacking wieners, was dethroned again by Nakajima, the methodical assassin. Using the revolutionary method of eating dog and bun separately, Nakajima broke his own record, eating twenty-four and a half. Adding insult to injury, another Japanese eater, Kazu-toyo "the Rabbit" Arai, took second with twenty-four. After the competition, Nakajima, a twenty-two-year-old, soft-spoken furniture deliveryman from Kofu, Japan, refused to reveal details about his training and tactics, offering only, "You have to concentrate."

In the wake of a devastating third-place finish with twenty dogs and buns, Krachie seemed bewildered. "I don't know where they put it," he said. "Both of those guys put together weigh less than me." Spurred on by a vocal, pro-Krachie crowd, Ed had kept pace with the Japanese challengers early on, but at the nine-minute mark Krachie had slammed face-first into that insuperable obstacle known as the wall, and his chewing ground to a near halt. Afterward, the thirty-four-year-old American champion was so dejected that he announced his retirement. The mighty Krachie had struck out, and there would be no extra innings.

It didn't hit him all at once. In the weeks and months after July 4, 1997, what began as a thought slowly crystallized into a theory. Ed Krachie, now a licensed engineer and blessed with a keenly analytical brain, began researching an insight into human physiology that would change the sport of competitive eating.

While many in the American competitive-eating community were biased by paranoia and even racism, Krachie tried to remain objective. It would prove difficult, especially since Krachie's friends had their own conspiracy theories. Some speculated that high rice consumption led to increased stomach capacity. Immediately after the competition, one friend, having downed a few too many beers, spotted a suspicious wire and decided to lift up Nakajima's T-shirt. It turned out to be a TV Tokyo microphone wire.

Then, a few months after the competition, Krachie claims he received an anonymous call from a man claiming to be a doctor. "Listen, I'd rather not give you my name," the man said, "but this guy might be taking drugs to stop him from regurgitating." The doctor went on to describe a muscle relaxant that could suppress the muscles that contract during regurgitation.

Krachie wasn't convinced by such convenient explanations. There had to be some natural explanation for Nakajima's abilities. Ed thought back to his own record-breaking win at Coney Island and remembered how trim he had been. Was it possible that skinny people actually had an advantage in eating competitions? What if, hypothetically, having a gut restricts one's stomach capacity?

Krachie talked to doctors, surfed the Internet, and bought a slew of medical encyclopedias. His research seemed to confirm his hypothesis. The adipose tissue of which a belly is composed lies between the abdomen and the skin. This belt of fat, known colloquially as the gut, pushes directly against the stomach, especially when it is distended. With this in mind, might excess belly fat weigh down the stomach muscle, inhibiting its ability to expand? What if—again, hypothetically—Nakajima had once weighed three hundred pounds himself, then went on a diet? Could he maintain a big man's stomach capacity within a small man's frame?

A steadily forming thesis crackled in Krachie's brain. He called George Shea, who received the theory enthusiastically. Shea suggested they submit it to scientific journals, including the prestigious *New England Journal of Medicine*. They worded the theory in the proper format and submitted it. Then they threw a rollout party to celebrate the public unveiling of the Belt of Fat Theory.

Ultimately, though, while a few New York newspapers covered their attempt to make science history, no journals accepted the thesis for publication. Krachie remembers the rejection letters with dismay. "They said, 'While it might be very valid in your sport—and it sounds steady—your theory really doesn't have real-world medicinal value. It's not something the medical community can use.'"

. . .

In the spring of 2000, Krachie received another call from TV Tokyo. The producer said he wanted to fly Ed to Japan for another New Year's Eve segment. This time, the event would be a "triathlon of eating," in which Ed would attempt to break three records in one day, in three different cities—ramen noodles in Kobe, Japanese pizza in Osaka, and shabu-shabu in Tokyo. While the free travel and healthy stipend sounded enticing, the sheer amount of food was staggering. He would have to consume fifteen pounds of food in less than twenty-four hours.

Were he not familiar with the extreme nature of Japanese fringe sports, Krachie would have been suspicious of TV Tokyo's motives. Eating fifteen pounds of food in a day, on top of travel and jet lag—it seemed a laughable proposition, but Krachie had seen excerpts from a Japanese TV show that illustrated just how sadomasochistic their entertainment could be. One segment involved two men lying on a metallic rooflike surface in the hot sun, wearing nothing but underwear. The roof tilted back and forth at increasingly extreme angles, and the men slid back and forth, burning off layers of skin. He who didn't fall off the roof or scream out for relief was declared the winner.

After weighing the pros and cons of the eating triathlon, Krachie decided the travel and cash would be worth the punishment. In exchange for his compliance, Krachie was treated like royalty. He and George Shea flew first-class to Kobe. When they arrived at the airport, they were so spent that Krachie told George he wasn't sure he could handle waiting in the customs line. At that point, a police officer jogged up to Krachie. "Hot darg man! Hot darg man!" the excited officer yelled out. Within seconds, Krachie was surrounded by jabbering well-wishers and autograph seekers.

A band of policemen escorted Krachie to a line marked VIP. After a genial chat with the customs official, Krachie entered the main terminal to find several dozen Japanese fans awaiting his arrival. Cameras flashed. Autographs were signed. Krachie, unaware that he was big in Japan, was stunned. Just as he began to fret that the mob would start tearing his clothes for souvenirs, a driver emerged from the crowd and whisked him away to a waiting limousine.

The next day was consumed by production meetings, sightseeing, and a fabulous sushi dinner. At around 6:00 A.M. the next morning, George and Ed were driven to a restaurant so small it could be a corner deli back in Queens. Ed was directed to sit at what looked like an old-fashioned soda fountain counter. The chef was directly across from him, boiling ramen noodles and adding them to the broth, then doling them out in half-pound servings. The goal was to eat six servings, or three pounds, in less than a half hour. The record stood at twenty-two minutes.

The clock started, and Ed slurped down his first few noodles. They were so hot they burned the roof of his mouth. He requested a glass of ice water. On the next bite, he twirled a swirl of noodles on his fork as if it were pasta. He dunked it in the cold water, sucked it down. The crowd oohed and aahed at the crafty American—it was a technique they'd never seen before.

Soon Ed was chasing the record. One half-pound serving to go, and he was just starting to feel full. The shouts of fans, camera crew, and wait staff transformed the shoebox restaurant into an echoing micro-stadium. "Come on, Ed!" George Shea urged. "You got this record!" Dunk, slurp, dunk, slurp. Ed was feeling it. This was why they called him the Animal, because he came up with a plan and executed the foodstuff. He ate one last forkful, lifted the bowl, and drank the broth. The clock stopped, and the place filled with cheers. Elapsed time: 12 minutes, 53 seconds. In Ed's words: "Totally annihilated the fuckin' record. So they're thinking . . . We got *the man* here!"

More pictures, more autographs. The owner framed Ed's picture and placed it on the wall next to the three Japanese eaters who had broken the record before. They drove to the airport, flew to Osaka, and checked into a five-star hotel. Krachie made a few phone calls, showered, and it was off to the next event at another hole-in-the-wall restaurant, with a six-foot-high door that Ed had to duck to get through. The place was famous for a type of Japanese pizza that doubtless wouldn't go over in the States—its toppings include cabbage and fish, and instead of baking it, they fry it into patties. Each pizza patty weighs four pounds, and Krachie was obliged to eat two pizzas in two hours.

Ed's reaction to the first bite was utter revulsion. "I'm like, 'Oh my God. What is this shit?' It's terrible. I mean, I can't believe this is a fast food here, and I can't even stomach it." He threw salt and pepper on it, then requested Tabasco. Still, Krachie couldn't hide his disgust. Ten minutes into the eating, the announcer, a talk show host roughly equivalent in Japan to Dave Letterman, said aloud to Ed, "You're insulting the chef!" *Uh-oh.* Even the dullest of dolts knows better than to insult a Japanese chef. "Just tell him I like the food spicy," Ed told the announcer. "I like it real hot."

Ed knocked one pizza down in an hour, but the repulsive flavor, combined with the gaseous effects of the cabbage, was almost too much to handle. He stepped away from the table, telling George he needed a ten-minute break. The cameras shut off, but the clock kept ticking. Part of the deal was that he could not, during the allotted two hours, use the bathroom.

With fifty minutes remaining, he started on the second pizza. Were it a four-pound Sicilian pizza or a flaky-crusted apple pie, well, no problem—but all this fried fish and cabbage was really getting to him. He ate a half pie in a half hour before the pain really set in. Ed's innards roiled and churned, audibly protesting this unnecessary punishment. He ate on, but each bite took its toll. Finally, only four forkfuls left. *I just gotta get these down,* Ed told himself. *And then I can run to the bathroom.* He ate three forkfuls in what felt like protracted, make-believe time. Less than a minute left. As he lifted the final forkful to his mouth, teetering on the precipice between victory and defeat, Ed exploded.

And *explode* was the operative term here. Eleven pounds of noodles, cabbage, dough, and fish reemerged in a much less pleasant form. The projectile fountain covered the food, the announcer, the cameraman, and the chef. It was everywhere. Usually, before one regurgitates, the body issues some sort of warning, but Ed swears there was none. "I guess there was so much in there that it didn't have time to warn me." He told George he had to go to the bathroom. *Now.*

Once locked in the bathroom, Ed's suspicions were confirmed: When he exploded, it came out in all directions. He took off his clothes and was relieved to see that the mess below was pretty much contained. He cleaned himself up. There was a glut of paper towels, but for reasons unclear, no garbage pail. And there was the matter of his soiled Skivvies, which could neither be worn nor kept as a souvenir. Anyone would agree that this was a real dilemma.

Ed surveyed the bathroom and spotted an opportunity. The bathroom ceiling was one of those drop ceilings, with panels. He wrapped the evidence in a nest of paper towels, stood on the toilet, pushed a tile up, and hid the bundle up above the tile. "I'm a crude American, I guess," Ed explains later, laughing. "What can I tell you? I didn't know what to do."

And so, in the end, Ed Krachie unintentionally exacted his revenge on the Japanese. They had duped him into eating against a champion and lured him to their country to perform an inhuman feat, but it was he who got the last laugh. Indeed, he stashed a crap-laden diaper in a restaurant infrastructure in Osaka, where, God willing, it still rests today. Though he did not continue on to the last leg of his journey, to Tokyo, he also was not forced to stuff down another obscene portion of food. Interestingly, though Japanese television producers have deemed footage of naked men burning their skin while sliding across hot metal acceptable, they apparently have no appetite for vomit. So regrettably, the most compelling footage from Ed's eating biathlon remained on the cutting room floor.

.   .   .

Ed Krachie's on a diet. He's lost thirty-four pounds in three months, and not from Atkins or that silly South Beach diet. "None of those fuckin' diets work," Ed says. "I realize I'm probably one of those guys with the fat gene, so I have to figure out what works for me." His formula is no pioneering breakthrough—he works out daily and eats light.

Krachie doesn't compete much these days. He's still proud of his accomplishments, but he admits that his ultimate flaw is that he's unwilling to train. The contests were only fun when he was the Natural, the big, loud guy from Queens who just showed up and won. He occasionally competes in local unsanctioned events, such as the benefit he did in the summer of 2004 for the Joe DiMaggio Children's Hospital near his home in Hollywood, Florida. He was so touched by the kids' bravery that he has started volunteering there.

That's not to say he's out of the game. There have been job offers that would bring him back to New York, his hometown and the hub of the sport. Instead of competing this time, Ed has visions of becoming a "player liaison" for the American eaters. He's convinced the Americans need to go in a different direction if they are ever to have a chance at Kobayashi. "I think we really need to maybe set up a *camp,* if you will, like at George's little conference room at the IFOCE." A primary goal of the camp would be to study Kobayashi and figure out what it is about his technique and his body that makes him so unbeatable. "Being an engineer, maybe that's a process for me to work on. But physically and mentally, I don't wanna be the guinea pig."

Krachie's scientific breakthrough, the Belt of Fat Theory, has already made a huge impact on the sport. In the November 2003 issue of *Popular Science,* the theory was finally published. "The size of the stomach at rest is inconsequential," the article states. "All that matters is the stomach's ability to expand, to adapt itself to the amount of food being shoved down the esophagus. . . . A skinny man's stomach has little fat to push against it and fight the food for space." In the ultimate cruel twist of fate, the article failed to mention Krachie as the theory's progenitor.

Does Ed feel vindicated, now that his theory's been published and the top three eaters in the world—all of whom weigh under 155 pounds—seem to be living proof of its validity? Somewhat, but he's not satisfied. He won't be until he can use the theory to help his fellow American eaters dominate the sport once again. Of course, he wouldn't turn his back on a little recognition. "Maybe in the future, with competitive eating getting so big, the *New England Journal of Medicine* will publish it. And that will be like my crowning achievement. I'll definitely get a signed copy of that and hang it on my wall somewhere."

8

CORNED BEEF, CABBAGE, AND CHARACTERS

There is no sincerer love than the love of food.

—George Bernard Shaw, Irish playwright and essayist

MARCH 16, 2004

Right before the 2004 Freirich Corned Beef and Cabbage Eating Championship, it occurs to me that maybe I'm losing perspective. The reason? For the first time in my brief stint on the circuit, I'm feeling starstruck. I mean, I admit to having felt slightly awed in the presence of Badlands and Sonya Thomas after having heard so much about their eating prowess. But I stand in the back room of Moran's, an Irish restaurant in Manhattan, conjuring up the courage to introduce myself to Hungry Charles Hardy, an old-school eater who has attained legendary status in my mind, I am suddenly, painfully aware that my idolatry may be less than healthy.

Trying to exude outward calm, I introduce myself to Hardy, whose authentic coolness quickly shatters my façade. His hair is done up in cornrows and he's all blinged-out in a thick, shiny necklace. Larger than life at 340 pounds, he moves laconically, speaks with a deep, raspy voice, and has a confident, commanding presence that, to me, approximates that mysterious quality known as star power.

Like a groupie finally meeting an adored rock star, I have to bite my tongue not to betray how much I know about Hungry Charles's career. Such as how he missed winning the Mustard Yellow International Belt back in '99 by a mere quarter of a dog. Or how he's traveled three times to Japan, where he was allegedly taught the "secret of Zen eating," which he steadfastly refuses to reveal. Or the fact that he's an NYPD officer who has been a bodyguard for the rapper Cam'ron, and how he helped out at the World Trade Center rubble pile . . . I want to ask about all these things, but the risk of freaking Hungry Charles out seems too high.

He's not the only veteran gurgitator I'm meeting for the first time. I notice Krazy Kevin Lipsitz, a Staten Island native whose exaggerated facial features and humpback give him the look of a caricature come to life. He's wearing a T-shirt, sweatpants, and a baseball cap with a dog's fuzzy muzzle on the bill. I know the lucky dog cap symbolizes his love for his two dogs, Sabrina and Lynn, who train with him for contests. In fact, because my research has outdistanced my experience on the circuit, I know enough about Krazy Kevin to loosely qualify as a stalker. (I even know he has an *actual* stalker, a young woman from San Francisco, because she e-mails me updates from her Krazy Kevin fan Web site.)

Both on and off the circuit, Krazy Kevin's profile intrigues me. Having won only one major title, the 2000 Carnegie Deli Pickle contest, Lipsitz's competitive-eating rep revolves more around perseverance than success. He boasts to reporters about his records for "most overall second-and third-place finishes," as well as "most times entered" in the Ben's Deli Matzo Ball Eating Competition. He has claimed that his performances in Nathan's Famous contests have at times been compromised by an obscure malady known as Hot Dog Delirium. When HDD takes effect, at around the seven-minute mark of contests, Krazy Kevin's mind goes blank and he slips into a hazy netherworld of half-conscious chewing.

George Shea announces the tight battle between (from left) Badlands Booker, Cookie Jarvis, Hungry Charles Hardy, and Leon "Justice" Feingold, while the author checks the official time. *(Courtesy of Matt Roberts/IFOCE)*

But the thing that intrigues me most about Krazy Kevin is his *spam*. Though he has never eaten it competitively, it's the first topic that comes up when you Google-search his name. Turns out that, in 1997, several disgruntled customers of Kevin's online magazine subscription service approached the New York State attorney general's office. The complaint became a case, and the case went to trial. The customers claimed Lipsitz was spamming hundreds of mailing lists with false testimonials for his subscription service. Krazy Kevin's lawyer argued that New York lacked jurisdiction because the customers were not New York state residents. He lost the case. The resulting *New York vs. Lipsitz* judgment is considered a landmark case in Internet legislation because, according to an online abstract, a "New York State judge upheld the state's right to enforce consumer protection laws against advertisers who use the Internet to distribute false and misleading advertisements."

With all this in mind, I walk up to Krazy Kevin and introduce myself. He is pleasant, if a little wary of my pregnant gaze. Unable to contain myself, I admit that I've been wanting to meet him since I saw the documentary *GutBusters.*

"At the end of that show," I say, "didn't you say you wanted to do a contest with one of the kosher meats, like corned beef or pastrami?"

"Uhhh. . . ." Krazy Kevin looks at me as if *I'm* crazy. "Yeah, I think so."

"Well, now you've finally got one," I say, "you must be *so* psyched."

Krazy Kevin nods agreement, and then the moment drifts awkwardly. He says it was nice to meet me and moves on. I walk over to Don "Moses" Lerman, the eater I'm most excited to meet. He is dressed like a pre-bout prizefighter, wearing a hooded terry-cloth robe with his name embroidered into it. His butter-eating record is one of my favorites, and from what I've read, he's one of the more quotable eaters on the circuit. He once described the Nathan's Famous contest as follows: "You're gonna see an eating frenzy the likes of which you never saw. Maybe if you were at the aquarium during shark-feeding. And I caution the public, please do not attempt this at home. This is for the trained gourmand only."

I arrange an interview with Don, then walk up to Ed "Cookie" Jarvis, who, at six feet eight inches, 460 pounds, isn't difficult to locate. I've met Cookie before, but his magnitude still overwhelms me. Cookie and I discuss today's competitive foodstuff—he tried the corned beef and thinks it may be a little dry. He asks me a favor: Could I go get him a bowl of cocktail sauce from the kitchen? Without hesitation, although I should be overseeing the preparation of dozens of one-pound plates of corned beef and cabbage, I amble out of the banquet room in search of cocktail sauce.

As I wade through the crowded room toward the kitchen, I notice that most of the eaters are talking to each other. The sociology of the circuit interests me, and I have often grilled Dave Baer about the details. Most of the eaters in the top twenty get along. Naturally, groups have formed, but they overlap considerably. For example, Badlands and Hungry Charles are particularly close, but this alliance seems self-evident because they're the only major black eaters on the circuit, and both New Yorkers. Cookie Jarvis, Krazy Kevin, and Don Lerman—known as "the three amigos" in *GutBusters*—seem to share a bond. All three of them got started on the circuit at around the same time; Lipsitz and Lerman are Jewish; and Cookie is, well, Cookie. He is by all accounts the eyes and ears of the circuit, a one-man rumor mill. Among the other eaters in attendance, Crazy Legs gets along with everybody, but seems particularly close with Badlands and Hardy. Beautiful Brian Seiken is a roving satellite, a friend to all the eaters but ultimately a lone wolf. His main attachment to the circuit is his inside-dope competitive-eating news Web site.

Though their chatter seems friendly enough, I sense an undercurrent of tension in the room. All the top gurgitators are extremely competitive and will do whatever it takes to get an edge, before and during the competition. Word has it that Hungry Charles goes with a silent, no-nonsense, intensely focused approach beforehand. Badlands does the Zen warrior thing, closing his eyes and centering himself, often visualizing his performance while listening to his iPod. Sonya Thomas, who isn't here today, has already gained a reputation for feigning fatigue and illness. I'm told Cookie Jarvis goes with a slightly more boastful, I'm-hungrier-and-more-prepared-than-thou psych-out approach. When I spot him engaged in a pleasant chat with Krazy Kevin and Beautiful Brian, I think, *I'll bet he's not telling anyone about this cocktail sauce plan.*

Fifteen minutes before the competition, it looks as if all systems are go. Dave Baer and Freirich rep Phil Percoco have spent hours doling out one-pound portions of corned beef and cabbage on foam plates. The eaters are still milling around, chatting with reporters and each other, catching occasional glimpses of the plates gathering behind the stage. George Shea is doing his thing, waxing ludicrous for a horde of local news stations about the sport he helped invent.

It's around this time that Nancy Goldstein, an IFOCE employee, walks up to me with a problem: The EMT hasn't shown up. Tardy EMTs have long been the bane of IFOCE announcers, because no event can start without them. I tell Nancy to keep calling the guy, and I go report the bad news to George. The thing is, George Shea, despite his silver tongue and equanimity under pressure, suffers from a bit of tension. This probably has as much to do with the fast-talking, hyperkinetic world of New York public relations as with any congenital defects. But when I pull him aside from his verbal flight of fancy to announce our lack of an EMT, I notice that his right hand—the one gripping the microphone—starts to shake. "Okay, okay. . . . It's no problem. I'll just buy some time, and you keep calling that EMT. And have 'em send another one if they can't find him."

I check back in with Nancy, who is outside on her cell. The EMT dispatcher swears the guy is like ten minutes away. Nancy says he made this ten-minute claim before, about twenty minutes ago. I run back inside, moist with sweat, only to discover that George has started the introductions. The room is so crammed with cameras that I have to push my way through. As I approach the stage, George flashes me a questioning look. A couple of the eaters gesture for me to get them more water. I run toward the bar and ask for glasses. The annoyed bartender says they've already sacrificed most of their pint glasses, but he'll try to wash a few more.

By the time I get the extra glasses to the table, George has finished his introductions. The eaters are standing over the table, waiting to eat. I haven't been on the circuit long, but I know that the proper rhythm for an eating contest is to raise the expectations to a fever pitch with the intros, then start the contest with minimal delay. The timing is off. Reporters are checking their watches and looking around. George pulls me aside. "Is he here yet?" he whispers. I shake my head. "Would you mind taking the mic for a second while I go see what's going on?" he says. My eyes pop open. "Uhhh . . ." The blood rushes to my face. I've got nothing prepared and am not feeling altogether calm. "I mean, yeah, sure, I guess."

George saunters back toward center stage, pulling me with him. "Folks, I would like to introduce my fellow announcer and head judge today, Mr. Ryan Nerz. Ryan's going to talk briefly about the rules of today's event."

Dear Lord, I think, as he hands me the mic. *The rules!* I haven't put a moment's thought into the rules, which in this case seem bland and self-evident.

"It's a ten minute event," I say, then mutter something about strength and stomach capacity. Instincts tell me to pace across the stage, that the motion will provoke ideas, but there's no room with all the cameras, so I just stand there, cornered. "Each plate is one pound and has been weighed to the nearest ounce, with corned beef and cabbage in equal proportions. Each eater has three plates before him, with more waiting in the wings. The eaters have been advised to eat all of the corned beef and cabbage on a plate before moving to the next one. Dunking is allowed; preapproved utensils and condiments are also permitted. Again, the competition will last ten minutes. . . ."

I have nothing more to say. The few sounds in the room—muted chatter, shuffling feet—seem damn near deafening. Everyone is looking at me. I am staring blankly at a small crowd and maybe a dozen cameras, but it feels like a paparazzi circus. If there is a quadrant of my brain that realizes this is no big deal—*it's just an eating contest—* that quadrant has shut down. Behind me, I sense the impatience of the eaters, standing over their heaping plates of increasingly lukewarm food. For reasons I can't explain, I need to make a good impression on these guys, and I feel that I'm blowing it. *Where the hell is George? Where's that EMT?*

"So as George said . . . we've got an incredible cast of eaters today, representing not only New York's finest gurgitators, but the finest in the country, even the world." The crowd already knows this, and I'm sure they don't care. *Help!* "We've got Crazy Legs Conti from the East Village, Hungry Charles Hardy from Brooklyn, Badlands Booker, originally from Queens but now representing Long Island . . ."

I spot George, coming toward me at a fast clip. Instead of trying to make a smooth transition, I abandon ship, ducking away from the spotlight while speaking into the microphone. "And here's George Shea, here to give you the final updates before the competition starts."

"We're fine," he whispers as I hand him the microphone. "He's here." As George launches into his spiel, I abscond into a side room and take deep breaths to still my pounding heart.

For the first five minutes of the competition, it looks like a six-way tie for first. Cookie, Badlands, Hungry Charles, Crazy Legs, Beautiful Brian, and Leon "Justice" Feingold are matching each other bite for bite, plate for plate. I notice Allen "Shredder" Goldstein, a Cookie Jarvis protégé, eyeing Tim Janus, a fellow promising rookie on the circuit, while he eats. It almost looks as if Goldstein is mimicking Janus's bite speed, using him as a pacer. I make a mental note of a potential future comment: *Goldstein is widely considered the most talented counterbiter on the circuit.*

Since condiments are generally eschewed by gurgitators as excess baggage, I keep waiting for Cookie's cocktail-sauce plan to backfire on him, but as other eaters start hitting the wall, Cookie takes a commanding lead. The corned beef is sliced thin, but it's lean and salty, a smidgen dry and quite chewy. Jarvis dips each beef slice in the cocktail sauce, and the lubrication seems to be reducing his chewing time. As for the cabbage, it goes down fast out of the gate but sits heavy as the contest wears on.

In the end, Cookie Jarvis takes the $1,000 first-place prize with six pounds in ten minutes, cementing his narrow lead over Sonya Thomas as the top-ranked American eater. Second, third, fourth, fifth, and even sixth place are separated from each other by a few ounces. Leon Justice Feingold, a lawyer who only shows up for exclusive events, takes second with an impressive four pounds three ounces to narrowly edge out Hungry Charles by a single ounce. Beautiful Brian Seiken takes fourth with a nibble over four pounds, and then come Badlands, Crazy Legs, Krazy Kevin, and Allen Goldstein, all with over three pounds.

After the contest, a more festive atmosphere replaces the tension prior to the competition. Except for the ever-present accusations of cheating or poor judging, eaters seem to interact gregariously after competitions. Or maybe the eaters are just stuffed and taking the path of least resistance. Stuffed or not, several eaters grab what's left of the samples that the J. Freirich Company have left for the press. I notice Don Lerman filling up a bag like a trick-or-treater on Halloween.

A reporter from the New York *Daily News* walks up to Cookie Jarvis and asks whether his ethnicity played a role in today's win. "Yeah, I'm Irish," Jarvis says.

"That's funny," George Shea interjects. "At the pasta-eating contest, you were Italian."

9

MOSES OF THE
ALIMENTARY CANAL

America. The fruited plains, the land of milk and honey, the home of the Whopper. Yes, this is the land of plenty. And plenty isn't nearly enough for competitive eater Don Lerman.

—Stephen Colbert, from *The Daily Show with Jon Stewart*

Don Lerman, disguised as either a 1930s-era gangster or the "Hamburglar," poses for the paparazzi before an eating contest.

SEPTEMBER 25, 2001.

Hundreds of rabid fans have assembled inside the Barker Hangar, a gargantuan soundstage in Santa Monica, California, to cheer on the world's premier gurgitators for the biggest televised event in competitive-eating history: the Glutton Bowl, a two-hour, multidisciplinary chowfest produced by the Fox network. The crowd has just watched Badlands Booker win the first round by decimating thirty-eight hard-boiled eggs in ten minutes.

The second-round eaters have been introduced and are now awaiting the arrival of the competitive foodstuff, the specifics of which they have been given no prior knowledge. A giant barrel descends from the ceiling and slowly tilts forward. As hundreds of yellowish sticks fall from the sky to collect in a Lucite bucket at the front of the stage, the crowd emits a collective groan. Unsure whether to believe their eyes, the announcer confirms their suspicions: The competitive foodstuff is *butter.*

From the moment the bell rings, the bearded eater at the far left end of the table jumps to a commanding lead. While the other eaters are waging a one-on-one battle with their gag reflexes, the bearded man eats with reckless, almost terrifying abandon. "He's eating very quickly now," announces George Shea. "Watch that! He has a sort of rabbitlike jaw movement."

The man is Don "Moses" Lerman. A five-foot-eight-inch, 172-pound Long Island native, Lerman is one of the IFOCE's most dedicated and fearless eaters. With an unruly black beard and a gaze of almost animalistic intensity, Lerman's nickname seems oddly fitting. Judging from his outfit—a T-shirt with a silk-screened picture of himself as the biblical Moses, and a baseball cap with the Ten Commandments tablets embroidered on it—Don has apparently embraced the nickname with his entire being.

The JumboTron screen behind the stage focuses briefly on an eater known as Justin "Lean Mean Eating Machine" Connoly. His discomfort is painful to watch. The crowd stares transfixed as he staves off the urge to retch three times within a matter of seconds. The effect on the watcher is that of absolute empathy—you feel yourself retching with him and can't wait for this torture to end.

Don Lerman, however, almost seems to be enjoying himself. He attacks each stick with a rapid-fire succession of minibites, coming at it from all angles. *Pow pow pow pow pow!* Like that, he's ingested a half stick of butter. He takes a few chews, swallows, then goes at it again. "Watch how Lerman gnaws away at that butter like a squirrel!" Mark Thompson, Shea's co-emcee, exclaims.

By the three-minute mark, he has built such a substantial lead—two full sticks ahead of the nearest competitor—that you can't help but wish he would just go easy. But not Don. Trying to capture the extent of Lerman's commitment for the wide-eyed audience, George Shea describes Lerman's daily training routine. "He eats one meal a day, and he eats it competitively. Six hot dogs, fourteen hot dogs. He sets a timer, and when he steps away from the table, he's done eating for twenty-four hours."

As the final seconds tick away, and with a commanding three-stick lead, Don masochistically rifles down an entire half stick of butter. After the buzzer sounds and the referee grabs Don's shoulder, he licks all ten fingers clean, evidently to give himself a sense of closure. He is about to go in for one final lick when the referee forcefully grabs his hand and lifts it to declare him champion.

"Folks," George Shea announces, "this is a man dedicated beyond all reason."

It's June 28, 2004, and Don Lerman has just picked me up from the Long Island Rail Road station in a car-truck contraption that looks remarkably like a space rover. Just as I begin to imagine us entering a parallel universe with Lerman as my guide, we pull into the driveway of his Levittown, New York, home. It's a nice white two-story house that seems especially spacious considering its only other resident is a French bulldog named Cammie. In fact, the house is so nice, with alabaster lions and pristine topiary bushes guarding the driveway, that I can't help but wonder what kind of dough this day-old-bread-shop owner was pulling in before he retired. But that can wait. For now, I just want to hear about the butter record.

"It's not like you're eating ice cream or whipped cream, where it gives you some great taste," Don explains. "Eating butter is much harder than it seems."

"I somehow doubt that," I say. "Seems pretty hard."

Don explains that the hard part wasn't that he dislikes the taste of butter—quite the contrary—but that he's used to eating it in much smaller quantities, and as a complement to other foods. The grease, he explains, is overpowering, which comes as no major surprise considering that the 7½ sticks of salted butter he ate in five minutes contain 3,750 calories, 49 grams of fat, 113 milligrams of cholesterol, and 26 grams of saturated fat (130 percent of the recommended daily allowance.) Cholesterol-wise, eating two pounds of butter has the same effect as downing twenty quarter-pound burgers with cheese. Saturated-fat-wise, it's like guzzling a jug of melted Crisco. On a positive note, however, it *does* contain 30 percent of the RDA for vitamin A. I ask Don what the aftereffects were like. Butter in mass quantities, it turns out, is an extremely effective laxative: "Everything went out. I mean, I had a piece of undigested fruitcake from six Christmases ago."

If the IFOCE had an award for Lifetime Gastric Distress, it would go to Don Lerman. His biggest titles include some of the most grueling disciplines in competitive eating: butter, jalapeño peppers, and baked beans. The record he set on that historic day at the Glutton Bowl is so staggering that it will likely never be broken. In the documentary *Crazy Legs Conti: Zen and the Art of Competitive Eating*, Crazy Legs attempts to match Lerman's butter feat, only to fail in a graphic and audible way. After a series of heavy sighs and penetrating belches, Conti gives up. *"No más,"* he says, throwing up his hands. "Don definitely has the mental stability to eat as much butter as possible, whereas I didn't enjoy it so much."

Jalapeño peppers were similarly challenging. Don has won two separate jalapeño-eating contests. In one contest, held in the border town of Laredo, Texas, Don ate 120 peppers in fifteen minutes. His nearest competitor ate 60. Don trained daily for the contest, eating peppers and downing multiple bottles of Tabasco sauce.

Though he had the intestinal fortitude to handle the heat *during* the competition, that was just the beginning. The real work of a jalapeño-eating contest comes afterward and can last for days. After the jalapeño victory, in his Laredo hotel room, Don's burning gullet kept him up all night, moaning and praying for mercy. When he awoke the next morning, his body was still *en fuego*. Not until a giant buffet dinner that night did he start to feel some relief. "It's the only contest on the circuit that's an endurance contest," Don says.

He did another jalapeño contest in Milwaukee, and the peppers there were even hotter. They were served in glass bowls because they were acidic enough to burn holes in metal. Halfway through the contest, Don claims his lips and tongue were completely numb: "You could have done dental work without the Novocain, no exaggeration."

When it comes to postcompetition elimination, Don is a purist. "I don't use no laxatives, and I don't throw up my food. I do the water, and I let it come out naturally." To describe the unique aftereffects of attempting to eliminate so many jalapeños, Lerman offers up the following joke: On a dare, a guy eats a fiery jalapeño, underestimating its power. Afterward, his friends give him ice cream to cool off. Later, while going to the bathroom, it burns so bad that he yells out, "Come on, ice cream!"

Don discovered the extent of his iron constitution as a young man, when his stomach passed the ultimate test. His grandmother was in the hospital in Brooklyn, extremely sick, with only a few weeks to live. Don's mother made some chicken soup—"Jewish chicken soup . . . penicillin." The family drove from their home in Queens to visit his grandmother daily for three weeks. One day, Don's mother called from the hospital and asked if he'd had anything to eat. "Yeah, I had some of that chicken soup in the fridge," Don said.

"What soup?" his mother yelled. "I made that like a month ago!"

Panicked, Mrs. Lerman drove home and picked up her son, grabbed the soup from the fridge, and took them both to the hospital. When she showed the soup to the doctor, he was stunned by its green tint and gelatinous consistency. "Talk about penicillin," Don explains. "That chicken had turned to penicillin." The doctor took one look at the soup and said that the chicken had turned to ptomaine. If Don had eaten it recently and wasn't already feeling deathly ill, then his innards were something of a minor miracle. A digestive system like that, the doctor explained, could tackle the local diet in most Third-World countries. Many years later, in Lerman's chosen sport, this innate talent would prove extremely useful.

From a young age, Don tells me, he was a *fresser,* the Yiddish term for a "big eater." His mother, however, was a lousy cook. "I just couldn't take her food. She put no love into it." By some cruel stroke of misfortune, his mother's mother was even worse. Though his father's side of the family had better skills, Don learned the hard way that being finicky wouldn't get him fed. When I mention my Flavor Advantage Theory—that it's easier to eat food competitively if you enjoy the taste—Don adamantly shakes his head no. A true professional gurgitator should be able to eat all foods with equal speed and dexterity, he says, regardless of flavor.

As a kid with a hearty appetite, it was tough going. From the age of eleven, Don worked at various businesses around his Queens neighborhood—a drugstore, a dry cleaner, a grocery store—to get cash for take-out food. After work, he stalked all the Italian and Chinese take-out joints, looking for the best deals on the biggest portions. His favorite meal was the "Dinner for Five" at a local Chinese restaurant. He would set up shop at a table while the courses came in waves—egg-drop soup, two egg rolls, two shrimp rolls, a lobster dish, ribs, lo mein, chicken wings, roast pepper Chinese vegetables, four ice creams, and huge mounds of complimentary fried rice. Afterward, he felt full but not uncomfortable, and his metabolism was such that he always remained trim.

After high school, Don moved out to Long Island with his family and took on a succession of jobs. He worked at a warehouse, became a bank teller, and eventually started his own business, the day-old-bread store. He also served six years in the Marine Reserves, including a few years of stateside active duty during Vietnam. This experience inculcated a deep patriotism in Don, a sentiment that continues to motivate him in international eating competitions today.

At the urging of his nephew, Lerman entered his first eating contest in January of 2000: the Ben's Kosher Deli Matzo Ball Eating Contest in Manhattan. With no training, he broke the record, downing twelve half-pound, baseball-sized matzo balls in two minutes and twenty-five seconds. Don loved the adrenaline rush and the shock that onlookers expressed at his lightning speed. "Look, he's like a machine!" someone had yelled out. Afterward, Mayor Rudy Giuliani presented Don with the trophy and check. When describing the post-contest press conference, Don's face lights up as if remembering a glorious halcyon day from his youth. "It was like a presidential press conference. It was a sea of cameras. You've got no conception. Reporters were everywhere."

Don was hooked and began training. Already a heavyweight "buffet buster," Don decided to up the intensity of his eating sessions at local buffets. He'd hit the buffet off 110th and Huntington for lobster and shrimp. Sometimes he'd hit the Indian buffet, "because it goes right through you . . . It fills you up very quickly, and there's no weight gain." He claims that every Chinese buffet restaurant within a six-mile radius of his home knows him by name. In terms of poundage, he estimates his capacity for a Chinese buffet meal at around ten to thirteen pounds. "No buffet ever made a dime off me," he boasts. (When I imagine Don throwing this line out to single women, it seems suddenly less mysterious that he doesn't have offspring.)

Don soon learned that buffet-busting alone wouldn't suffice. He would have to devise eating techniques to keep him a step ahead of his opponents.

With hot dogs, Don found that the limiting factor wasn't technique or stomach capacity, but swallowing. He needed to learn how to swallow larger amounts faster, without getting nauseated or triggering the gag reflex. Over time, aided by the expertise of his nephew, Don developed a theory about how to train his body not to get nauseated. "There's a muscle at the end of the esophagus, the cardiac sphincter, which is the epicenter of nausea. That's why you get nauseous in a contest." Don's nephew had discovered the cardiac sphincter in college, while trying to improve his skills with a beer funnel.

So how could Don train his cardiac sphincter? With water, or as he pronounces it in his New York accent, *woitah*. Don trained himself to down a gallon of water in under three minutes. He initiated a daily ritual: Each morning, he'd wake up, drink some coffee, then chug a gallon of water, fast. The first few times, Don described the cleansing effect as that of a "reverse enema." Once that effect subsided though, he found he'd not only gained control of his cardiac sphincter, but his fast-paced stomach capacity as well. He liked to think of his training sessions as "internal workouts."

Internal workouts still weren't enough. Don felt that the physical duress of contests was such that overall fitness was important as well. He started running. The combination of water training and running, ironically, got him into the best shape he'd been in since his time in the Marine Reserves. Who'd have guessed that, to eat huge amounts of food, the best option would be to get into tiptop shape? Having quit smoking, Don's competitive-eating training became a sort of replacement compulsion. When questioned about Don's regimented lifestyle, even George Shea admits to being awestruck: "Here is a man who's been eating fourteen hot dogs and buns every day this season, and then running four hours a day. No one asked him to do it. No one understands exactly *why* he's doing it."

Indeed, outsiders might consider Lerman's commitment to the sport extreme. During our interview, I brought up a quote I'd read that was attributed to Lerman: "I'll stretch my stomach until it causes internal bleeding. I do it for the thrill of competition." Before I could finish, he tried to interrupt, waving the question away. "My promoter didn't like that," he explained. "It was a joke. It was a joke. I don't use that line anymore."

Another aspect of Don's intense commitment is that he seems to enjoy establishing and perpetuating rivalries. At the 2001 matzo-ball-eating contest, when Hungry Charles Hardy took the crown from Lerman, Hardy claims that one of Don's relatives heckled him during the contest, and that Don himself wasn't entirely amiable. They later patched things up at the Glutton Bowl, but only after a few chilly contests.

During our interview, Don mentioned that he'd like to go head-to-head with Jed Donahue, the perennial Laredo jalapeño-pepper-eating champ, who had missed the contest Don won because he'd broken his arm. Soon thereafter, I noticed that Don posted a picture of himself on his Web site in a cowboy hat and holding a gun, with the following caption below it: "Jed Donahue, I'm Gunning for You."

Don reserved his most acrimonious words for a female bean-eating champ I'd never heard of. He had read about her bean-eating victory on Beautiful Brian Seiken's Web site and was interested in a one-on-one challenge. Don's prediction: "I'm gonna go against huh. I'm gonna destroy huh. I'm gonna pulverize huh. I'm gonna break huh."

Say what you will about Don's commitment to the sport, but you can't question his sincerity. In a world of filthy rich athletes who seem put-upon when asked to show up for a practice or charity event, his attitude is refreshing. "This is my sport," Don says. "Some people are good at baseball or golf, or they play the piano. This is what I do well. And I believe in it. I want to pursue it. I want to nurture it every day. I wish I could be the heavyweight champion of the world in boxing. Or Olympic decathlon. But I can't. This is what I do well. I practice, and I take it real serious."

. . .

Don keeps checking the toaster. Every time he gets up from the table, he mentions something about "checking on the dogs," and at first I'm not sure what this means. I know for a fact that one dog need not be checked upon—Cammie is beneath the table, scratching my legs if I stop petting her for even a moment. Then suddenly, midinterview and with no segue, Don gets up, grabs a plate from the kitchen, and leads me outside to the back deck. It's sunny out and crickets are chirping.

Now I realize what we're up to. When I'd set up the interview, I vaguely recall having mentioned wanting to watch him train for the Nathan's Fourth of July contest. Judging from the oversized digital timer on the table, I'm about to be involved in a training session, and I must admit I'm pumped. It occurs to me that we're outside in the June heat to simulate game-day conditions. Don explains that, in fact, he often puts the dogs in the shower for a steaming effect that approximates the mugginess down on Coney Island. I'm tempted to ask what he does to simulate that distinctive boardwalk *stench,* but it's no time for jokes. Don's got his game face on—I don't want to snap him out of the Zone. He neatly folds each dog into its bun with the care a mother uses to diaper an infant. Then he stacks them on a paper plate in a pyramid formation. "I've got nine dogs here. And I'm gonna time it."

Don is instantly poised over the mound of weenies, bent forward with his hands in the ready position. I figure this is my cue to start the countdown. When I say "Eat!" he's off like a rocket. He gobbles down a dog, dunks the bun, and downs it. There's minimal chewing involved—it's just dog, dunk, bun, dog, dunk, bun, in rapid succession, his hands churning from plate to mouth like a windmill. Don claims he's got "the fastest hands in competitive eating," and this is apparently no idle boast. Forty seconds in and he's on his fifth dog. I'm so caught up in the moment, swept away by the momentum of Don's passion, that it seems suddenly natural and right to be sitting on a grown man's porch on a Monday afternoon watching him speed-eat hot dogs. I find myself even slightly envious, convinced that I could train for a decade and never maintain this pace.

"Wow!" I say. "Wow. Nice work . . . wow!" I want to say something more inspiring, but the repetitiveness of stuffing and chewing defies any attempt at eloquence. He finishes the last dog and I stop the clock—nine in just under two minutes. After taking a moment to catch his breath, he confides that he's not satisfied. "I felt I coulda went a little fastuh," he says.

"What do you think slowed you down?" I ask. "Was it the swallowing?"

It's the rhythm, he says. This is becoming a pervading theme. Badlands mentioned rhythm as an essential component, as did Kobayashi. In *The Doughnut Dropout,* a now out-of-print children's book about competitive eating that Jed Donahue suggested to me as an essential read, the following was dispensed as crucial advice for an aspiring eater: "The great art in eating . . . is in using every muscle, head to toe, to establish the rhythms." Don explains that he didn't have the right chewing/swallowing rhythm at first, and it took him several seconds to adjust.

"Well, I was impressed." I pat Don on the back. "Nine dogs and buns in two minutes . . . that's a Kobayashi pace! So then, explain to me, what happens in the second half of a contest that limits your total consumption?"

Don doesn't hesitate. "When it gets hot, you get what they call the meat sweats. The protein and the fat starts gettin' to ya. The fat turns to lactic acid, and you just get tired. It just puts you to sleep."

Aha! The meat sweats. I've heard this term before, even used it myself, but I'd always assumed it was some BS that George and Richard made up to amuse themselves. (Actually the Sheas claim that their friend Dave Kreizman, the headwriter for the soap opera *Guiding Light,* coined the term after watching eaters sweat profusely after sucking down Rocky Mountain oysters at the Glutton Bowl.) An online search reveals that there's no official definition, but the term is posted on www.urbandictionary.com as a slang word, defined as follows: "To consume an obsene [*sic*] amount of meat resulting in perfuse sweating." "Perfuse" meaning, of course, "to force a fluid through an organ or tissue by way of the blood vessels." (The Meat Sweats, unsurprisingly, is also the name of a lesser-known indie rock band.) When I press Don about what the meat sweats feel like, he says, "The fat and the grease and the protein from the meat gets to ya, and it just knocks you out. You get so tired and disgusted you can't wait for them to ring the bell."

After the hot dog demonstration, Don leads me to a shiny, well-kept room in his basement. The trophy room is twelve feet by twelve feet and stuffed to the brim with Lerman's competitive-eating memorabilia. Along the wall and sitting on top of a large TV are myriad trophies and belts—five Nathan's Famous qualifier trophies, second place in the Philly Wing Bowl, the bean trophy, the pelmeni trophy, the jalapeño trophies. Don glows with pride as he recounts each contest. Interestingly, I have found that many competitive eaters seem almost as excited about trophies as prize money. This phenomenon, I believe, helps confirm my theory that many gurgitators compete mainly for the fundamental human desire to receive a pat on the back. Money comes and goes, while trophies remain as lasting reminders of a hard-won accomplishment. Don seems particularly proud of the Cloud Burger Belt, which he says is worth $800 and is now on display in a $400 Plexiglas shadow box.

There are as many pictures as trophies, and the pictures give a thorough account of one man's fifteen minutes of fame. Here's Don with Mayor Giuliani; here he is with Bloomberg. Here's a shot from the news show *20/20*. Here he is with Sally Jessy Raphael, and there with Drew Bledsoe. There's a shot from the set of *GutBusters,* and one from *The Glutton Bowl.* Here is the infinitely jolly Al Roker, post-gastric-bypass, and a bearded man that looks like a genetic hybrid of Don Lerman and the pre-bypass Roker.

"Look at me," Don says, noticing the picture I'm fixating on. "You can see how heavy I was."

"That's *you*?" I say, unable to hide my shock.

Don explains that his weight fluctuates so severely that it's sometimes difficult to recognize him from one sighting to the next. He admits this freely and speaks of his weight as if it's being controlled by some external source. At the Glutton Bowl, he weighed 172. During our interview, he weighs 206. But not so long ago, during the time of the Al Roker picture, he was up to 230. These fluctuations, which can be gauged by the puffiness of his cheeks and the roundness of his paunch, are so extreme that I cannot help but feel that he's got shape-shifting abilities.

This shape-shifting metaphor can be extended to other areas of Don's eating persona. Like Dale Boone and Badlands Booker, Don has alter egos that he likes to assume for eating contests. His most common identity, naturally, is Moses. The official IFOCE line is that Don earned the nickname for his ability to part the buffet line, but the actual story is more prosaic. In 1979, Don's aunt gave him the nickname because of his beard, or "beeahd," as he says it.

Unmoved by the fact that the biblical Moses was more renowned

Don "Moses" Lerman, wearing a personalized Don Lerman T-shirt, points at the commissioned portrait of himself as Moses in his competitive eating trophy room.

for his holiness than his appetite, "Moses" is a competitive-eating identity Don has wholly embraced. The centerpiece of his trophy room is a framed portrait he had commissioned of himself as Moses. A Moses action figure, which he intends to sell on his Web site, is displayed nearby. Don's favorite movie is *The Ten Commandments,* and he has fashioned two tablets into exact replicas of Charlton Heston's from the movie.

Beyond the Moses obsession, Don has a clear affinity for costumes. At the corned beef and cabbage contest, he showed up in a boxer's robe. At the jalapeño contest in Laredo, he dressed up as a gun-slinging cowboy. He once showed up to a matzo-ball-eating contest dressed as a Prohibition-era gangster, complete with vest, hat, and pencil-thin mustache. Next to the Moses painting in his trophy room is a picture of Don as the king of Prussia. In the back room of the IFOCE, there's a framed picture of Don dressed up as a gray-haired old man. In the caption beneath is Don's joke about eating competitively until he's ninety years old: "If the PoliGrip holds . . . I'll have a good day."

Don is similarly obsessive about using embroidery to personalize his stuff. His car has DON "MOSES" LERMAN embroidered into all the seats. The towels in the bathroom are embroidered likewise, except for the one that says FOR GUEST USE ONLY. His closet is packed with embroidered jackets. They all feature his name, along with slogans like EL PRESIDENTE: THE JALAPEÑO EATING CHAMP and THE JIM THORPE OF COMPETITIVE EATING. Another one reads DON LERMAN: FASTEST HANDS IN COMPETITIVE EATING, next to a logo of a hand holding a lightning bolt. "I've got that one patented," he explains. He has nearly a dozen of them total, all of which he plans to auction off and give the proceeds to charity.

After checking out his jackets, the last thing Don and I do is watch a videotaped segment from the *Daily Show with Jon Stewart.* The episode is called "What So Proudly We Inhaled." It begins with an appeal to America to embrace our best competitive eaters: "In this time of crisis, Americans appreciate the heroes amongst us. Not just America's finest, America's greatest, but America's *fullest*." The reporter, Stephen Colbert, casts Don as a patriotic hero who is "as American as fifty apple pies."

"Don . . . ," Colbert asks earnestly. "How about the vomit? What do you say back to your body when it says, 'I'm gonna throw up.'"

"I do it for America," Don answers. "I fight the vomit for America."

Colbert gravely states that, on the Fourth of July, "on the island of Coney," Don fell victim to a hot dog sneak attack by Takeru Kobayashi, who used his "secret karate esophagus" to exact a sort of gustatory Pearl Harbor. After grilling a dietitian for ways that we can eat more food faster, Colbert ends with a somber appeal to the American public: "Ask not what your country can do for you. Ask for seconds."

Though this segment gently mocks Don and satirizes competitive eating in general, he shows it to me with pride. This adds to my wonder about the extent to which certain competitive eaters *get it*. Competitive eating as presented by the IFOCE hovers somewhere between earnest sport and cultural parody. The Shea brothers, it seems, are able to balance the dead serious with the deadpan because they believe that much of American culture is absurd, and within that context competitive eating is perfectly viable entertainment. With the eaters, it's difficult to distinguish the earnest from the ironic, the tongue-in-cheek from the wide-eyed stuffed cheeks. So, while Don Lerman is intelligent and has a refined sense of humor, I can't tell whether he's playing to his audience or playing it straight when he says things like "It is an American sport, and we want to win it for America. It's like the Olympics. Everyone wants to win for themselves, and for their country."

Then it dawns on me: *Who cares?* Who cares whether Don Lerman has a sense of irony about competitive eating? The important thing is that it has transformed an aging bachelor and retired day-old-bread-shop owner into a D-list celebrity with a roomful of accomplishments and a cell phone full of friends. It has given a man with a fertile imagination an outlet for expression. Yes, believe it or not, competitive eating can lend meaning to a man's world and make him feel alive, in the same way that paintball and poker can. In a way, if Don Lerman isn't being totally earnest about his competitive-eating career, I don't want to know. Because his sincerity is so contagious it makes me want to forgo all sarcasm and irony for a few glorious victories and a world record all my own.

10

THE EMPEROR
OF ICE CREAM

The only emperor is the emperor of ice-cream.

—Wallace Stevens

The Coat is made of black denim, extra long, with enough fabric to craft drapes for a bay window. A trench coat, technically. It took him six weeks to find it, at a flea market near his home in Long Island. He would rather have gotten blue denim, for added contrast, but when purchasing a trench coat in size 6XL, one can't be too picky.

Airbrushed on the front of the coat is a smaller, mini-me rendition of the oversized man within. The right hand is clutching the trademark spoon. In the outstretched left palm is a house, symbolic of his job as a Realtor, and disproportionate in a way that brings to mind the globe on Atlas's broad shoulders. At the bottom of the coat are flames, reaching upward as if to set the whole scene ablaze. And on the left lapel of the coat-within-the-coat, the one the airbrushed man is wearing, is one of the most feared names in competitive eating: Ed "Cookie" Jarvis.

Though this frontal image is arresting, and not lacking in useful metaphors, it's the back of the Coat that draws more attention from fans and onlookers. (And not merely because it provides a posterior view of the six-foot-eight-inch, four-hundred-pound Jarvis, which has its own merits.) Listed in chronological order from top to bottom are the many titles held by one of the circuit's most seasoned veterans. A quick glance reveals that the Coat's wearer is among the best cross-eaters in the sport, boasting titles in a cornucopia of foodstuffs—pizza, zeppole, meatballs, pickles, steak (chicken-fried and regular), dumplings (Chinese and Russian), hot dogs, burgers, pasta, ribs, french fries, and chicken wings.

So what's the secret behind Cookie Jarvis's cross-eating success? It includes most of the standard ingredients for the recipe of competitive-eating greatness—voracious appetite, dogged determination, immense stomach capacity, and an almost unhealthy desire for media attention. But the X-factor that separates Cookie from his contemporaries is his scientific attention to detail. He is an eater's eater, a clever tactician who uses every advantage he can unearth—from utensils to condiments to psych-outs—to wrench victories from the jaws of defeat.

The man, the myth, the legend—Cookie Jarvis, wearing "the Coat," approaches the competitive eating table. In his right hand, he holds the trademark Cookie Spoon (as does the air-brushed Cookie on "the Coat"), and in his left hand, he holds a knife (while the airbrushed Cookie holds a house). *(Courtesy of Matt Roberts/IFOCE)*

. . .

"The french fry title was actually a few days after my dad passed away. George Shea didn't want to call me at the time, and I said, 'No, no, no. My dad would want me go.'"

Cookie Jarvis and I are seated in the basement of his Long Island home, cataloging the titles listed on the back of his coat. He has just explained how drinking Aloe Vera, a bottle of which I found in his kitchen, makes his stomach more stretchable. On the wall to my right, Jay Leno is smiling down at me. The framed picture of him with Cookie is surrounded by dozens of gleaming trophies and belts, the spoils of his gurgitory dominance, as well as an authentic Shaquille O'Neal basketball shoe that would comfortably fit Sasquatch. The basement also features an extensive collection of Beanie Babies, a huge aquarium filled with tropical fish named after fellow eaters, and an elaborate indoor playset for his two young children. We are only on his fourth title, and already I am shaken by the sentimentality with which he describes these early victories.

"I ate two pounds, eight ounces of *pommes frites*, which is a tougher fry than a regular fry, 'cause they're greasy and narrow, so they're very chewy," he says. "I dedicated that title to my dad."

I shake my head. "Wasn't it hard, having that sort of emotion going into a contest?"

"I use it as fuel," he says.

Sensing that he is too emotional to elaborate, I decide to move on. "So tell me about ice cream."

Cookie immediately peps up. It so happens that the 2001 Max and Mina's Ice Cream Eating Championship was a watershed moment in his career. After a practice run in which he was soundly defeated by Don Moses Lerman, Jarvis realized he was making a crucial error. Specifically, he was hampered by brain freeze. So he went home and, with the help of a few pints of Max and Mina's vanilla, figured out how to avoid brain freeze.

The secret to staving off the paralyzing effects of brain freeze is to turn the spoon over. That way, Cookie says, the ice cream makes contact with the tongue, as opposed to the roof of the mouth. "Your tongue can get frozen. It doesn't even affect you at all. Plus, your tongue pulls the ice cream off the spoon. The top of your mouth doesn't do that—you've gotta use your teeth."

Employing the double whammy of this groundbreaking technique along with the now famous Cookie Jarvis spoon, he blew away the field, knocking down six pounds, fourteen ounces of ice cream in twelve minutes. It was his first major pro victory over a field of celebrated eaters that included Don Lerman, Badlands Booker, Krazy Kevin Lipsitz, and Leon Justice Feingold. Producers from the BBC were on hand to film the contest for a segment on sweet eaters, giving Cookie his first taste of big-time media exposure. Ultimately, the ice cream title, along with titles in zeppole, pizza, and fries, propelled him to the first-ever IFOCE Rookie of the Year award, presented on July 4, 2001.

In his first competition of 2002, Cookie continued to use strategy to his advantage. At the first ever Cannoli Eating Contest, held in Manhattan's Little Italy as part of the San Gennaro Festival, he showed up with a mysterious paper bag. "What's Jahvis got in the paper bag?" Cookie remembers other eaters murmuring. The secret weapon was four cups of steaming-hot coffee, which provided just enough moisture for him to dunk his way to a half-cannoli victory over Badlands Booker, twenty-one to twenty and a half.

Perhaps the event most suited to Cookie's ability to manipulate multiple foodstuffs was the Battle of the Buffets, a competition televised by the Travel Channel. The competition, held in Las Vegas, a city known for its bounteous buffets, involved five courses—breakfast, lunch, appetizers, dinner, and dessert. Cookie's strategy was to come in second in each round—just enough to advance—and then to seal the deal in the final dessert round, his specialty. This tactic proved crucial in the second-to-last round, when Rich LeFevre pulled way ahead of Cookie, only to be disqualified after suffering a Roman incident. The dessert round featured ice cream, which Cookie "whipped through like it was nothing."

(Appropriately enough, Jarvis's nickname represents a perfect blend of his cerebral eating style and his sweet tooth. In sixth grade, renowned for his insatiable appetite for cookies, his classmates dubbed him Cookie Jarvis, after the name of the wizard on the box of Cookie Crisp cereal.)

Recognizing that preparedness was the key to victory, Cookie continued to outsmart opponents. In buffalo wings, he kneeled to shorten the distance between hand and mouth. In pelmeni, a type of greasy Russian dumpling, the Jarvis spoon kept the dumplings from slipping away. In pasta, he tipped the bowl and used the spoon to shovel his way to victory in Little Italy. In chicken-fried steak, he used cocktail sauce to counteract the thick gravy, a tactic he would later employ in his corned-beef-and-cabbage victory.

By the end of 2003, his confidence soaring, Cookie had set the circuit ablaze, accruing thirteen titles, including a nine-for-ten streak to close out the year. He was the number-one-ranked American eater, and the American hot dog record holder with thirty and a half. The trench coat was so filled with titles that they were almost stretching into the airbrushed flames. The future, it seemed, could only hold more success, more cash prizes, and more media attention. Cookie Jarvis felt invincible. At this rate, it seemed that, when the American Competitive Eating Hall of Fame opened its doors, the Jarvis trench coat would likely be its centerpiece.

Initially, the Coat was intended for two purposes. The first was strictly informational. At events, or whenever he told someone he was a professional competitive eater, people always asked the same question: What have you won? So he started small, embroidering his titles on the back of a jean jacket, but it was soon filled to capacity, forcing Jarvis to think bigger. (The mind reels at the potential value of that prototype jacket on eBay.)

The Coat's second purpose was sponsorship. Cookie envisioned it as a sort of mobile advertising unit, not unlike how brand names are emblazoned on NASCAR cars. "I'd like to have Tums sponsor my jacket," he explains. "Home Depot. Whoever! Just walk around with it. A walking advertisement. I mean, the race cars do it and I'm almost as big as them. And I'm all over the place."

This idea gives a glimpse into Cookie's tireless entrepreneurial spirit. On the front of the jacket, he's holding a house not only to exhibit his preternatural strength, but to show that he's a real estate agent. Though he stopped short of adding his agency's name—ReMax—to the jacket, he admits that his competitive-eating fame in no way detracts from business. "I made a closing today, and all they could talk about was competitive eating," he says with smug laughter. "It's like, they forgot about the closing."

Real estate is just one of his businesses. When asked, he reels off a list of side businesses with descriptions that hover somewhere between impressive and perplexing. He "does travel part-time." He's a marketing consultant for a product brokerage company. He sets people up in home-based Internet businesses, where they can earn a six-figure residual income out of the home. He is the customer manager of a Web site, www.bigmoney.unfranchise.com, which is associated with an entity called Market America and seems to do just about everything. Jarvis explains the endless possibilities of the Web site. "You can buy gift certificates or you can buy products. You can get 'em shipped or you can get 'em not shipped. You can shop at eight hundred stores with only one checkout. I can sell Web sites. I can sell custom vitamins. Pretty much anything you can think of. Custom gloves, custom whatevah."

Rich Shea once told me that Cookie tried to interest him in a "binomial." I ask Cookie what this means. "That's the Market America business. It's a binomial product, meaning it's not a multilevel marketing company." *Hmm.*

One can't help but be impressed by the magnitude of Cookie's ambition. From day one on the circuit, his goal was to be the number one competitive eater in the world—and even that wouldn't be enough. The plan beneath the plan was to use competitive eating as a vehicle to fame, if not international superstardom. "Guys like Stone Cold Steve Austin and Hulk Hogan used wrestling as something they made a lot of money in, to get them to the movies. And basically my concept is the same thing."

The skeptic might be tempted to snicker at such lofty ambition, but the extent of Cookie Jarvis's media exposure suggests he's not so out there. One of his goals was to get on *The Tonight Show with Jay Leno*—mission accomplished. He's also been on the *John Walsh Show, The Morning Show with Al Roker, The Daily Show with Jon Stewart, Fox and Friends,* CBS News, CNN News, ESPN News, as well as a half-dozen cable specials on competitive eating. He was on the front page of the *Wall Street Journal,* complete with illustration. He was the feature of a *Playboy* article, the wet dream of many a red-blooded American male, and perhaps most notably, he landed a speaking role on a 2004 episode of the NBC TV show *Las Vegas,* starring James Caan.

Though his exposure is indisputable, some might contend that Cookie's yen for self-promotion borders on pathological. Before contests, he throws T-shirts into the crowd featuring his name and his three Web sites. After most contests, especially victories, he is the last one to leave the horde of reporters. Without any trace of irony, he ranks the rush of getting media coverage "between a good piece of chocolate cake, and sex."

Cookie and the media make natural bedfellows, because he is among the most avid talkers I have ever met. During our two-and-a-half hour interview, he receives no less than seven phone calls, and he answers each one. If a sport were made of phone talking, Cookie would be neck and neck for the top ranking with some teenage girl. Every eater on the circuit has stories about getting multiple voice mails from Jarvis, often in the following format: "Hey, [insert name], it's Jahvis. Gimme a call on my cell." The amount of daily Cookie calls to the

IFOCE averages around a half dozen, and there have been unconfirmed rumors that a special board was once dedicated to the daily tally.

Say what you want about his unlimited cell phone minutes, but Cookie's incessant phoning has made him the eyes and ears of the circuit. Everyone calls Cookie, and Cookie calls everyone. Within minutes of the end of any given contest in which Cookie has not competed, he will call one of the participants. His timing is uncanny, a sixth sense.

This constant communication has both positive and negative sides. It powers the circuit's rumor mill, but also establishes a constant touchstone of communication. One major draw of the circuit, as with all teams and organizations, is the common human desire to be a part of something greater. Outside of the IFOCE, Cookie is the unifying force that connects the individual eater to the circuit, and there is nary a secret, rumor, or training technique that hasn't been stored in his mental file cabinet. "I'm like the interconnection between the world of eating," Cookie explains. "I consider myself one of the pillars, or the foundation of the IFOCE."

NOVEMBER 26, 2003

It's the day before Thanksgiving, the American holiday that best reflects the values of competitive eating. A collection of the finest gurgitators in the known universe has gathered at Mickey Mantle's Restaurant on Central Park South in Manhattan for the Thanksgiving Meal Invitational. The field, which includes the winners of eight Harvest Series events, are bent over plates piled high with a unique and demanding foodstuff—"turducken," a semiboneless turkey stuffed with a boneless chicken, duck breast, and layers of sausage stuffing. Unbeknownst to fans, eaters, and journalists alike, in a matter of minutes, the course of American competitive-eating history is about to change dramatically.

When the final whistle blows, the Shea brothers announce a stunning upset. A hundred-pound rookie, Sonya Thomas, has edged out the number-one-ranked American eater, the 409-pound Edward Cookie Jarvis. The final count reveals a photo finish. While Jarvis has consumed seven and a half pounds of Thanksgiving meal (featuring turducken, green beans, cranberry sauce, and yams), Sonya has eaten seven and three quarter.

It is Sonya's first major win over a field of top-ranked eaters. The loss halts Cookie's ongoing dominance for the 2003 season and lodges a wrench in the spokes of his confidence. Though the appearance of the Japanese at Coney Island has lent credence to Krachie's Belt of Fat Theory, the sight of a hundred-pound woman snatching a Thanksgiving eating crown over hundreds of pounds of raw masculine eating prowess is all but confirmation of the theory.

In the next few meetings between Cookie and Sonya, Cookie wins only one, a mano-a-womano chicken-wing challenge at Hooters in Manhattan. He maintains his number one ranking, but Sonya's takeover feels imminent. This transition is so radical that it defies sports analogies. It's as if Michael Jordan's NBA scoring title was usurped, not by Kobe Bryant, but by a five-foot-two-inch female point guard. It's as if a one-armed amputee edged out Tiger Woods for a major PGA title. It is, in a word, unthinkable.

Since the gradual shift in the competitive-eating power structure that began in late 2003, Cookie Jarvis's attitude toward the circuit has soured somewhat. It's not that he has any less affection for the sport, or for the eaters, but he does not like to lose, and he doesn't seem to be acclimating too rapidly. Though he has always been constructively critical of the way the circuit is conducted, his protests have grown more frequent.

When asked what rule he would institute if he were George Shea, Jarvis doesn't hesitate. "My biggest improvement would be professional scales at every event." The Jarvis Amendment would require weighing each competitor's food before each event, then weighing the leftovers and subtracting the difference for the official count. Cookie claims that not weighing the food invites unjust rulings in close contests. Specifically, he felt that his Thanksgiving turducken squeaker loss to Sonya was too close to call without extensive weighing. "If you don't do something about it," he says, "then the guys are all pissed off, like myself." It occurs to me that some of Cookie's bitterness stems from his constant contact with other eaters. He is the unofficial complaint receptacle of the circuit.

Cookie thinks IFOCE eaters should be pursuing advertising contracts with more tenacity. "I told George that I'd like to get a second agent for just *that*. 'Cause I think I'm missin' the boat on that. I could be doin' like a 'Pizza! Pizza!' commercial for Little Caesars. Or maybe Rolaids . . ." Cookie smiles for an imaginary camera. "After all these competitions, take Rolaids."

He'd like to see drug testing implemented in the IFOCE. He has made allegations of the use of "throat relaxers" on the circuit, which he feels should be investigated. "Hey, if a horse wins by some exorbitant amount, they take him to get tested right after the race," he explains. "Kobayashi should have been tested the first year he came. I'd like to do a sonogram on him, see what his stomach looks like. And a drug test. They might even have some herbal thing in Japan that I don't know about."

Though his relationship with his "nemesis" Sonya Thomas is relatively cordial, Jarvis feels that her presence dilutes the fraternity-like camaraderie of the circuit. While many of the guys hang out with each other after the contests, Sonya—partially due to her gender, partially to her difficulties with English—often sticks to herself or heads straight to the airport with her winnings.

Cookie also thinks that the Nathan's Famous competition should be restructured. The Japanese could bring over a half dozen eaters and have their own competition, while the Americans stage their own. One way or another, the American champs should be recognized. Regardless of who wins, Cookie feels that the contest should introduce cash prizes, which it presently lacks. "I mean, you eat thirty hot dogs, and you've got nothin' to show for it," he explains.

In fact, Cookie has felt so dismayed at times by the state of the circuit, he's even considered hanging up the spoon. That's right—retirement. Has it come to this? Any gurgitator will agree that a Cookie-less circuit is a difficult reality to swallow. Without the thick pillar that is Cookie, the circuit's social nexus, would the competitive-eating circuit collapse under its own weight? Other eaters have begged him not to go, even threatened to boycott his departure. "It's like when Hulk Hogan left wrestling," Cookie explains. "Then they dragged him back in. Then he would leave and they'd drag him back in again. A lot of these guys are like, 'Come on. You're one of the great eaters in the world.'"

Cookie Jarvis is a man at odds with himself—a lumbering paradox—and his personal crossroads is suggestive of the modern American gurgitator's many frustrations. He seems satisfied to have leveraged his eating greatness to become a media darling, then expresses frustration at not having an advertising contract. He is considered cocky by some, always talking smack and playing precontest mind games, and yet he is generally well-liked and bighearted and inclusive. One moment, he's professing his dogged determination to be the best eater in the world, even if that requires Kobayashi tossing his cookies at Coney Island. Then the next moment, he's talking about retirement. Now he's saying his training cuts into his family and career, and then he's saying the sport will be in either the X Games or the Olympics in ten years, and he wants to be around for the big show.

One message remains consistent, though. Jarvis has accepted the Belt of Fat Theory and is committed to losing weight. Having slipped in the rankings behind svelte gurgitators like Kobayashi, Thomas, and LeFevre, the writing on the wall is like a mural in neon graffiti. He's hoping to interest Subway in a sponsorship deal, under which he would shed pounds eating exclusively at Subway for a series of commercials, much like the "Subway Guy," Jared Fogle, who weighed 425 pounds before his Subway diet.

Call it a hunch, but I don't see Cookie retiring anytime soon. Undoubtedly among the most gifted cross-eaters eating today, he will continue to dissect foodstuffs, psych-out opponents, and talk reporters' ears off. Though there has been speculation about his health, Jarvis claims that he undergoes frequent checkups and is in good health. He's doing his damnedest to lose weight, and when he succeeds, world beware. "When I'm thin, I'm tellin' you . . . watch out. It's gonna be trouble. There's gonna be a new sheriff in town. Jahvis is gonna be back in action."

11

DOWNING DEEP-FRIED
ASPARAGUS

*You needn't tell me that a man who doesn't love oysters and as-
paragus and good wines has got a soul, or a stomach either. He's
simply got the instinct for being unhappy highly developed.*

—Hector Hugh Munro

APRIL 21, 2004

Being an emcee out on the circuit is like being a rock star on tour.
That is, a rock star without the groupies, the posh travel arrange-
ments, the stalking paparazzi, the raucous bouts of drug-fueled sex,
the divalike demands, and the screeching hordes of fans.

But for a few hours aboard my JetBlue flight to Sacramento, I
am able to suspend disbelief and almost be a semistar of sorts. The
woman seated next to me has taken such an interest in my job that,
after interrogating me extensively, she confesses that despite being a
successful real estate mogul, she isn't particularly happy with her
job. To sense envy from such a well-dressed woman buttresses my
already warm feelings toward my job and this trip. Our conversation soon leaks to nearby passengers, and before I know it I've developed a four-person fan base in the vicinity of seat 21D. One of
them, an older man, even vows to come see the competition at the

Stockton Deep-Fried Asparagus Eating Championship, my present destination.

Upon touchdown, the illusion dissolves into disappointing reality. I drive to my buddy Luke's off-campus house near the University of California at Davis, where I spend the night on his couch. The next morning, I call James "Big Ox" Martin, a local rookie, to confirm his appearance on the UPN morning news show *Good Day Sacramento*. Big Ox explains that he is unable to get his work shift off. *Sweet.* There is a special variation of Murphy's Law that applies to hosting eating contests, which takes into account the unreliability of eaters and EMTs, as well as the difficulties of preparing and weighing immense quantities of food. Adding insult to injury, a flurry of phone calls to my list of registered local eaters results in one air ball after another.

The upshot is, as of 6:00 A.M. the morning of the TV spot, I sorely lack an eater for the on-air asparagus eat-off we've planned against a news anchor. That isn't the only fun part. Moments after I lock myself out of my friend's house, I realize that my jacket, camera, and stopwatch are still on the couch. After my window-banging elicits suspicious glares from a neighbor walking her dog, I abort the mission, hop in the rented OldsmoPlymouth and head south on I-5, knee-steering, one hand on my coffee cup, the other pressing cell phone to ear, explaining to various producers that things aren't looking as good as we'd hoped for this eat-off thing.

In a stroke of good fortune, the UPN anchor for the segment is Mark S. Allen, a freethinking young lad who once hosted Comedy Central's *Short Attention Span Theater* and has a history of pulling wacky stunts. (He once lived on a billboard for a month, which he fell off of, breaking both legs.) By the time I meet up with him, at the Civic Auditorium of the Stockton Asparagus Festival, he has already recruited some young Filipino guy to eat against him for the segment. After briefly interviewing me on camera, Allen talks to the kid, who clearly has a strong competitive-eating pedigree.

"So you've won many awards yourself?" Allen asks.

"Exactly," he answers. "At home."

"Wait. Back up a minute," Allen says. "What kind of stuff are you doing at your home? Competitions with your family?"

"Well . . . you know, we eat government cheese, or anything free."

Allen nods. "I have experience with government cheese, but today, my friend, will be my first experience with an asparagus-eating competition."

They discuss how the asparagus will be prepared. The Filipino kid has no preference, and defers to Mark S. Allen's South Beach diet, which demands that the asparagus be steamed. Before we begin the one-minute exhibition, Mark S. Allen asks me what Kobayashi does to prepare. When I say that Kobayashi reportedly talks to his stomach, Mark asks me to talk to his. At this point, my unfamiliarity with news media becomes suddenly, glaringly obvious. In a high-pitched, vaguely Asian voice that sounds like a gay swami after sucking down a balloonful of helium, I pretend to rub Mark's stomach and say, "Come now, Mark's stomach. Eat, Mark's stomach, eeeeat much asparagus." When I finally snap out of it, I notice Mark has pulled away, red-faced, and the camera has already turned away. I imagine hundreds of bewildered viewers reaching at once for their remote controls.

Later that day, I meet up with Cookie Jarvis at the Asparagus Festival. He has arrived a day early to scope the scene and present what I like to call the Cookie Show. When I arrive, Cookie is talking up some young thing working the tent of a local radio station. He is—*astoundingly*—wearing-the Coat. I say astoundingly because it's a cloudless ninety-six degrees, the world highlighted bright yellow by the inescapable California sun. If social conventions permitted, I would be shirtless and in Skivvies. So it strikes me as odd that, despite having his fair share of insulation, Cookie has on a black trench coat and a black baseball cap. But such are the sacrifices required for the Cookie Show.

The Cookie Show is a fairly simple ritual. It basically involves sauntering around in the Coat and seeing what happens—and something always happens. Interactions. The magnetism of the Coat is not to be underestimated. Judging from the reactions of the Stockton festivalgoers, the Coat's effect is equivalent to the allure those glowing blue bug-zappers have on flying insects.

Which explains why, within moments of meeting up with Cookie, we are surrounded by onlookers. They gather behind the Coat, where they squint and point at the titles, waving family and friends over for a look. Then come questions, photographs, and autographs. To his credit, Cookie is kind and forthcoming with fans. Some folks recognize him from the local newspaper ads that featured him with hands raised, his right hand clutching the trademark Jarvis spoon.

Even without the Coat, I think Cookie attracts attention by dint of his sheer magnitude, which makes me oddly aware of my relative smallness (five feet nine inches, 165 pounds). The crowd seems to perceive me either as Cookie's stunted sidekick, the Teller to his Penn, or as some utterly anonymous runt. In fact, I feel almost physically deformed and begin to see how embracing your weaknesses in bold ways can turn them into strengths. In other circumstances, what may well be overtly negative attention—*Check out the fat dude!*—has been channeled by the Cookie persona into mild adoration.

Once the crowd dies down, Cookie says he wants to sample the asparagus. As part of his general commitment to preparedness, he takes a hands-on approach to precompetition negotiations. He has already raised several concerns to me in phone conversations. Would the asparagus's deep-fried batter shell become a cheating problem? Would it fall to the ground, or into the water during dunking? Will the $1,000 prize money be given as a lump sum to the victor, or will it be split up? And how will the plates be weighed? Cookie says he prefers five-pound plates to one-pound plates.

To facilitate his prep work, I call up Cathy Schieberl, the assistant to Kate Post, the executive director of the Stockton Asparagus Festival. Cathy, a cute Filipina-American college student, picks us up on her golf cart. She weaves through the crowd on "Spear-It Lane" and drops us off at "Asparagus Alley."

In the Asparagus Alley inventory tent, the Cookie Show starts up anew. The festival workers all seem to know about Cookie and act downright starstruck in his presence. More pictures are taken, and two heaping batches of deep-fried asparagus are delivered. They are like no species of asparagus I've ever seen. Each spear is at least eight inches long, with tips as thick as Sharpie markers and bases the circumference of quarters. They are dipped in golden brown batter and deep-fried, then topped with a healthy dose of Parmesan cheese. The tips are moist and chewy, highly bitable and quite tasty. But as you move toward the base, they become increasingly stubborn and stringy, a bit of a chore to chew. No less than four spears down, and I'm completely full, surveying the area for a trashcan inconspicuous enough not to draw contempt from the workers. I look at Cookie, who's chewing with a focus rarely associated with such a mindless act. The asparagus tips meet with his approval, but his expert assessment of the other end is far more critical. "These bottoms are brutal," he says, bobbing his head a little as he chews. "They're like an inch thick . . . and so dense!"

The moment of truth. It's just after 11:00 A.M. and already hot as Hades out here at the main stage of the Weber Points Event Center. Waivers are signed, the EMTs accounted for, and my girl Cathy is weighing the last of the sixty-odd one-pound plates of asparagus. (Despite Cookie's insistence on larger plates, I have overruled him on the grounds of less complicated judging.)

A calming Marvin Gaye tune oozes from the speakers, but the tension in the air is palpable. West Coast eating fans are newcomers to the sport and don't seem to grasp the significance of the matchup they're about to witness. Sonya and Cookie certainly do. They are avoiding each other self-consciously, over by the registration tent. Cookie's blinking and doing neck rolls; Sonya is smiling with her arms crossed. Head-to-head, they are 3-2 at this point, in Cookie's favor. Sonya's got Thanksgiving Turducken and Wing Bowl, while Cookie's got the two wing wins and Nathan's. Whoever takes asparagus will gain the upper psychological hand, and if Sonya prevails, she'll be one step closer to overtaking Cookie's precarious number one American ranking.

I'm sweating my nuts off, and it's not just the unfortunate combination of my wool suit with this tropical weather. I've got stage fright. This is basically my first big gig alone. I look out with trepidation onto an endless circular lawn that's starting to fill with people. Cathy has just informed me that I will be up on the stage, high above the eaters, whose tables are near the crowd on the lawn. This sermon-on-the-mount positioning psychs me out. Furthermore, I have just discovered that a couple of the eaters are noticeably absent. Suddenly, the Marvin Gaye chorus coming from the speakers seems to be mocking me. "What's goin' on?" it keeps asking. "What's goin' on?"

It's go time. I grab the mic, introduce myself, and welcome the crowd. I give shout-outs to the mayor, the sponsors, and my Uncle Mike Nerz, a local doctor. "And a special shout-out to my friend Luke Barton," I say, "a former mushroom-eating champion at Yale University."

This, of course, is not true, but it's a harmless lie. The unknowing crowd cheers, which loosens me up a tad. I'm wearing a suit, so they assume that I'm legit. Just as the momentum is going my way, I fall into some meandering digression about today's competitive foodstuff, asparagus. It goes on and on.

I say we know asparagus has been cultivated for about two thousand years. We know that King Louis XIV adored it so much he built special greenhouses so he could enjoy it year-round, which is why it's called the food of kings. We know it's nutritious, that it's high in folic acid, vitamins A, C, B$_6$, and thiamine. We know it's high in the cancer-fighter glutathione, and in rutin, which strengthens the blood vessels. *(What am I talking about?)* We know it comes in several colors, from white to purple. We know that California is the Asparagus State . . . (finally, some cheers) . . . that this state grows 80 percent of the U.S. domestic supply, around fifty metric tons every spring.

"So we know a lot about asparagus. But what we don't know, and what we are gathered here today to find out is"—I do my best dramatic pause—"how much asparagus can one human eat in ten minutes?" My excruciatingly long setup is finally rewarded with a relief-sigh of cheers. "And I say *human* because, unlike other sports, which are overtly sexist, in competitive eating women compete alongside men." I explain that the IFOCE's egalitarian spirit will prove particularly interesting today, because the two top-ranked gurgitators in America will be competing against each other. One is a four-hundred-pound man, and the other is a hundred-pound woman.

My attempt to explain the Belt of Fat Theory is met with confused silence. I'm not sure why I'm taking this didactic approach, lecturing like a professor, when clearly a WWF-barker style would be more effective. Luckily, it's time to bring out the eaters, so I can revert to the old standards.

"Our first contestant, weighing in at 175 pounds, five foot ten. He is presently unemployed and considering competitive eating as a career choice. . . . His name is Jonathan 'the Qrusher' Quok!" The crowd cheers. The Qrusher—a patently normal Asian twentysomething with a buzz cut—has taken my suggestion to make a strong entrance. He pulls his T-shirt up, showing off a prize-winning belly.

I knock down the list of local eaters. Bennett "the Bellybomb" Ouchi is a former amateur Cap'n Crunch eating champ from Davis. James "Big Ox" Martin is a 350-pound man-mountain whose life is a continual training session. (Big Ox also lifts his shirt on his jog to the table, and it must be said that he looks to have more natural talent than the Qrusher.)

Then it's time to pull out the big guns. I rattle off Sonya's records and claim that she is the fulfillment of an age-old prophecy about the arrival of the One Eater. She walks out, waving her hands and smiling. The crowd eats it up, all the more so because of how impossibly skinny Sonya is. Her jeans, which appear to be somewhere between a women's size one and a children's XL, are quite literally falling off her.

Our next eater, the number-one ranked American gurgitator, needs no introduction. I mention each of Cookie's many titles, but draw particular attention to his mayonnaise-eating feat, sixty-four ounces in five minutes. The crowd gasps. Cookie jogs out to the table, his drooping teardrop of a belly bobbing rhythmically.

"Ed-*die*! Ed-*die*! Ed-*die*!" someone chants.

"All right, Stockton," I say, "are you ready?"

Stockton yells out yeah, and I'm starting to feel the love. I explain the rules and advise the crowd to watch the flip numbers of our celebrity judges. The eaters are all seated, a rare sight for a pro competition. Once the competition starts, I sense as an emcee both the awkwardness of silence and the tragic mistake of cloaking that silence with drivel.

"This is the healthiest competition on the circuit," I say. "These people are gonna add a month to their lives, at least, with all the nutrients in asparagus."

Sonya's quick out of the gate, knocking down her first plate in a minute flat. I point out that she is a phenomenon, superhuman, and claim that skeptics have inaccurately theorized that she swallowed a tapeworm.

"Don't worry, folks," I announce. "We have advised all the eaters not to use the Porta Potties afterwards. There's been a lot of talk about the potentially pungent aftereffects."

It's a cheap joke, but it pays big laughter dividends. There are intermittent yelps of "Go, Sonya!" The guitarist of some rock band—apparently the next act—is behind me on the stage, tuning his guitar. This strikes me as disrespectful but adds a strangely appropriate sound track to the steady, furious munching.

"Folks, ten minutes might not seem like a long time to you, but it's like ten years to them. Help 'em out!" The crowd claps and woo-hoos. It's funny. You work hard to think up one-liners, but ultimately the straight-up rah-rah stuff is most effective. "How 'bout a little chant," I suggest. *"Eat! Eat! Eat! Eat!"*

Approaching the four-minute mark, Sonya and Cookie are both working on their third plates. Ron "the Drain" Davis and James "Big Ox" Martin are the local front-runners with one and a half plates apiece. I remind the crowd that there's never been a world record with asparagus, and therefore we're witnessing history. Whoever wins today will not only set a new world record, but take home a $1,000 check and the coveted Asparagus Trophy. I have developed verbal tics while emceeing. Today's front-runners for Words of the Day are "man-mountain" and "Stockton's finest." A little over six minutes into the contest, Sonya reaches for her fifth plate and appears to be pulling away. A group of fans are now ceaselessly chanting, "Let's go, Son-ya!" *Clap clap, clap clap clap clap.* "Let's go, Son-ya!"

At the seven and a half minute mark, there is a much needed dramatic development: Cookie stands up. I immediately pounce. "He's up! That's important. It helps to stand. Standing stretches out the alimentary canal, making peristalsis a little easier." The general policy of the IFOCE is to disdain chairs during competition, and this is for good reason. When gurgitators sit, there is an odd rushing-through-dinner undercurrent that dilutes the athleticism of the event.

"Unloosen your belt, Cookie!" someone yells out. Less than two minutes left, and the crowd's getting involved. Rival factions lob dueling Cookie and Sonya cheers. When Sonya finishes her fifth plate, the crowd goes insane, and I do my best to capitalize. "Five pounds of deep-fried asparagus, my Lord! It's divinely inspired. . . . Oslorf, the Norse god of consumption, is shining down upon this spot! Look at Sonya Thomas go!"

Sonya's still sitting, steadily stuffing. Endowed with extremely capacious cheeks, she is employing a technique known as chipmunking.

(Though Coondog O'Karma lays claim to the term, its etymology is unknown.) Chipmunking is a way of using the cheeks to temporarily store the foodstuff while the esophagus is busy swallowing.

"We're at eight and a half minutes, with two and a half minutes to go," I announce, so absorbed by the action that I've lost rudimentary subtraction skills. "Our local eaters seem to have hit a wall." This gets a big laugh, because the locals are slumped over, looking ready for a nap. Ron the Drain has stopped entirely and is leaning forward in his chair to get a better glimpse of Sonya. Cookie's on his fifth plate. It's not looking good, but I try to bolster the audience's hopes. "Don't count him out, folks. Cookie always surges late in the game."

Thirty seconds left, and the crowd keeps getting louder. "We are getting there! Do you feel it?" The cheers drown out the cacophonous tuning of that damn guitarist behind me. When they start to drown out my voice, I'm forced to scream myself hoarse. "Do they have the willpower, the stomach capacity, the hand-eye-mouth coordination?" We do the countdown, and, just like that, it's over. I command the eaters to put down their asparagus, let out a deep sigh, and lean against the railing. "Dear Lord," I announce. "This is an emotional moment."

The thrill of victory is more viewer-friendly than the despair of defeat. Sonya waving at the crowd, me comparing her intestinal fortitude to that of Joan of Arc, an asparagus trophy that looks roughly the size of its new owner . . . these are the images the world wants to see. The Stockton crowd confirms this sentiment, howling wildly at the announcement of her new world record: 5.75 pounds of deep-fried asparagus in ten minutes.

But it's the other eaters that intrigue me most. What's in it for them? And what about Cookie Jarvis, an extremely competitive human being, who has flown across the country with the expectation of confirming his status as America's best eater? In this sport, not only

Sonya Thomas lifts the fabled Asparagus Trophy while discussing her victory with an aspiring gurgitator. *(Courtesy of Loukas Barton)*

does the loser suffer the letdown of having tried and failed, he is also extremely—even unpleasantly—full. He is physically exhausted, but without that sense of dull-muscled fatigue that adds some consolation to having just lost, say, a soccer match. Although this is changing as the circuit gains clout, it's often winner takes all, money-wise, so the consolation prize is a free lunch, a stomachache, and a pat on the back.

But let's not break out the Kleenex just yet. The local eaters are all smiling, getting hugs and high fives from family and friends. Cookie is signing plenty of autographs and doing multiple interviews. As tempting as it is for an eater to feel self-pity, to blame the coldness of the foodstuff or the weather, the pro eaters generally congratulate the winner and move on. In this case, Cookie moves on . . . to the airport. Within hours of the end of the competition, he has boarded a flight to Florida, where he'll participate in the Sweet Corn Eating Competition in West Palm Beach the next day.

It just goes to show, you can never count out Cookie. Fifteen hours after his asparagus loss, with four hours of sleep and a full belly, he pulls off one of his greatest strategic coups ever. Ten ears of corn into the contest, with Jammin' Joe LaRue and Ray "the Bison" Meduna nipping at his heels, Cookie gets lockjaw. Unable to open his mouth, he starts doing smaller rows. Soon enough, this isn't working and he starts ripping the kernels off with his hands and throwing them into his mouth. This messy technique leaves his plate piled high with a mound of kernels. With one minute left, Cookie shovels the mound into his mouth. He ends up taking first place, breaking Gentleman Joe Menchetti's old sweet-corn record by more than a dozen ears. So when all is truly said and done, less than a day after his loss to Sonya, Cookie is three thousand miles away, smiling a big, yellow-flecked smile.

12

THE NADER DISPUTE: FOR AND AGAINST COMPETITIVE EATING AS SPORT

To the haters, the people who write derogatory comments about competitive eating, I just say, 'Hey, don't knock it till you've tried it.' And hopefully, you'll change your mind and find the good things about the sport to stay with it."

—Badlands Booker

In the April 20, 2004, edition of the Stockton *Record* there's a quarter-page advertisement for the Deep-Fried Asparagus Eating Competition that features Cookie Jarvis and the following tagline: "There's 1,000 bucks at stake, and the competition is huge." The article directly above this ad announces that Ralph Nader, the independent candidate for president, has called for the total withdrawal of U.S. troops from Iraq within six months.

To the layperson, it may seem that these two media artifacts are irrelevant to each other, but there is some correlation. On his Web site and in the *Philadelphia Daily News*, Ralph Nader has openly attacked competitive eating. He has called eating competitions a sign of societal decay on par with the excesses of former Tyco CEO Dennis Kozlowski, who wrote off his wife's $2 million fortieth birthday party in Sardinia as a deductible business entertainment expense. Here's an excerpt from the article on Nader's Web site:

Gluttony literally is rapidly becoming a competitive sport. In fact, out-gorging has become a contest with the gourgers [*sic*] riding circuit around the country performing in what its euphemists call "competitive eating." No longer the seven deadly sins in this field, "Crazy Devin" [*sic*] Lipsitz, winner of the 2000 year United Carnegie International Pickle Eating Contest in New York City, describes his skill as "a sport" played by "athletes."

There is even an International Federation of Competitive Eating which presides over dozens of events a year where contestants inhale hot dogs (the champion swallowed 50 hot dogs in 12 minutes), matzo balls, chicken wings and who knows what's next—mayonnaise?

While the competitive-eating community is not known for taking stances of any kind, it has reluctantly been dragged into the political sphere. His spelling and research errors aside (mayonnaise has been done and is among the IFOCE's finest records), Nader makes a few presumptuous assertions here, foremost of which is that competitive eating is *not* a sport. His stance has been seconded by Bill Maher, who said, "Competitive eating is not a sport. It's one of the seven deadly sins. . . . What's next, competitive farting?" In light of these assessments, some may even bristle at my insistence on calling competitive eating a sport throughout this book. Let's hash it out.

The *American Heritage College Dictionary* defines the word "sport" as "an activity involving physical exertion and skill, governed by rules or customs and often undertaken competitively." Is competitive eating an activity? Clearly. Does it involve physical exertion? Check. It only takes witnessing one IFOCE event to note the physical distress that eaters display in terms of heightened heart rate and excessive sweating. Take it from Don Lerman, a reliable primary source, "You put the body through more trauma in an eating contest than, let's say, a heavyweight boxer after three rounds."

Does competitive eating involve "skill"? This would likely be a sticking point for nonbelievers, because "skill" is a subjective term. Judging from my experience on the circuit, the average man on the street would not stand a chance in a contest against the top twenty IFOCE-ranked eaters. Topflight gurgitators rarely lose to local trenchermen in contests around the country, which implies that they have a "skill" that allows them to perform above and beyond average—even naturally talented—speed-eaters. Therefore, it's a skill, and one that is increasingly rewarded by society. Finally, is competitive eating governed by rules and customs? Absolutely. So by definition, competitive eating is a sport.

For the sake of argument, let's take into account factors outside this definition by which some might contend that it's not a sport. Some feel that activities like figure skating, diving, and gymnastics are not sports because they are entirely subjective—based on the decisions of judges. (This criterion breaks down in the case of boxing, which is both subjective and objective.) Competitive eating is usually timed and weighed, so it still meets this requirement.

Some might say it's not a "real" sport because it's not popular enough. Such naysayers might even call competitive eating a "fringe activity." If this is indeed the case, how can one explain Wing Bowl, which annually fills a sports arena with over twenty thousand fans? And what about the annual broadcast of the Nathan's Famous competition on ESPN, the "total sports network"? Doesn't this suggest popularity bordering on mainstream legitimacy? (Of course, ESPN covers nonsports like poker, too, which complicates the argument.) Furthermore, don't Sonya Thomas's total 2004 earnings—estimated at over $50,000—suggest a market for competitive eating?

George Shea draws a parallel to snowboarding, which was, not long ago, viewed with scorn. "Fifteen years ago, snowboarders were assholes. They were the morons of the mountain. People hated them. They were universally reviled. . . . But now that they've broken through the resistance, everybody goes, 'Oh, great sport.' It's in the Olympics. It's a great sponsorship moneymaker."

The debate rages on. As competitive eating steadily gains a groundswell of support in America and abroad, a handful of detractors remain. Baseball manager Lou Piniella succinctly captures the skepticism of many old-school sportsmen with his flip dismissal of Kobayashi's feat: "Fifty hot dogs in twelve minutes? That's not a sport. That's stupidity." To Rich Shea, the comment reeks of territorial pissings. "Lou Piniella is trying to protect a sport that drives dollars into his pocket. And that is a sport called baseball, and we're pulling eyeballs away from that sport. So for Lou Piniella, it may be a knee-jerk reaction. He wants to protect his sport, baseball, because he's threatened by our sport."

Perhaps the reason skeptics like Piniella can't reconcile themselves to the athletic nature of competitive eating is that, unlike in most sports, the real physical skill takes place internally. Unlike, say, soccer or basketball or football, where the playing field is decidedly external, much of the talent involved in what a competitive eater does is invisible to the naked eye. Another bias against the sport is the culturally reinforced assumption that the main function of eating is nourishment and enjoyment. This attitude has its place, but most competitive-eating supporters believe that this Europeanized view will be replaced by a more expansive take on eating. In the future, perhaps the world will look at a hot dog and see it not merely as a delicious snack, but as a piece of sporting equipment no different from a tennis ball or a hockey puck.

"There is a parochial and elitist attitude in sports," says George Shea. "But in what way is this not a real sport? Pick any sport. Minigolf, which is in the World Games, or curling, which is in the Olympics. Curling, what is that? My point is competitive eating is a very fundamental sport. The fundamental sports are running, jumping, pushing, and fighting. Eating is even more fundamental: Who can eat the most and in the quickest time, when that mattered in terms of whether or not you survived? There are rules. We have a governing body, and we keep track of the records."

. . .

The airtight case that competitive eating is a sport will not, however, silence the detractors. Nader's other allegation—that competitive eating is sanctioned gluttony—is a more complex and moralistic one. "Gluttony" is defined as "excess in eating or drinking." Even the most loyal fans might concede that eating as much as possible in a timed interval would fall loosely in the category of "excess in eating." Touché.

There is a difference, however, between eating immoderately and eating competitively. The first implies a lack of discipline, the inability to restrain the urge to eat. This sort of day-to-day gorging rises from the wellspring of greed, of reveling in pleasure. Competitive eating, on the other hand, requires considerable discipline. Gurgitators don't come to the table to enjoy a big meal, then find themselves unable to stop. They push themselves well beyond the point of moderation into a realm of physical discomfort, even pain, similar to the discomfort all athletes feel at the height of competition. "We are not eating like this every day," says Badlands Booker. "This is a sport. It's a skill that we exhibit for people who appreciate it. We're not tryin' to go out and just gorge every second. There's a purpose to it, so it's not gluttony."

Whether it is gluttony or not, the critics—or "haters," as Badlands might call them—continue to attack from all angles. Unsurprisingly, the most vocal critics are foreign reporters, who see the sport as a negative sign about American culture. Charles Laurence, a reporter from South Africa's *Sunday Times,* tosses out statistics about the obesity epidemic in America and adds, "Critics see the contests as a grotesque metaphor for America's consumer society." While this is indeed a tempting metaphor, it conveniently disregards the fact that nearly everything in contemporary America is a metaphor for consumerism. We walk around in $100 brand-name sneakers and jeans, toting shopping bags, iPods, and BlackBerrys: there are armadas of SUVs on every road and two hundred cable TV stations in each household; advertising and marketing are so ubiquitous as to be downright inescapable. These are all metaphors for the grander concept of consumption, and most of them are just as commonplace in any other country with a somewhat robust economy.

But the haters keep hating. John Sutherland, a reporter from the *Guardian* in the United Kingdom, takes this "consumerism gone awry" metaphor a step further. He uses the sport as a launching pad to denounce all of contemporary American culture.

> Competitive eating is, like World Federation Wrestling, a sport for our degraded times. It coincides with an unprecedented boom in the American economy fueled by rampant "consumption." If the American consumer stopped consuming, it would be 1929 again. America must gorge or die. But gorging is killing America.

So according to Sutherland, competitive eating—or the rampant consumption it represents—while keeping us from another Great Depression economically, is a catch-22 in terms of health. Hmm. It's a compelling theory, but by no means novel and a tad simplistic. It makes one wonder just how well capitalist British society, filled with chain-smoking, beer-swilling fried-fish eaters, is maintaining the balance between wealth and health. Other pundits take Sutherland's doomsday rhetoric a step further, saying that the rise of competitive eating in America brings to mind the fall of the Roman Empire. This apocalyptic view of America eating itself alive has been promulgated for over a century now, since the industrial revolution took hold. Why should we assume that this phenomenon represents the tipping point?

And to what extent is competitive eating an American phenomenon? There are eating competitions in Germany, England, Australia, New Zealand, Thailand, the Czech Republic, and Japan. As the Japanese circuit seems to wax and wane, America has emerged as the leading market internationally for the sport. This may have more to do with American sensibilities than our eating habits. Our fascination with guilt-laden pleasures—sex, eating, shopping, and leisure—fueled by our twin legacies of consumerism and a puritanical morality/work ethic, has prompted us to explore our own taboos in an uninhibited way. Further, the extremely competitive nature of American society has led to the view that almost any activity, from Rollerblade basketball to Texas hold 'em poker, can be transformed into a sport.

Associating competitive eating with obesity, however, is fallacious, as Sonya Thomas, Rich LeFevre, and every Japanese eating champion will attest to. That the best eaters are thin, bolstered by the Belt of Fat Theory, is a dashing blow to those who try to correlate the sport with America's obesity epidemic. Naturally, these provincial reporters rarely discuss thin gurgitators, but instead use more rotund eaters like Badlands, Cookie, and Hungry Charles as the objects of their contempt. What they don't mention is that these gurgitators didn't become big men *after* their eating careers started. They've always been big guys. It's not the dozen ten-minute contests per year that establishes a competitive eater's frame, but the calories-consumed versus calories-expended ratio over his or her lifetime. In fact, now, thanks to the demands of competitive eating, they are all trying to lose weight to catch up with the front-runners.

The harangues of these editorialists often take on a hateful tone. Nick Sargent, a reporter from www.spectatornews.com, repeatedly spits venom at Jarvis and Jed Donahue for being "fat," then adds that competitive gluttony is among "the top seven ways to ensure your fate in hell." John Sutherland, the *Guardian* reporter, calls Cookie a "human garbage grinder . . . an unashamed 420 lbs of all-American lard (432 after the contest)."

While obesity is clearly an American health problem, this sort of fat phobia suggests a related problem. In his book *Fat History: Bodies and Beauty in the Modern West,* Peter N. Stearns, a history professor and provost at George Mason University, dissects America's obsession with fat. He attempts to explain why the French have more success staying trim than Americans, despite dieting less. Professor

Stearns attributes this disparity to America's tendency to equate thinness with moral rectitude. He says that this attitude is exacerbated by America's increasing indulgence in sex and materialism, which leaves the population with a guilt complex and a proclivity for snacking. Indeed, the visceral "disgusted" reaction that some might feel in watching an eating contest has as much to do with this culturally ingrained association of free eating with laziness and obesity. Interestingly, for a true competitive-eating fan, the reaction of watching a skilled gurgitator in a contest is akin to the enjoyment one might feel watching a world-class orchestra play, or a fluid hitter swing a baseball bat.

Most of these outspoken critics have a dyed-in-the-wool vision of what an athlete looks like: he or she is thin, fit, and muscular. Period. At times, of course, the media makes exceptions for charismatic athletes like Babe Ruth, Mo Vaughn, or William "the Refrigerator" Perry (who, it should be noted, competed in the 2002 Nathan's Famous competition and was a talentless speed-eater). Generally, America cannot accept the image of an overweight athlete.

Why not? Why not appreciate a gurgitator's talent, even if he or she is overweight? In this day of rising salaries for spoiled, steroid-addicted pro sports stars, why not have a sport for Everyman? In this era of liposuction and salad-picking, all-protein diet fads and anorexic supermodels, where nearly every American feels insecure about his or her body, would it not be healthy to exalt the overweight man, or the woman who gorges openly? At a time when meals are laced with the bitterness of guilt, what harm is there in letting loose at the dinner table, if only for a ten-minute timed interval?

Even the thin gurgitators aren't immune to verbal attacks. On his Web site, Jim Rome, sports journalist and former host of *The Last Word with Jim Rome,* refers to Sonya Thomas (a woman half his size) as a "freak." "What a lady," he says sarcastically. "The female Babe Ruth of competitive eating. I'll bet her family is very proud."

The debate continues to divide the very fabric of our nation. A protective mother says competitive eating sends a bad message to her kids about overeating, and another counters that the message implicit in most women's magazines—*emaciated is beautiful*—is even more harmful. Some bleeding heart calls competitive eating a waste of food, and a devout fan stands up and says, "But at least they clean their plates!" Another one chimes in, "I don't see you complaining about NASCAR being a waste of fuel!" Indeed, this national argument has become so rancorous that Ralph Nader, who is usually willing to verbally duke it out with his many opponents in hopes of publicity, now refuses to return phone calls from anyone associated with the IFOCE.

What Nader and other critics overlook about competitive eating is that elemental factor that has led to the sport's meteoric rise: It's *fun*. That's right. It's fun for the crowd and the participants and the announcers and the reporters covering it. Not yet tainted by the poison of big-time money, it's still just a dozen or so regular mortals who have gathered at the table to answer that most fundamental of questions: How much can you eat?

The competitive-eating community may be a fun crew, but they can also hold a grudge. At times they're tempted to step up and say, "Either you're with us, or you're with them." George Shea dismisses Nader's comments as the blather of a madman. "This is a man who, in an effort to protect the environment and America, destroyed Al Gore's chance of being president and still doesn't recognize that fact." Don Lerman also has no time for Ralph Nader and his gurgitator-hating cronies. "He's just a killjoy, because we work hard at it, and it's good old-fashioned family entertainment. People like to watch it. It's fun. It's entertaining. And every media outlet—the local, the cable, the independent, the print, the radio—are in hot pursuit to pick it up." Lerman pauses to catch his breath and think this through. "He's just a spoiler. Like he was in the presidential election."

There is a precedent in the competitive-eating community for how to deal with adversarial politicians: They eat them. At a peaceful protest during the 2004 Republican National Convention, Badlands

Booker and Crazy Legs Conti ate a life-sized mashed-potato version of Dick Cheney at a downtown Manhattan bar. Hordes of young New Yorkers, who had gathered to launch a magazine for which Crazy Legs had written an article, urged the gurgitators on with "Eat Dick! Eat Dick!"

With that precedent in mind, perhaps it only makes sense to eat Ralph Nader as well. Not in the living flesh, but in effigy. If the American competitive-eating community must be pulled into the political sphere, then let the world hear the gnash of their teeth. As for the potential ingredients of an edible Ralph Nader, a number of foods come to mind that are suggestive of Nader's disposable political viewpoint—bologna, pork rinds, cheese puffs, or potted-meat food product.

13

ESCAPE FROM THE
POPCORN SARCOPHAGUS

Having to eat your way out to stay alive, out of a giant amount of food that's weighing you down and crushing you, seemed like a very good and a very bad idea at the same time.

—Crazy Legs Conti

MAY 2, 2004

The phone rings. It's George Shea, calling to give me the rundown on tomorrow: In a never-before-attempted stunt, Crazy Legs is going to eat his way out of a popcorn-filled sarcophagus as a promotion for the premiere of the documentary *Crazy Legs Conti: Zen and the Art of Competitive Eating,* at the TriBeCa Film Festival. My job is to dress up as a priest—no, make that a pastor—and just be there for Crazy Legs' spiritual support. I should wear all black, including a blazer and some black slacks, and I'll need a dickey, one of those collars that priests wear.

"You can say you're from the Brooklyn Episcopal Unitarian Church," George explains. "Located in East Flatbush."

I laugh. "But I think maybe if you're Episcopal, you're not Unitarian. Those are like two different denominations."

"Right. Maybe Brooklyn's not good anyway. Too close to home. You can be from the Hauppauge Unitarian Church, in Long Island."

I grab a pen and a scrap sheet. "How do you spell that?"

"H-A-U-P . . . I'm not sure. Doesn't matter. Just find a town in Long Island."

"Got it."

"So you're Reverend . . . what's that name you go by, your alter ego?"

"Manning," I say. "Roscoe Manning."

"Love it. So you're Reverend Manning, the pastor at Hauppauge Unitarian . . . no, junior pastor! You're the junior pastor, just got out of the seminary and took a position there. The reason you've come down to the theater is because you heard about Crazy Legs' stunt, and you're concerned because the danger level is so high."

"Right."

"Quite frankly, you're concerned for his life. You think there's a chance he might not emerge from the sarcophagus, so you want to be there to perform last rites if necessary."

"Okay."

"Before he goes into the sarcophagus, you'll consult with Crazy Legs quietly, hold his hand and console him. You might even ask aloud if he's ready to meet his maker."

"Got it."

"Say that you object to what Crazy Legs is about to do. You think it's insanity, that it's testing fate, testing the will of God. You disagree wholly, but you're not gonna abandon Crazy Legs at this crucial juncture just because you disagree."

"Naturally," I say. "And what's my background again, I mean, besides the Unitarian Church?"

"You trained in Bangor, Maine, and did your missionary work in . . . I don't know . . ."

"Bangalore?"

"Bangalore," George says. "Perfect. So I'll have Yesenia get you a collar. You can pick it up at the office in the morning."

"All right then. Game on."

"I have the utmost faith in you, Reverend Manning. See you tomorrow morning."

You can tell Crazy Legs is nervous because he won't take off the goggles. Red marks are forming around his brow, cheeks, and nose from the suction. You can barely see his eyes beneath the fogged-up lenses. He looks even more cartoonish than usual, a goateed white guy with reddish brown dreadlocks wearing a tuxedo, shorts, top hat, and a pair of swimming goggles with the attached snorkel flapping beneath his chin. Actually, Crazy Legs explains, it is two snorkels duct-taped together to ensure that it reaches the oxygen above the popcorn.

A movie-theater concession stand is not a place typically associated with tension, but this isn't your average concession scene. Danielle Franco and Chris Kenneally, the filmmakers and Crazy Legs' friends, are all over the place, handing out press clippings to reporters, advising cameras where to set up, checking in on the handyman. It's a matter of minutes till go time, but the handyman is still on his knees in the corner with an assortment of tools, feverishly working out the kinks of the sarcophagus. Popcorn-filled trash bags are piling up next to the concession stand like a family of fat ghosts. George Shea—whose outward cool on the mic at events is doubly impressive considering the frenetic mind state it masks—is fully bugging out. He keeps walking over to check with the handyman, who doesn't look up from his toil but assures him that everything's cool. George's main concern, as he's mentioned quite a few times, is carbon monoxide poisoning. The only one who seems vaguely composed here is Rich Shea. Feeling guilty about my uselessness in the beehive, I walk up to Crazy Legs.

"You might wanna take those off," I say, pointing at the goggles. "You're gonna be wearing those for a long time."

"Oh, right." Crazy Legs takes off the goggles and stretches out his face. Big red rings encircle his eyes. It's disorienting to see him even a little rattled, a rare sight. Despite the misleading name, Crazy Legs is generally levelheaded and self-possessed. I've come to think it's precisely this quality that allows him to surround himself with such an off-kilter crew of friends and never lose his sense of self.

"How you feelin'?" I ask him.

"All right. I felt fine until I talked to George."

"You ready to eat some popcorn?"

"Yeah. I'm ready. I just hope they don't have to use that ax."

I pat him on the shoulder. "You'll be all right."

"Thanks, man," he says, smiling. "That's reassuring coming from you, Father."

Cynics might say the word "sarcophagus" is a bit dramatic for what Crazy Legs has just lowered himself down into. "Chamber" might be more accurate. It stands approximately nine feet tall, a good three feet taller than Crazy Legs, who is six feet two and 213 pounds. It's about four feet wide and three feet deep, open at the top, and has been fashioned of plywood into the shape of a box of theater popcorn.

As garbage bags of popcorn are being dumped onto his head, George and Rich Shea attempt to give the hundred or so reporters and fans gathered in the theater lobby a sense of the magnitude of Crazy Legs' stunt. I might be tempted to take the Shea brothers' hype with a grain of salt, but the behind-the-scenes tension today makes this feel momentous. They explain that Crazy Legs has been rigged with a color-coded emergency communications system. On his thumb is a strip of green tape, for "all systems go." There's a strap of red tape on his right wrist, for "danger," and the other wrist is yellow, for "alert/need more butter." In the unfortunate case that Crazy Legs flashes the red signal, there is an ax handy for destroying the sarcophagus. An EMT is on standby for any medical emergencies. When the final bag of popcorn is dumped, all you can see of Crazy Legs is his goggled face in a square Plexiglas window.

"He is the David Blaine of the competitive-eating community," Rich belts out. "The Evel Knievel of the alimentary canal, the Houdini of cuisineee . . ."

"Like George W. Bush before him," George chimes in, "He enters the chamber numb, bereft of an exit strategy."

As Crazy Legs' face is slowly submerged beneath white-and-yellow kernels, George introduces Reverend Manning, the junior pastor who has taken it upon himself to help Crazy Legs in this time of need. As often happens in scenarios like these, George immediately disregards our agreed-upon backstory. He says that before I went to Brooklyn Unitarian I did missionary work in Bulgaria, and then he hits me with a non-sequitur question.

"So then, Reverend Manning . . . Bulgaria. Is that near the Hague?"

"Uhh, I don't believe so."

"And what exactly is The Hague? Is it a country, a territory, or some sort of commonwealth?"

I try to cover up my panic with outward spiritual calm. "I couldn't say actually. That wasn't covered in my studies at the seminary."

"No matter," George says. "What is the church's take on a stunt like this?"

"Officially, the Old Testament would call this gluttony. But I'm not concerned with such labels. My only concern is that this young, foolhardy man makes it out of that sarcophagus alive."

"And how old is the Old Testament, Reverend?" Rich asks. "When was that published again?"

"It's very old," I say.

"Because I understand that it has been through several reprintings," Rich adds.

Crazy Legs is now fully submerged and has wriggled his way to the front of the chamber. All we can see are fogged-up goggles and a few dreadlocks. He looks like a termite buried in its own wood-gnawings. I make eye contact with Crazy Legs, then press my hand against the Plexiglas window. He does the same. We share a moment, one that can only be described as tender.

"Ladies and gentleman," George says. "Witness one last moment of contact between a holy man and a man submerged in sixty cubic feet of popcorn. May both of their prayers be answered."

When Chris Kenneally and Dani Franco first met Crazy Legs in 1999 while all three were working at the film studio the Shooting Gallery, they were stunned by the extent of his obsession with competitive eating. "We used to go to his house," Franco remembers, "and he would pull out these competitive-eating tapes. This was way before he ever competed. He was a superfan. He knew every single eater's stats. And he got us really excited about it after a while because he was so into it."

Kenneally remembers Crazy Legs doing spontaneous eating challenges at work. While waiting for the elevator one day, Kenneally ran into Conti, who was carrying a huge McDonald's bag. Kenneally followed Crazy Legs to the roof of the building, where he performed a stunt called Nug Nug Ninety-nine in front of a dozen other employees. In ninety-degree heat, wearing a huge fuzzy hat, Crazy Legs ate sixty-eight Chicken McNuggets in forty-five minutes.

Another time, while working on the set of a film in Little Italy during the San Gennaro Festival, Crazy Legs made a bet with a fellow worker, a teamster known as Tommy the Teamster. While eating a pasta lunch, somebody ordered the all-you-can-drink Guinness special with lunch. "You know, Guinness has a lot of nutrients," Crazy Legs said. "I bet you could live on that for a week." Minutes after the comment came out, the bet was on. If Crazy Legs lived on Guinness for a week, he would earn a free lunch at the Corner Bistro, a West Village bar known for its delicious hamburgers. He won the bet, drinking about seven bottles of Guinness a day out of coffee cups while working. After the first day, he no longer felt any intoxicating effects beyond the delirium of malnourishment. By the time he redeemed his victory meal, he had lost five pounds.

Considering his affinity for such non-film-related activities, it's perhaps not so shocking that Crazy Legs soon lost his job. He worked freelance production-assistant gigs for a while, before having an epiphany one morning on a movie set. It was 4:00 A.M., and Conti had been ordered to find a place to dump the leftovers from a meal. "And I thought, 'What am I doing?'" Crazy Legs says. "I didn't come to work in film to be out here at four in the morning fending off transvestite hookers so I could dump clam chowder while the residents scream at me about rats."

A Johns Hopkins University graduate from its Writing Seminars program, Crazy Legs decided to quit the film biz and start writing a screenplay. To pay the bills, he took odd jobs such as posing nude for student art classes and donating semen at a sperm bank. While working as a short-order cook, a fellow worker told him about a job washing windows. It soon became his steadiest gig.

One day in late March of 2002, while watching television with Kenneally and Franco, Crazy Legs got a call from the manager at the ACME Oyster House in New Orleans. On February 3, 2002, Conti had broken the restaurant's oyster-eating record while watching his favorite team, the New England Patriots, win the Super Bowl. The ACME folks explained that they would like to pay for Crazy Legs to come to New Orleans and compete in the Big Easy Oyster Eat-Off speed-eating championship.

Kenneally and Franco, who had just bought a video camera, decided to follow Crazy Legs and shoot his quest to upgrade from fan to pro eater. They shot him training with butter and oysters, then filmed his first visit to the IFOCE office, where they were shocked to see that George Shea recognized Conti.

They shouldn't have been. Every year from 1996 on, Crazy Legs had made the annual trip to Coney Island to pay homage to his favorite eaters. He remembers the days when the contests weren't crowded and how a person dressed in a pea suit showed up each year to advocate vegetarianism. He was bummed to have missed Krachie's dominant years but psyched to have caught the Japanese takeover of Arai and Nakajima. When the Shea brothers retired Mike "the

Scholar" DeVito's mustard-stained jersey to the rafters, Crazy Legs had been hanging from a pole to get a better look.

Franco and Kenneally had no particular ambitions for their project. They just wanted to have fun and maybe get a short film out of it. But when Crazy Legs won the Big Easy Eat-Off on April 13, 2002, they realized something bigger was in the works. Having started his gurgitating career with a bang, Crazy Legs decided to go after the grail—qualifying for the Nathan's contest. So they followed him to the Boston qualifier, interviewing his parents along the way. What might have been throwaway footage turned into a revealing look at his food-obsessed parents—an artistic mother who had bronzed her son's pacifier and a father who cooked incessantly when not working as a rocket scientist on the Patriot missile program.

After losing the Boston qualifier, Crazy Legs decided to give it one last shot at a remote qualifier in Seattle. He won. Realizing that he would be competing in Coney Island now, Kenneally and Franco decided they had a feature-length documentary on their hands. They recruited friends from their film jobs to help with the editing and friends from open-mic nights to help with the score. Crazy Legs told them he wanted to be a pure subject with no influence on the film. The first time he saw the final product was at its first screening, which Kenneally and Franco arranged by renting a theater for a hundred people in Boston.

When *Crazy Legs Conti: Zen and the Art of Competitive Eating* was selected as one of the feature-length documentaries for the TriBeCa Film Festival, a New York City event founded by Robert De Niro, Kenneally and Franco were overjoyed. Here they were hoping to make it in the world of entertainment, only to get their biggest breakthrough in the form of a unique friend.

Although the movie contains all the elements of a compelling story—the quest of an interesting protagonist, obstacles, a villain (Cookie Jarvis), and redemption—the story ultimately succeeds on the basis of Crazy Legs' character. He is enigmatic, in many ways a nice, normal guy, but with a host of peculiarities. He wears shorts 365 days a year and only owns two pairs of pants. His nickname has become his real name such that only his closest friends know the real one (Jason), yet he refuses to explain the story behind how "Crazy Legs" came about. He is highly intelligent and articulate, well-read in acclaimed literature, yet chooses only low-paying jobs and has an obsessive collection of lowbrow eighties movies, especially those starring "the Coreys"—Feldman and Haim. Though he has a clear sense of irony, his interests in eighties movies, obscure foods, and competitive eating seem entirely earnest.

Perhaps most interesting is Crazy Legs' social life. He is a self-appointed social events coordinator who is constantly e-mailing notices of group activities to his many friends. The events include the ongoing open-mic night known as Doctor Jellyfinger's Paradise Jam, New York bike tours and bar crawls, kickball games in Central Park, and parties at "Coleman's Bar & Grill." This is the name Conti has given to his East Village apartment, which is jammed with books, VHS movies, liquor bottles, an industrial stove, a Door of Fame, and a neon COLEMAN'S BAR & GRILL sign. The people who travel in Conti's circle are artistic by temperament and go by strange names. There's the Drunken Poet, Little Jimmy (a little person from Coney Island), Dinshaw, Sandwich, Bourbon, Wet Levi, and Doctor Jellyfinger. The common tie that binds them is their love of a good time and their allegiance to Crazy Legs.

So it was probably inevitable that somebody in this motley crew of artists would ultimately recognize that their de facto leader was an obvious subject for a film or a book or a song (or all three, as it has turned out). Like many writers, Crazy Legs leads a double life as a character worth writing about. In the tradition of beatniks like Ken Kesey and Neal Cassady, he has been added to the canon of youthful American protagonists who reflect their surroundings in meaningful ways.

· · ·

The problem with distance eating is that it takes so long. Crazy Legs has been steadily munching for a solid hour; we can now see his face and upper torso. The goggles are off, his dreadlocks are matted with popcorn shrapnel, and his once white tuxedo shirt is stained a chemical-butter hue of toxic yellow. As Crazy Legs requests a tube of Chap Stick, the Reverend Manning strikes up a conversation with a woman named Elyse HF Maxwell, the founder of the Burger Club, a group of New York residents who meet twice a month in search of the perfect hamburger. The reporters are beginning to tire of the whole spectacle, but Crazy Legs is determined to continue eating until his film premiere—six hours from now. The "We love you, Crazy Legs!" cheers have died down. The only thing sustaining the crowd is the on-going banter of the Shea brothers.

GEORGE: It appears to be awkward, Rich, this eating one's way through sixty cubic feet of popcorn.
RICH: There's something gerbil-esque about his movements that's both beautiful and disquieting.
GEORGE: When things slow down, I'm going to talk about how the Indians called it maize.
RICH: They introduced it. I understand we introduced taxes.

Reporters from the *Daily News,* the *New York Times,* Knight Ridder, Reuters, and the Food Network are moseying around, trying to decide whether to wait it out. Jeanne Moos, an anchor from CNN, has resorted to reaching down into the sarcophagus to wipe off Crazy Legs' goatee. One reporter is so desperate he interviews the Reverend Manning and inquires about the strange name stenciled on his Bible: RYAN NERZ. An argument sparks up between a few television reporters and the Shea brothers. The reporters want footage of Conti's exit, for closure to the piece. The Shea brothers, in defense of Crazy Legs' wish to continue eating, have run out of relevant comments but continue to buy time.

Crazy Legs Conti, submerged in the popcorn-filled sarcophagus, keeps munching while the cameras keep snapping. *(Courtesy of Reuters/Chip East CME/ JDP)*

GEORGE: I was watching the Weather Channel last night. You know, it's horrendous what earthquakes can do . . . the *damage*.

RICH: You know that Matt LeBlanc, from *Friends*? He sure is a cutie.

GEORGE: Speaking of that, you know, *Friends* is ending. *Frasier* is ending. It's all ending.

RICH: Did I mention that Patrón is sponsoring tonight's after-party?

Finally, the reporters take a stand. At their insistence, Crazy Legs reluctantly emerges from the Popcorn Sarcophagus, "like a turtle emerging on the beach," as George describes it. Crazy Legs has eaten down to his waist, which, to the observers who've been watching his efforts, qualifies as an escape. Crazy Legs, who's noticeably annoyed that he's been cajoled into quitting, seems physically fine if a little wobbly. "It's not the corn that gets you," he says in summation. "Or the pop. It's definitely the *butter*."

Little does he know that this stunt will gain him almost as much media attention as the documentary itself. Within hours of his escape, he receives interview requests from Australia, England, and Israel. A segment on Crazy Legs's escape appears on CNN's *Anderson Cooper 360°*, and pictures by a Reuters photojournalist are posted on Web sites across the world. But most significantly for a former college high jumper and basketball player, the footage of Crazy Legs's escape is ranked number six on ESPN *SportsCenter*'s Plays of the Day.

14

THE SECESSIONISTS

Gentleman Joe is clearly a victim, almost a Christ figure.

—George Shea

The TriBeCa Film Festival premier of Crazy Legs's documentary was not merely a gathering of his New York posse, but an opportunity for several prominent gurgitators to walk the red carpet. Because the IFOCE eaters are a tight-knit bunch, it was touching to hear Crazy Legs, clad in a dashing lavender tux (with matching shorts), give shout-outs to the likes of Cookie Jarvis, Badlands, Beautiful Brian, and Hungry Charles Hardy. Many insiders, however, were shocked to hear him mention another eater in attendance, one seated dangerously close to the IFOCE crew—Gentleman Joe Menchetti.

Several months before, Gentleman Joe had boldly seceded from the IFOCE to strike out on his own in the hardscrabble field of independent eating competitions. The focus of Menchetti's rift with the IFOCE was not new to professional sports—a contract dispute. Having been a featured gurgitator for a couple years, Menchetti, like most eaters in the top twenty-five, had signed the IFOCE contract. The contract establishes an eighteen-month relationship wherein the eater agrees to compete only in IFOCE-sanctioned events unless consent is given by the IFOCE brass. Though most gurgitators are happy to sign the contract, some second-tier eaters feel that it restricts their ability to earn prize money in unsanctioned contests.

In late 2003, Gentleman Joe opted out of the IFOCE contract, establishing himself as the circuit's prodigal son. He cooked up an ad hoc Web log, www.speedeat.com, a low-budget affair without graphics or photos that billed itself as "THE source, for up to date, speed eating news!" The log lists the results of eating competitions, both IFOCE and otherwise, while laying out an ongoing critique of all things IFOCE.

Perhaps taking its cues from the civil rights movement, speedeat.com rejects the language of its oppressors. Gentleman Joe, who narrates his blog in the first-person plural (as in the royal *we*, or "We here at speedeat"), calls the Shea brothers "the $hea $i$ter$" and their eating organization "the Fed." Instead of using the traditional terms for vomiting—"reversal of fortune" or "urges contrary to swallowing"—Menchetti has coined the term "bulemic behavior" (brazenly rejecting accepted notions of spelling). He has even created a few nicknames, such as Carlene "Madam of Etiquette" LeFevre and Dave "Unworthy of a Nickname" Baer.

In keeping with the maverick journalistic style associated with blogs, speedeat.com is unabashedly subjective. It lists Menchetti's opinions on the issues that concern Americans most, such as how the Fed is "as corrupt as Louie the Prefect in Casablanca," and how Beautiful Brian is the "BIGGEST LOSER!" On occasion, it is even delightfully mean-spirited, with conclusions like " 'El Wingador' loses to some Hick!" He has been particularly harsh on Crazy Legs at times, whom he calls "a game show host masquerading as a competitive eater." When Conti failed to win a stew-eating contest in New Mexico where cash and pottery were offered as prizes the blog said, "We guess Crazylegs' mom doesn't get any indian [sic] pottery for Christmas."

The posting of IFOCE contest results are often so prompt that there have been accusations of an intelligence leak among the IFOCE eaters. (The source is difficult to determine, but some fingers point at phone man Cookie Jarvis.) Sometimes speedeat.com's paragraph-long pieces are objective statements about who won what, but a particular focus is placed on IFOCE mishaps and Gentleman Joe's victories and prizes. When writing about his own triumphs, Menchetti often refers to himself by the Alex Rodriguez–like nickname Gjoe. Of his cicada-eating victory in Washington, D.C., Gjoe writes, "If you don't know what a cicada is, its [sic] a flying insect that shows up every 17 years. Many chefs & nutritionists recommend eating these creatures as a free source of tasty protein. 'Gentleman' Joe Menchetti won this 1 minute contest by eating 89 seasoned & fried Cicada's [sic]." Gjoe does provide some compelling personal confessions, such as the incident that occurred after his victory in a paczki-eating contest. "Gentleman Joe admitted to a rare incident of 'bulemic behavior' caused by a massive coughing fit, 1.5 hrs after winning the $200 prize." Menchetti is never bashful about his own gurgitory prowess. In the rankings section of speedeat.com, Gjoe ranks himself above Hungry Charles Hardy, Oleg Zhornitskiy, and Nobuyuki Shirota.

On January 22, 2004, I got my first taste of corporate espionage. I attended the Frank's Red Hot Sauce Battle to the Bone, a chicken-wing-eating competition held in a conference room at Madison Square Garden. In 2003, the IFOCE had produced a wing-eating circuit for Frank's Red Hot Sauce, but negotiations broke down the following year, and the IFOCE didn't get the contract. In a remarkable (if slightly suspicious) turn of events, Frank's Red Hot chose Gentleman Joe Menchetti to help out with the refashioned circuit. After the announcement that the kickoff event would be at MSG, the Shea brothers suggested that, as a writer, I might want to go check it out. Before the competition, I bought a microcassette recorder at RadioShack. At the arena's entrance, I was greeted by a smiling young lass in a Frank's Red Hot shirt.

"Hello. What is your name, sir?" she asked.

"Roscoe Manning."

"And what media outlet are you associated with, Mr. Manning?"

"The Yale School of Journalism. I'm a grad student."

This seemed to please her. With this Roscoe Manning routine, I was beginning to enjoy the same liberating character transformation that eaters must feel when they shift into their onstage gurgitating personalities. She handed over a press packet and ushered me into the conference room. It wasn't your typical competitive-eating scene, but more like a lavish corporate conference. A buffet lunch was set up—salads and hot wings and wraps—and tables were scattered about for dining. The crowd was sparse, consisting mostly of well-dressed corporate types, a handful of journalists, and several dozen eaters. With the exception of Hal Schimel, a quirky eater whose profession is stalking celebrities and pro athletes for autographs, I hadn't heard of any of the eaters.

I sat down, turned on my tape recorder, and watched three rounds of qualifiers. For the first time (and with some admitted bias), I began to see just how essential the commentary and pageantry of an eating competition is to its entertainment value. Because the play-by-play was limited to quips like "He's eating pretty fast," I found myself feeling bad for the eaters, wishing that they could enjoy the wings at the leisurely pace with which I was eating them. If not infused with dramatic narrative and humor, eating competitions can be tedious to all but the most dedicated fans.

That said, the female British journalist seated beside me found the competition fascinating. She analyzed the competition like a cultural anthropologist, unaware that her opinions could be construed as condescending. "I believe it has something to do with the immigrant experience," she theorized. "It must be deeply rooted in American culture to gobble up as much food as you can before it disappears."

After the qualifiers, the deejay announced a special guest: Gentleman Joe Menchetti. My ears perked up. A broad-shouldered, dark-haired, goateed man in a tuxedo took the stage. Reading in monotone from note cards, Menchetti reeled off his eating records. "I'm also currently ranked number seven in the world by speedeat dot com," he said. He dropped training techniques such as chewing gum for jaw strength and demonstrated the "one-pass swoop" and "rotating umbrella" methods of stripping wing meat. Before the competition, the judges, Menchetti included, recited a lengthy oath promising objectivity and fairness.

Once the final competition started, things picked up. People gathered around the stage. Arnie "Chowhound" Chapman, a bearded guy wearing a baseball cap with dog ears, looked as if he had talent. He was knocking them back pretty quick.

"Strip and swallow," Gentleman Joe called out. "Don't chew it."

"Go Chowhound!" I yelled, impressed by this young upstart.

Chowhound Chapman won, with two point five pounds of chicken meat in eight minutes, no shabby tally. When I interviewed him afterward, he said he was ranked thirty-seventh by the IFOCE, but that he should be ranked higher. He said he used to train with ramen noodles but wasn't sure how effective it had been. He had really started getting into speed-eating, he claimed, when his son was born. "This is kind of a way for me to carve out some of my identity beyond work and being a father," he added.

I walked over to Gentleman Joe and introduced myself. Tape recorder in hand, I did my best impression of a reporter. "So you said you're ranked number seven with . . . what is it?" I asked.

"Speedeat dot com."

"So that's like a Web site or is that like a league?" I asked.

"It's hoping to become a league."

I asked if he was competing much these days.

"I did a qualifying stunt for the Wing Bowl in Philly. Completed my stunt—it was ten Big Macs in twenty-five minutes. But the two guys that run that contest perceived—actually, accurately—that comments on speedeat dot com that they thought were negative came from me."

"Ah," I said. "I see . . ."

"So you're from Yale?" he asked, breaking the awkward silence.

My heart thumped. *Is he onto me?* "Yeah, I'm a graduate student there, in journalism."

"I grew up right down the street in Hamden."

"Oh, okay. Yeah? Cool."

"I made an attempt at the Yankee Doodle burger challenge."

"Oh, right." I knew about the Doodle challenge. The Yankee Doodle is an old-school hole-in-the-wall diner right near campus. The challenge is, if you can eat more burgers than whatever the standing record is, you get them for free. If not, you pay.

"The record was twenty-eight," Joe said. "And I got twenty-seven before I had a little bit of bulimic behavior."

"Right," I said, giggling. "I know how that works. Urges contrary to swallowing, as they say."

"Right," said Gentleman Joe. "But I try not to use that one . . . because I know who invented it."

A week after the Frank's Red Hot episode, Gentleman Joe gained a lasting ally in his war against the Fed. After the Frank's Red Hot event, George Shea warned Arnie "Chowhound" Chapman that he would have to sign an IFOCE contract if he wanted to compete in the Ben's Kosher Deli Matzo Ball Eating Contest finals. George e-mailed the contract, but Chowhound refused to sign it.

The contract felt fishy, Chowhound explained. "What? You mean I can't go to some local thing and win two hundred bucks for my family? I mean, who are you to tell me that I got this talent, but I can't go use it?" At the same time, the thought of not being able to compete in matzo balls was almost too much to bear. After the Frank's Red Hot win, Chowhound was feeling like "someone who could make noise in competitive eating."

He had only competed in a handful of IFOCE events and felt that matzo balls would be his breakout performance. After buying matzo balls in bulk, he had trained for months. "And I don't even like matzo balls," he said. "I think they're disgusting. But I ate *so many* matzo balls. I ate more matzo balls than anybody should eat in a lifetime in getting ready for this." Chowhound called the Ben's Deli PR rep to complain about the contract dispute, but was told that nothing could be done. "Do you realize that you've just made a deal with the devil?" Chowhound responded.

It was a day that would live in competitive-eating infamy: January 27, 2004. Aware that he wouldn't be allowed to compete, Arnie Chowhound Chapman showed up at Ben's Deli anyway. "And of course, I was steaming," he said. "I was extremely angry. And I'm gonna be honest with you, I was angry with the other eaters." He felt that they should protest to George and stick up for his right to compete. But the other eaters had all signed the contract and were thus short on sympathy.

Chowhound decided to actively boycott the contest. As the competition began to unfold, with George laying out the precompetition hype, Chowhound's bark became his bite. He started walking up and down the table, trying to get under the skin of various eaters. He approached Crazy Legs.

"Cut off your dreadlocks, man!" Chowhound remembers saying. "Because dreadlocks are supposed to be about consciousness. It's supposed to be about doing something positive. And what you're doing right now, in going along with this bullshit, watered-down contest, is not positive. Your dreadlocks are doing you no good. *Cut 'em off!"*

As Badlands Booker remembers it, the words were even more provocative, such that Crazy Legs, who's not the brawling type, was ready to fight. But the other eaters calmed him down. When nothing came of the confrontation, Chowhound, incensed, approached Badlands.

"Hey, Booker!" he yelled out. "I thought slavery was over!"

Whoa. Though I wasn't there, I imagine a record scratching and the place going silent. As I understand it, the S-word, like the N-word, is not something you use lightly around African-Americans. Badlands, for his part, was dumbfounded. "I'm up there with the IFOCE shirt on, you know, representin' the clique," he explains. "And he says *that.* I was like, 'Ohhhhh! You went *there.*' "

Chowhound defends the comment, saying it wasn't meant to be racist, that his intentions were misconstrued. He claims that the word "slavery" only came out because, in certain eating circles, the IFOCE contract was commonly referred to as "the slave contract." He says he grew up in Red Hook, Brooklyn, and knew his share of black folk. "The thing that's really ironic about this whole thing is that I'm like a reggae fanatic," Chowhound says. "I love black culture. I know more about black history than most black people do."

Badlands maintained perspective, as is his wont. He had met Chowhound before and thought he was "a great guy." In fact, Chowhound had competed in Badlands' first Nathan's contest in Long Island. "If I didn't know the man, I would think he was probably a racist. But I actually knew what he meant. He thought that because I was with the IFOCE . . . that I was a slave to them. That's why I didn't wig out on him or nothing like that. And you know, that's not my nature. I'm not gonna stoop to the level to kick his ass, mess around, and get arrested."

When the imbroglio boiled over, Badlands performed a few rap tunes for the delighted audience. Then, employing a Zen mind trick that allows him to funnel anger into raw ingestion, he won, swallowing twenty and a quarter baseball-sized matzo balls in five minutes, twenty-five seconds. "I'm not gonna let him steal my joy, competing," Badlands says. "I trained for this day. It's very important to me. So I'm not gonna let his little comments get me off of my focus."

The next day, Chowhound Chapman sent Badlands a letter explaining what he meant. He hadn't meant to offend, and if he had, he apologized. With twenty-twenty hindsight, Chowhound "wouldn't have put it that way." In the end, Badlands bears no ill will toward Chowhound, but can't guarantee that other IFOCE eaters share his compassion: "Sometimes the tongue is like a sword. The damage has been done. It's the talk around the competitive-eating watercooler. It's like, 'You heard what he said to Booker? You heard what he did to Crazy Legs?'"

Arnie Chapman's fixation with justice may stem from his having been dealt a bad hand early on. Growing up in a foster home, he became the self-appointed "barracks lawyer" for kids who got in trouble. In the army, he spent two years of active duty stationed in the demilitarized zone that separates North and South Korea. He was forced to listen to speakers belting out mind-numbing Communist propaganda, and the outrage he felt toward Kim Il Sung and his suffering constituents was seared indelibly into his memory.

Though his father claims he'd always been able to make food disappear, Arnie credits his impoverished youth for his appetite. He remembers going days without eating as a young boy. Later, as the youngest of three brothers in a foster home with dozens of competing mouths, Arnie saw the dining room as a battle zone. "I like to think that I've eaten competitively my whole life," he says.

What a pleasant surprise then to discover that he could eat not only for free, but for *profit*. Indeed, like many gurgitators, Chowhound started out as a mercenary eater. His first contest was back in 1991, when he was unemployed and living in Rockaway Park, Brooklyn. Riding by a Nathan's Famous hot dog stand, he saw a sign advertising a hot dog contest with a $100 prize. With dollar signs in his eyes, he snarfed down eleven and a half hot dogs and buns in six minutes to take the bounty.

As quickly as Chowhound's competitive-eating career started, it stalled. Disappointed at the small number of tournaments on the then fledgling eating circuit, Arnie decided to turn his obsession with justice into a job. Over the years, all of his caretakers had relayed the same message. "They all said I was a good advocate of people, that I was concerned about the underdog, and that I would make a good social worker." Inspired by this message, he got a bachelor's in social work, and then a graduate degree in vocational rehab counseling.

His competitive-eating career catapulted him toward righteousness as well. After narrowly losing a Long Island pickle-eating contest to a man named, appropriately enough, Marv Biteman, Chowhound decided to get hungry and focused. "At some point in 2003, I got this crazy idea, like, I'm gonna give it all I can. I had a mortgage, I had a kid, I had a wife. . . . I gotta have some kind of life outside all these responsibilities." He signed up for the Nathan's Famous Civil Service qualifier and didn't win, but showed some promise.

At the 2003 Cannoli Eating Competition in Little Italy, Arnie says he learned the hard way about the cutthroat nature of the IFOCE circuit. Just minutes before the contest started, the other eaters' wives and friends started handing them paper bags. From them they pulled a secret ingredient known to circuit veterans: coffee, for dunking. Arnie called out to his wife, desperate, but she was stuck in the crowd. "I learned from that experience. I'm, like, these are nice guys. But they weren't nice enough to tell me about that little trick."

Still, Chowhound remembers how his "heart swelled with pride to be a part of the IFOCE." He took a respectable fourth in a star-studded field in cheesecake. On the basis of such solid finishes, George Shea sent him out to Las Vegas for the Stagg Chili Eating Contest. Even then, though, he sensed the IFOCE's treachery. Of the chili-eating contest, for example, Chowhound says, "When I look back, I was one of the most least-deserving people to go." He also claims that, though his travel and lodging were covered, the IFOCE reneged on a promise of $100 in expense money.

The stage was set for the Ben's Deli Matzo Ball meltdown. Once that occurred, there was no going back. Chowhound came to a stark realization. "Shea wasn't gonna let me into any of his contests unless I signed a contract. So at one point, I said to myself, 'The only way I'm gonna compete against really good eaters is if I make my own contests.'" Destiny, it seemed, was in Chowhound's hands.

He launched a Web site, www.competitiveeaters.com. It started out as a spite site that, like speedeat.com, served mainly as an open forum to vent at the Fed. "At first, it looked like doctrine. And then some of the people around me told me there was too much anger." With the help of people like Coondog O'Karma, another renegade IFOCE outcast from Ohio, Chowhound began envisioning a potential revolution. They formed the Association of Independent Competitive Eaters (AICE), a loose affiliation of gurgitators that more closely resembles a union than a league.

Unlike the IFOCE, which Arnie sees as a dictatorship run by the Shea brothers, Chowhound and Coondog would run AICE by socialistic principles. Established by eaters, the league's core principle was the recognition of "eater sacrifice." AICE would acknowledge that eaters show up for contests, sometimes at their own expense, sacrificing time that could be spent with family. They prepare, train, and adjust their eating schedules for contests. Pencil pushers like George Shea don't understand this principle, he says, because he's not a gurgitator. "He talks about 'I do all the work.' But do you know what it's like getting behind a table of hamburgers or hot dogs and going twelve minutes? I mean, I've run marathons before. I've been an infantry soldier. But that's one of the toughest fuckin' things you can do . . . So to say that an eater's contribution to the whole thing is insignificant is totally devaluing what the eater does."

As the Web site's mission statement details, AICE stresses the importance of "Eaters' Rights." The most fundamental right is that eaters possess artistic control over their presentation. This means that all professional eaters shall be introduced based on their "professional identities." "So if I'm the knockwurst champion," Chowhound explains, "and I hold the record for that, I don't want you to forget about it. It's something I did. It's something I accomplished."

When discussing issues and planning contests, Chowhound and Coondog "seek input from all Stake Holders for AICE standards, values, and principles." This means that if AICE is contracted to produce, say, a steak-eating contest, all those who hold a stake in the contest will be consulted beforehand about how best to consume steak competitively. Stake Holders in AICE include, but are not limited to "the eaters, the family members of the eaters, the eaters' organizations, any of the sponsors doing the event, all the people that are connected to the contest, and the billions of eating fans out there." That's a lot of voices to reconcile, and at times Chowhound admits that he, being the CEO, has to step up and make a game-time decision.

AICE's most socialistic policy involves the sharing of revenue. At the 2004 World Chili Eating Competition, all of the eaters, representatives, and family members pitched in on the contest's production. Afterward, the eaters who placed in the top three "took the winnings, threw it all in the pot, and split it up," Chowhound says. "And the money we had to pay for lodging and all that was split up. And we got a fraction of the money that the Sheas would normally get for a contest."

This idealistic business model, which takes profit sharing to new extremes, seems to work for AICE. But if the core Stake Holders in the company exceed the present base of a half dozen or so, management difficulties are bound to follow. Already Chowhound has noted the difficulty of juggling roles such as CEO/gurgitator. At the chili-eating competition, for example, he set up the contest, did some emceeing, then took his place at the table and won the contest. Arnie admits that this setup detracted somewhat from the event's professionalism. "My own people told me that it just kind of looked weird."

But such are the growing pains of starting up a competitive-eating league/union based loosely on Marxist principles. And there has been growth. There was the chili gig, a hoagie-eating championship in Pennsylvania, a Coney Island hamburger-eating competition on the Fourth of July, and their biggest breakthrough yet, a New Year's 2005 gig at the Fiesta Bowl.

Though some contend that AICE's innovations have been minimal, the institution of "picnic style" eating rules is regarded by some as a breathtaking advancement. On September 12, 2004, at the Corn Beef Sandwich Eating Competition in Coney Island, Brooklyn, eaters were "required to adhere to picnic style eating rules which prohibits dunking, separating and/or desecrating the food item." This advancement, Chowhound says, is both a publicity gimmick and a reaction to the fact that most Americans associate competitive eating with footage from the Nathan's Famous contest. "And when they watch Nathan's, they see the guys dunking the hot dogs, and the buns, and separating them, and the various tricks connected to that." Because the victors are Japanese, American viewers inevitably think of them as "foreign invaders, with their tricky ways of eating food." Picnic-style rules maintain the integrity of the competitive foodstuff. It's an appeal to tradition, to eating the foodstuff "the way God intended."

Considering AICE's advancements and growing calendar of events, some members of the competitive-eating community are surprised that IFOCE eaters don't defect. One can't help but think of leagues like the ABA and the AFL, which changed their respective sports and were ultimately absorbed by the dominant leagues, the NBA and the NFL, respectively. But as of yet, no eaters have made the switch. Why is this? Some might say that eaters are held back by the inertia of breaking with tradition. Others cite the Shea brothers' skills as emcees, their public relations acumen, and the rising profile of the IFOCE. But more than anything, it's likely a by-product of loyalty. "How can you do it better than George Shea?" asks Badlands Booker. "He's competitive eating *personified*." Chowhound believes the reason no one defects is, in a word, *convenience*. "The other option is you have to be crazy like myself or Joe Menchetti or Coondog and be willing to travel to other places and compete in other events."

But the battle rages on. Allegations shoot back and forth. IFOCE members accuse AICE of sabotaging its events, of calling up their sponsors and lowballing IFOCE fees to pick up their scraps. AICE accuses the IFOCE of instituting a lifetime ban on all AICE eaters, of threatening lawsuits for breach of contract, and of freezing non-IFOCE eaters out of middle-ground events such as Wing Bowl. George Shea sees both sides of the argument, but opts for the middle ground. "There are those who have accused Coondog and Chowhound and Joe Menchetti of being mediocre imitators with no vision and a lot of bitterness. And while I disagree with all those words, I respect as an American people's right to say them. Because the First Amendment is the best amendment."

For outsiders looking in, the whole conflict probably seems ludicrous. A competitive eaters' union? A Web site whose primary goal is to malign the International Federation of Competitive Eating? The argument is so esoteric that most outsiders wouldn't even understand the cyber-barbs tossed back and forth on fringe competitive-eating Web sites such as those of Gentleman Joe Menchetti and Beautiful Brian Seiken. When Menchetti, who is loosely attached to AICE, writes that "the suicide/homicide watch is firmly on Beautiful Brian" because he wasn't picked for a select televised IFOCE event, it's an inside joke understood by fifty people, tops. When Beautiful Brian threatens on his Web site to stuff cheesecake up the ass of an AICE eater named Eddie "the Geek" Vidmar, many IFOCE members don't even know whom he's talking about. Only in this media-saturated age of blogs and vanity Web sites could such an obscure argument get so involved, and so heated.

Some claim the competition has been good for the sport, that IFOCE prize money has shot up considerably since AICE hit the scene, and some appeal, Rodney King–like, with that clichéd sentiment "Can't we all just get along?" Many IFOCE eaters claim that, were he given the opportunity, Gentleman Joe Menchetti would get back in the league in a heartbeat.

But one thing is clear: Chowhound will stand his ground. He believes America is filled with undiscovered gurgitators who never see the light of day because the IFOCE klieg lights never shine down upon them. There's "Big Dan," who beat Chowhound in a wing-eating contest in Dewey Beach. There's Tony "Hustler" Harrison, who edged Chowhound out for a Baltimore pasta-eating championship. These guys may be unknown, but he believes that they possess some of the greatest American appetites of the twenty-first century. If Chowhound has his way, if the quixotic dream that is the Association of Independent Competitive Eaters is realized, the future will belong not to the IFOCE, that Hollywood tyrant of competitive eating, but to the common man with his uncommon, oversized stomach.

15

NOODLES AND THE ROMAN INCIDENT

Slowly, a sound started to build in Lardass's stomach. A strange and scary sound like a log truck coming at you at a hundred miles per hour. And suddenly, Lardass opened his mouth. And before Bill Travis knew it, he was covered with five pies' worth of used blueberries.

Gordie, from the movie *Stand by Me*

Three days before the Zyng Asian Grill World Noodle Eating Championship, I become concerned that the client won't get its money's worth in publicity. Though I am scheduled to do some on-air radio gigs from my Brooklyn apartment, I sense that Columbus, Ohio, is too small of a media market to drum up much coverage. Fairly ignorant of how the publicity machine works, I come up with an idea. The Atkins diet has reached its zenith of popularity, so maybe we should use this to our advantage in publicizing the event. After a brief consultation with the Shea brothers, I invent a fictional group known as the Atkins Liberation Front, a.k.a. ALF.

The Atkins Liberation Front, I decide, flourishes on college campuses like that of Ohio State University in Columbus. Its radical members are sick of feeling guilty for eating carbs and have chosen the Zyng Noodle Eating Championship as a site for a major, potentially violent protest. The Shea brothers don't think my plan is workable and decide instead to pursue media outlets more aggressively, but I'm not so easily deterred. I make a few phone calls to friends in the Midwest to see if they will dress up in all-black outfits and make up some placards. They all think I'm nuts. When I explain my idea to Jay Sunderland, the owner of the restaurant where the contest will be held, there is silence on his end of the line. Frustrated at the failure of my one big PR stunt idea, I crumple up the press release I've written and toss it in the trashcan.

In my conversations with Jay Sunderland, I soon realize that he assumes the IFOCE is like a traveling circus. He tells me he's looking forward to having Kobayashi in town, as well as that Crazy Legs guy he recently watched escape from a box of popcorn on CNN. It's not the first time that a client presumes that our eaters travel in a pack, fed raw meat daily and let out only before showtime. Because of the low prize money ($250 for first, $100 for second), the competition is less a showcase of big-named talent than a celebration of Midwestern gurgitory prowess.

On the day of the event, May 21, 2004, it's a blazing eighty-five degrees and skin-sticky humid out. Fifteen eaters are lined up at a row of tables in the parking lot next to the restaurant. The turnout is solid—a hundred or so fans, several reporters, and quite a few local TV cameras. But I can't tell if they understand the significance of the event. This is where competitive-eating dreams *begin*, I explain, at the mail-room floor, the minor leagues, where individual greatness is discovered and cultivated, over years, into that of tried-and-true professionals.

Before introducing the eaters, I issue a safety precaution. At IFOCE headquarters, I say, we have received numerous threats from the Atkins Liberation Front, a militant left-wing organization firmly opposed to the strictures of the Atkins diet, to use this contest as a platform for their cause. So if anyone sees suspicious long-haired types skulking about the premises, please inform the authorities immediately. Zyng Asian Grill has beefed up the security detail in preparation for just such a clash. The ALF are a notoriously violent bunch,

I explain, as opposed to their mild-mannered counterparts, the Pro-Carb Congress.

I introduce the eaters, focusing on the locals first. There is Hungry Justin Henderson, an Ohio State med school student with an interest in gastroenterology, who may or may not be using this contest as research. There is Susan Bowlus, a registered nurse whose last name means "a soft mass of unchewed food." And there is Kevin "the Carburetor" Carr, a local favorite who recently appeared on the reality TV show *Are You Hot?*

I pit the locals against a couple of midranked interlopers. Big Brian Subich is an athletic behemoth of a man wearing an IFOCE T-shirt, who at six foot six, three hundred pounds, more than lives up to his nickname. Then the favorite, from the confusingly named city of Boston, New York, is "Buffalo" Jim Reeves. A humble man with an easy gap-toothed grin, Reeves is a chicken-wing specialist. Currently ranked eighteenth in the world, Reeves, who will compete alongside his brother Ed, once ate nine quarter-pound burgers and buns in five minutes.

We count down, and they're off. There is something primal about shoveling noodles into one's mouth. The eaters look like tapeworm-infested farm animals at the trough. The slipperiness and thick consistency of the Shanghai noodles make for a slow eat. Five minutes in, at the halfway mark, the contest is still up for grabs. Kevin Carr is in the lead, with Buffalo Jim Reeves and an unknown rugby player from the University of Michigan named Brett Barna trailing by a few noodles. "I am humbled to take part in an event of this magnitude," I say. "Never before in the history of this parking lot have the people of Columbus witnessed such greatness." The eaters are red-faced and looking abnormally stressed, so I caution them to take their time and drink more water, but Kevin Carr, a rotund writer with a goatee and a belly like a basketball, keeps stuffing with a savagery rarely seen on the circuit. It doesn't look quite right. I put my hand over the mic and advise him to pace himself.

As the last minute winds down, it feels as if something will have to give in this pent-up, sweltering feeding frenzy. Be it an orchestrated attack by the Atkins Liberation Front or a sudden thunderstorm, we are on the brink of something. Whatever it may be, Kevin Carr looks as if he might have something to do with it. He is really going for it. Following the gaze of the fans, I turn around. He looks like a human garbage disposal on turbo autopilot, cheeks puffed out in the same shape as his belly. Eyes shut. Hungry and focused. He just keeps cramming those noodles. There's a term in sports psychology known as flow, which describes the mind state associated with peak performance. Kevin Carr has reached that level, having pulled almost a full bowl ahead of the pack. Yet it still doesn't look quite right. "Ten, nine . . ."

Freeze-frame. Before we get to what happens next, let me just say that I'm reluctant to even go there. Because competitive eating is about more than just puking. Whenever people ask me about competitive eating, the same topics come up. The first thing they ask is How does that Chinese guy eat all those hot dogs?" The second thing people ask is "Do they just go and puke it up afterward?"

The answer is complex, but in truth most competitive eaters pride themselves in keeping it down. The top three eaters in the world—Kobayashi, Sonya Thomas, and Rich LeFevre—all solemnly swear they don't upchuck after contests. When I asked one prominent gurgitator how common it is for eaters to pull the trigger, he claimed that less than 20 percent of the top-ranked eaters purge.

The most common means of elimination, I'm told, is letting the natural digestive process do its thing. Of course, this results in wave after wave of bowel movements that can be both distressing and visually interesting. Some eaters use laxatives. When pressed about his postcontest ritual, Badlands Booker says, "I'm a gurgitator, man! I'm not into regurgitation." He's not afraid to use a laxative on occasion, but his more common postcontest ritual is pretty uneventful. He sits in his favorite armchair, watches ESPN, and drinks lots of seltzer water or diet Snapple. Every eater has a different technique for easing the digestive process. Crazy Legs Conti claims that bitters, the herbal ingredient used in mixed alcoholic drinks, is particularly helpful in digesting mass quantities.

The fact is, there's no way of knowing for sure what eaters do after contests. Purging is frowned upon, so eaters are unlikely to confess. As long as a reversal doesn't occur within the contest, it is beyond the domain of the officials. The only way to know for sure is to follow eaters to the bathroom after contests, which I am unwilling to do. I suspect that it's more common than most eaters will publicly admit. After watching a meatball-eating competition in Atlantic City, I overheard one midranked competitive eater announcing his plans for the day, "I'm gonna go puke and play blackjack."

One eater, Jed Donahue, the seven-time winner of the jalapeño-eating contest in Laredo, Texas, freely admits that he taught himself to purge as a necessary means of survival. After his first few wins, Jed learned the hard way that jalapeño-eating was an endurance event that lasted for hours after the contest ended. "The day after the competition, my colon was basically the seventh circle of hell," he explains.

By his fourth victory, his postcontest ritual became so rote that it bore about as much significance as a businessman's daily routine after a long day at the office. "I puke it all up and go to Dairy Queen," he explains. He's got it down to a science and claims that he could, at any moment, throw down a hundred jalapeños, bring them back up, and "go hit the town." The process is almost like a volcano erupting from within the body. It still hurts, he says, but "it hurts a lot less than letting it pass naturally." After the contest, he's not coy about slipping away from the press. "I'm almost like, 'Excuse me. I need to go puke,'" he says. In fact, he has found that people are intrigued by the thought of him vomiting up six pounds of peppers. "I like looking at it, quite honestly. It's a strange sight. It's just a bunch of seeds there."

After listening to Jed's candor about the subject, I wonder, Why are we so squeamish about vomit anyway? It's just the process of disgorging the contents of one's stomach, another bodily function like coughing or peeing. What's the big deal? In truth, culturally, we seem to have embraced vomit as almost mainstream. If we are so sensitive about the subject, why would we tolerate a Web site like www.ratemyvomit.com?

Besides, puking has been used to great effect in dozens of movies. The 1986 movie *Stand by Me,* which contains arguably the most famous cinematic competitive-eating scene of all time, focuses on vomit as its centerpiece. In it, an overweight character named Davey "Lardass" Hogan uses castor oil as an emetic to make himself hurl in the pie-eating contest, exacting revenge on his tormentors by causing the whole crowd to follow suit. There's also the famous scene in *The Exorcist,* where darling little possessed Regan vomits a pea-green stream onto Father Karras's face and shirt.

In recent films, booting has become so common that it's almost a cliché. Tom Hanks blows chunks in *Road to Perdition* after he finds out his wife and son have been murdered. Denzel Washington barfs in *He Got Game* and in *Remember the Titans.* Jamie Foxx does it in *Any Given Sunday.* In fact, Puke has almost become its own character, making guest appearances in *Memento, The Virgin Suicides, The Sixth Sense, Almost Famous, Clueless, 10 Things I Hate About You, The Rock,* and *The Matrix.* Perhaps the two most unabashed puke scenes in cinematic history occur in the Trey Parker–Matt Stone satire, *Team America,* and Monty Python's *The Meaning of Life,* in which the character Monsieur Creosote vomits nine times and then explodes.

In a slightly more extreme way, that unforgettable scene captures the effect that Kevin Carr's dramatic reversal of fortune has on the audience at Zyng Asian Grill. It is at once funny and gross and slightly tragic. In the waning seconds, Kevin spurts forth a sea of slimy worms, relinquishing his imminent victory. The audience is united under the common bond of having witnessed a man's body cruelly betray him. We feel sympathy and disgust in equal measure. I am so touched that I don't even have the heart to shout out the go-to IFOCE response, "Elvis has left the building!"

After disqualifying Carr, I naïvely assume the default winner will be Buffalo Jim Reeves—but the scales never lie. The remains are weighed, and we have an upset on our hands. Nineteen-year-old Brett Barna, a Worthington, Ohio, native whose only prior competitive-eating experience was his victory in a nonsanctioned collegiate Mongolian-beef-eating competition, has upset Buffalo Jim Reeves by a mere two ounces. He has eaten nearly two and a half pounds—no staggering sum, but impressive considering the adverse conditions and hearty wheat-based noodles.

Another competitive-eating dream fulfilled, another champion revealed. The crowd gasps at the upset by the blond, boyish-faced upstart. It's always exciting to watch a newcomer discover a previously unknown talent like this, a treasured moment that is more common in competitive eating than most sports. The press flocks to Barna, and

Kevin "the Carburetor" Carr sucks down noodles with reckless abandon before suffering one of the more stunning reversals of fortune in competitive eating history. *(Courtesy of Kelly Carr)*

he answers their questions with a wide-eyed expression like Macauley Culkin's post-aftershave look in *Home Alone*. "I was just doing this for a free meal," Barna says, seemingly shocked by his own performance.

In the end, though, the most compelling man of the day is Kevin Carr. Something about his carpe diem attitude and relentless noodle-attacking method makes you want to give him a hug. George Shea captures the essence of the thirty-two-year old father of two when he says, "I knew that I had met a man who was more than simply a man. He was a champion—a leader of men and women and athletes. He's an eater's eater." Kevin, for his part, is gracious in his postmatch press conference. "I just hit capacity. When your body says no more, you just kind of have to listen to it. If you're going down, you might as well go down in flames."

16

THE FIRST COUPLE OF
COMPETITIVE EATING

Those who break bread together, stay together.

—Ancient proverb

MAY 1, 2004

Twenty minutes till go time, and the Bacci World Pizza Eating Championship has all the makings of a complete fiasco. Dozens of locals have qualified by eating three jumbo cheese slices in twenty minutes at their local Bacci Pizzeria. Around forty eaters have signed up for the contest, and at least a dozen more are waiting in line to register. Over two hundred jumbo slices in boxes have been placed on four thirty-foot-long rows of tables. The tented area shading the tables from the blazing heat is choked with eaters, fans, and reporters. I've been assigned a crew of ten Bacci employees to help judge the event. It isn't nearly enough to ensure a fair contest, especially since I don't know who they are. My entire family, along with my girlfriend, is in attendance. Running my hands through my hair obsessively, I feel as if I'm on the verge of hyperventilating.

The publicity leading up to the event has been sensational. There was a huge front-page spread in the *Chicago Tribune,* and another article in the *Chicago Sun-Times.* I spent the day prior driving around to news shows with an eighteen-year-old recent graduate from Downer's Grove High School named Mark Skiba, who won last year's contest and the $1,000 prize. Mark and his father are proud of his victory and have predicted he'll take the $2,500 prize again this year. Beyond giving Mark vague warnings about a small Asian woman known as the Black Widow, I don't have the heart to tell him how slim his chances are.

Three angry-looking young men approach me. They're wearing official contest T-shirts, which read GOT PIZZA? I ask if I can be of assistance. They lay a paper filled with signatures in front of me. "This is a petition signed by thirty contestants claiming that Ed Jarvis, Sonya Thomas, and Rich and Carlene LeFevre are all ineligible for today's contest. It says on the Bacci Web site that all contestants must complete the pizza challenge in order to be eligible for this event. None of these eaters have completed the challenge."

I stare blankly at the signatures. My mind reels. This is the last thing I need, to have IFOCE eaters who have flown in from New York, Washington, D.C., and Las Vegas knocked out of the contest on a last-minute technicality. Competing with this concern is the thought of some Chicago-mobster type brutalizing me with a crowbar as I walk through the parking lot after the contest. I represent the IFOCE, however, so I have to stand my ground. "Listen, guys. I'm sorry if you feel betrayed that these professional eaters haven't completed the pizza challenge. But this is an IFOCE event, and that means the eaters you just mentioned will be competing in it. Period. If you still want to protest, then go talk to the owner, Bobby Didiana. He's the little Italian dude over there smoking a cigarette."

While seemingly a nice guy, Bobby is the brains behind the fiasco. The year before, he had organized a similar contest, an hour-long endurance match that turned into a highly amusing pukefest. It had gained the Didiana family business some nice publicity, so he decided to up the ante this year. I have urged him strongly to shorten the contest and organize it into qualifying heats. In return, Bobby has reluctantly offered a compromise of one contest divided into fifteen-, twenty-, and thirty-minute time limits. Prizes will be offered for first, second, and third in the fifteen-minute round, and for first place in the next two rounds. Bobby has also made it clear that his decision to import ranked professionals has been controversial, and that he'd love to see a local pull off an upset.

Time to address the crowd. I put on the carnival barker's hat and stand up on a chair. I explain that it's only appropriate that the first ever pizza-eating record should be held here, in Chicago, the city widely regarded as having America's best pizza. I tell the crowd to get behind their locals, who will have an uphill battle against four of the top competitive eaters in the world. I introduce Mark Skiba, the defending champ, and a college buddy of mine, Bob Greenlee, who I say has eaten nothing but pizza for forty days and forty nights in preparation for the contest. I then introduce the IFOCE eaters, and it's game on.

The contest is an orgiastic frenzy of pizza consumption. Eaters chomp and gnaw while I spout the usual fun facts peppered with play-by-play. Unlimited pizza—it's every kid's dream come true! When the fifteen minutes are up, Sonya is the clear winner with six and a half jumbo slices; Cookie takes second with five and a half. Just as I'm about to announce Rich LeFevre in third place with five and a quarter, Bobby Didiana comes up and says that, actually, a college student named Patrick Bertoletti has nosed out LeFevre.

Unconvinced, I walk over, grab Bertoletti's final slice and bring it over to LeFevre. I juxtapose the leftovers and stroke my chin. Overruling the restaurant's owner, I call it a tie and opt to use the next five-minute interval as a tiebreaker. Rich LeFevre handily wins the overtime period. His wife, Carlene, sticks with it into the thirty-minute round, only to succumb by one-quarter of a slice to a local rookie twice her size.

After the contest, Rich and Carlene LeFevre, the first couple of competitive eating, thank me profusely for my fairness. I've been looking forward to meeting them for months and can't help but swell slightly at their approval. They don't look the part of competitive eaters. Rich is over sixty years old, stands five feet seven, and weighs 145 pounds. A retired accountant, he looks exactly as I've seen him in countless photos, a small, gray-haired gentleman with thick, round glasses, wearing a Hawaiian print shirt. I have heard him described as a Mr. Magoo look-alike, and the analogy is fairly apt. His wife, Carlene, a retired teacher, won't disclose her age or weight, but she is allegedly older than Rich and svelte with an athletic build. She looks as feminine as a woman can look after an eating contest, with curly, feathered hair and freshly applied lipstick. "We just wanted to thank you for taking control of that situation," Rich says. "We're proud of you for sticking to your guns."

Sandwiched between Carlene and Rich LeFevre during the 2004 Bacci World Pizza Eating Championship, the author mugs a cheesy game-show-host smile. *(Courtesy of Amy Esposito)*

NOVEMBER 23, 2004

"I just wanted you to know that, after the contest, I went around and looked, and you can't know how many people didn't eat their crust," says Carlene LeFevre. "And you know that kid that beat me out for the last prize? Afterwards, he told me that in the qualifier, they didn't have to eat the crust."

Her husband agrees. "Yeah, we saw lots of crusts in boxes. You know when you have the boxes, they throw the crust inside, and nobody checks the boxes."

I thank Rich for the insight. It's nearly seven months after the Chicago pizza mayhem, and I'm talking with the LeFevres by phone from their home in Henderson, Nevada, which they call the Pink Palace. I have heard that Rich's success on the circuit is due in part to his obsessively meticulous nature, and his tone reflects this. It seems that, with twenty-twenty hindsight, I wasn't quite as effective a judge as I'd hoped. This crust issue remains a permanent scar on my official IFOCE record. Not that the LeFevres blame me. They understand it was an impossible contest to judge, totally understaffed and all, but the fact remains that those crusts were the hardest part to get down. "That crust, that rim," Carlene says. "I swear to God, it was like putting a leather belt in your mouth. It would not masticate at all."

If there were one thing the LeFevres could change about the circuit, they are quick to point out, it would be the quality of competition food. Carlene understands that it's hard to prepare food in such mass quantities, but still, it's a pity. "As much as I love to eat, and Rich, too, in a way I'm kind of sorry that I have to waste my calories on food that's not really high quality." The subject is particularly touchy now, because at a contest that Carlene recently won, the food was so repugnant she found herself sighing out loud. The foodstuff was posole, a type of spicy, fried hominy. "You know what it reminded me of? You know when the radiator in your car boils dry, and there's that smell? To me, it tasted like that smell."

They've earned the right to be finicky. Rich and Carlene LeFevre are now ranked third and seventh in the world, respectively, and are regarded by some as the most dominant married couple in professional sports. They also have a rather unique relationship to food, because outside of competitive eating, they are health and exercise nuts. Their go-to meal includes a combination of wheat germ, flaxseed, and oatmeal. Carlene was a Richard Simmons aerobics instructor for eight years, and Rich routinely competes in a spate of sports. Our last interview was cut short because they had to take off for Tuesday-night table tennis. By all accounts, the LeFevres are not your average couple. Even within the competitive-eating community, their story is unique.

If not for Willie Mays, Carlene LeFevre might never have met her husband. In the late sixties, Rich passed his navy written exam with such flying colors that he was given carte blanche to choose where he would be stationed. Out of abiding love for his favorite baseball player, Rich chose a naval base just south of San Francisco so he could go watch Mays play for the Giants.

In the fall of 1970, Carlene had just broken up with her boyfriend and was staying at home with her parents in San Francisco. A self-described daddy's girl, she didn't mind living at home, but her mother insisted she go hang out with people her own age. In the paper, they spotted an ad for square dancing. Carlene started going, and one evening in October, she saw Rich at the entrance. "Rich would peek in before he'd pay his entrance fee to see if there's anything other than old ladies and young girls to dance with."

What happened next remains the source of some debate. Rich claims that Carlene shot him come-hither looks and motioned him toward her. Carlene says it's a lie. "No, it isn't," Rich says. "She said, 'Why don't you come in? We'll have some fun.'" Rich paid his entrance fee and they've been square dancing ever since. They started out as pals, dancing and going to the movies, and before long became best friends.

From day one, Rich was attracted to Carlene's eating prowess. He had found that, when he took a girl out to dinner, she'd usually leave food on her plate—not Carlene. "With Carlene, I mean, we would eat, and I'd be interested in talking, and she'd be interested in eating. She'd be done, and I'd be half-finished." They grew ever closer, but Carlene had never seen herself as the marrying type. One day while talking on her front porch, Carlene misspelled Rich's last name. "You'd better learn how to spell it," Rich warned. "Someday it might be your last name."

Like many competitive eaters, Rich and Carlene shared interests not just in food, but in travel as well. Early on in their marriage, they began taking road trips. In 1985, while traveling through Amarillo, Texas, the LeFevres successfully completed the Big Texas Steak Ranch challenge for the first time. The challenge states that if you can eat the Big Texan, a seventy-two-ounce steak that now costs over $60, you get it for free. If you don't, you pay. The LeFevres both knocked it down, then topped it off with triple-decker ice cream cones. They enjoyed it so much that they came back to do the challenge annually for fifteen years.

In January of 2000, when Rich and Carlene returned from their annual New Year's trip to Reno, a message was waiting for them on their answering machine. It was from the producers of *Ripley's Believe It or Not* offering to televise them completing the Big Texan challenge as a couple. Carlene was reluctant at first. A steadfastly feminine woman, she worried that the show would make her look masculine and undignified, but Rich finally talked her into it. Three months after their *Ripley's* appearance, producers of the *Donny and Marie Show* came calling. This time, Rich ate a mind-blowing *two* seventy-two-ounce steaks—nine pounds total—in one sitting.

Competitive eating had discovered the LeFevres. In 2001, Japanese TV producers flew the couple over for a major televised competition. Rich bowed out early due to his distaste for sushi, but Carlene ended up tenth overall out of five hundred eaters. The contest's winner was a kid named Takeru Kobayashi, who would, in a matter of months, travel to New York for his first shot at hot dogs.

In the summer of 2002, Rich LeFevre competed in his first Nathan's qualifier, in Las Vegas. He went head-to-head against a roster of then heavyweight IFOCE eaters—Coondog O'Karma, Gentleman Joe Menchetti, Moe Ribs Molesky—all of whom had traveled West to seek out a weak field of qualifiers. George Shea announced Rich's odds at a hundred to one before listing the deep résumés of his opponents. "I heard all these numbers and accomplishments," Rich remembers, "and I kind of rolled my eyes. I thought, 'Gee, if these guys are so good, it might be tough.' But I still expected to win. I don't know why I expected to win." In his first hot dog battle, and without dunking, Rich downed twenty for first place. George Shea was blown away and told Rich that only seven people had ever done the deuce.

George had noticed Rich's unorthodox style, in which he was crouched to within inches of the table, and gave him a nickname he had long been hoping to bequeath. "He resembled a skinny insect feeding his maw with twitching mandibles, so I compared him to a locust during the contest. And there had been a legend in the competitive eating community about a breed of eater called the Locusts, freelance eaters who refused to compete in sanctioned contests, opting instead to set their records without an audience. It was a rare honor, George noted, for a Locust to join the circuit, and even rarer for a ranked eater to "go Locust."

Still, despite her husband's arrival on the circuit, Carlene was reluctant to compete. Not until Rich convinced her to take part in the *Battle of the Buffets*, a Travel Channel special, did Carlene give in to the lure of competitive eating. It was there that her now famous eating dance, known on the circuit as popping, or the Carlene pop, was first witnessed by the world. The Carlene pop (not to be confused with the Kobayashi shake) is a sort of side-to-side wiggle that aids digestion and helps burn Carlene's surfeit of nervous energy.

The Battle of the Buffets included five courses—breakfast, lunch, appetizer, dinner, and dessert—eaten over five days. On the second day, in the lunch round, Carlene won a hard-fought battle against Coondog O'Karma. Afterward, she admitted that she had hit the wall and wanted to surrender, but thought of her husband. "I knew he was gonna be so disappointed with me if I quit," she said.

Rich and Carlene have fundamentally different mentalities toward competition. Rich loves to compete and, despite his small size and unorthodox technique, always expects to win. As an example, Carlene discusses a tennis tournament where Rich was up against the odds. His opponents were, in Carlene's words, "all these macho guys looking like Dean Martin's son—you know blond, tan legs, six foot two, just drop-dead gorgeous guys. And here comes my little husband with his bowlegs and his one little cheapy racket. And I'll be darned if he didn't win that whole tennis tournament." Carlene adds that he nearly gave himself brain damage running down balls.

Carlene, on the other hand, is fueled by a fear of failure. Once, after undergoing arthroscopic knee surgery, Carlene's doctor told her to ride a bike as much as she could handle. Carlene came back a week later, her knee swollen up like a grapefruit. The doctor shook his head, told her to settle down, and added a red flag to her folder to remind himself that she was a pathological overachiever. "That made me realize I'm kind of nutty," Carlene says.

Often, before a competition, Carlene will admit to Rich that her goal is just not to finish last. It drives Rich nuts. "It's like Tiger Woods saying, 'I hope I don't finish last in the tournament,'" he explains. "It's ridiculous." Because of their difference in attitudes, Rich is not afraid to go into football-coach mode. He says Carlene often needs a push in the right direction, be it through positive or negative reinforcement. After a 2004 Krystal hamburger qualifier in which Carlene struggled, Rich didn't pull any punches. "I just told her she did terrible, that's all. I mean, if she was doing the best she could and she ate twenty-four, I would say, 'Nice job, honey.' But she stunk!"

When Carlene does her best, though, Rich is the first to shower her with praise. At the 2004 Sky City Casino World Posole Eating Championship, in Acoma, New Mexico, Carlene shocked the competitive-eating world by beating her husband for the first time. She ate 109.75 ounces (almost seven pounds) of posole in twelve minutes, and Rich ate only 96.25 ounces. Afterward Rich's disappointment was totally overshadowed by pride. "She whipped me! I mean she whipped me like Sonya does. . . . That's never happened before so I feel really good about that. Maybe this will be the beginning of something great for her."

Indeed, there is a beautiful undercurrent of gender equality to their eating exploits. In late March of 2004, amidst one of their many driving trips, Rich and Carlene stopped by Pointer's Pizza, located in a St. Louis suburb, to attempt the Pointersaurus challenge. The Pointersaurus is a ten-pound, twenty-eight-inch, two-meat pizza. To successfully complete the challenge, two people have one hour to finish the pizza. It costs $42 up front, and the reward for eating it is $500. Over five hundred teams had attempted the challenge, but only five had been successful, none of which included a woman.

When the Pointersaurus was prepared, Rich decided to make a point. He cut the pizza in half and stipulated aloud that they would each eat half. He didn't want anyone claiming that he'd shouldered the load. Rich explained to his wife in the form of a sweet nothing, "This way, if two of *you* had come in here, you would have been successful, too." They dropped the Pointersaurus in a half hour, all the while chatting with their niece, who lives in the St. Louis area. Afterward, they split a gallon and a half of ice cream.

The next day, before they left town, Rich dropped by the Crown Candy Kitchen. He'd heard about the malt challenge, which required drinking five twenty-four-ounce malts in a half hour. He did it in sixteen minutes, licked his lips, and shook off the brain freeze. Didn't have to pay a dime. Since there was still time left, he struck a deal. If he knocked down a sixth one, would they throw in a free mug and a T-shirt? Carlene had mentioned repeatedly how much she loved the mug and T-shirt. They agreed. Rich inhaled the last one in four minutes and, like a high school kid winning a stuffed animal for his girl at the fair, walked out with a smiling woman on his arm.

The LeFevres are a new breed of retiree. While most elderly couples are playing bingo, Rich and Carlene remain in active pursuit of the next adrenaline rush. Carlene says they live an extreme version of the lifestyle prescribed by *Prevention* magazine. "We bungee jump, we've white-water rafted, we rode those donkeys down the Grand Canyon. We go to the amusement parks and ride the roller coasters, the crazy rides, over and over till we have whiplash in our necks." They don't need children, Carlene says, "because we are each other's child." After winning the posole-eating contest, she described the thrill of their extreme lifestyle. "We like to do those things where you could die, 'cause if you don't die, oh my, what a rush."

The LeFevres epitomize the new breed of competitive eater—thin, active, and obsessed with healthy food. Competitive eating is just another adrenaline rush, one that provides exciting travel, prize money, and media exposure. Contrary to the common preconception, competitive eating is an organic part of their healthy lifestyle. "In order to do this you have to be even more healthy," Rich says. "In order to make up for what you're doing in the contests."

Rich and Carlene claim to have low cholesterol, low blood pressure, and low tolerance for salt, fat, sugar, and simple carbohydrates in their diets. After contests, they don't take laxatives and they don't vomit. The only time they've ever gotten sick was after the 2004 SPAM-eating contest, affectionately known as the SPAM Cram. Had it been a SPAM-burger-eating contest, as they'd been promised, they would've been fine, but a dearth of buns changed that. "They just took the SPAM out of the can and dumped it on the counter and you just ate the whole slimy block. It was gross."

If their doctor ever says they are prediabetic or plagued by high blood pressure or cholesterol, they have vowed to quit, but for the time being, they're going to continue to up their game. Both have overcome serious impediments to get to where they are. Rich, originally a distance eater with poor cheek capacity, had to teach himself how to swallow and stuff for the speed-eating discipline, and Carlene had to get over the self-consciousness of eating in public. Now she relishes the spotlight and has been known to fix her lipstick in the reflection of her knife after a contest.

They rarely train for eating events, but discussions of strategy are ongoing. As for next year's pizza contest, they will learn from their mistakes. "I'm going to tear off the cheese and start chewing that," Rich explains. "And while I'm doing that, I'm going to have six cups of water in front of me and I'm going to take that pizza and I'm going to rip it up and put in the water." Carlene disagrees. "I don't see any sense in eating the cheese by itself. But you know that rim around the edge that's like a leather belt? I'm going to rip that off and put it in the cup and let it sit there for at least two minutes while I'm eating the other parts." As for my part, both Carlene and Rich agree that I better check those boxes for crusts. "Next time, either have more judges or not as many eaters."

17

THE WING TOUR WITH
THE BLACK WIDOW

*Black widow is female spider, right? And then, when I go to eating
contest, I am the woman, female. And the female spider kill the
male spider.*

—Sonya Thomas, in the documentary *You Swallowed What?*

As an IFOCE employee, I'm given info on a need-to-know basis.
All I know about the present mission, which George has vaguely
dubbed the Wing Tour, is that I'll be going on a one-week expedition
throughout the Midwest with Sonya Thomas and Drew Cerza to promote Cerza's brainchild, known as the National Buffalo Wing Festival. Drew, who owns a food promotion company, got the idea for the
festival from the animated film *Osmosis Jones*. In the movie, the character voiced by Bill Murray is a fried-food addict. Murray's daughter,
concerned for his health, suggests a hiking trip. Instead, Murray wins
tickets to the National Chicken Wing Festival in Buffalo. The movie
prompted Buffalo newspapers to question why such an event didn't
exist. Cerza stepped up to the plate, and on Labor Day of 2002, the
first Wing Festival took place.

On June 21, 2004, I arrive at the Buffalo airport. While waiting
for Sonya's plane to arrive, I unwisely order a dozen buffalo wings in
the airport terminal. She arrives, and we take a cab to City Hall,

where a kickoff ceremony celebrating the fortieth anniversary of the invention of the buffalo wing awaits us. As our cab pulls up at the monument circle in front of City Hall, we find ourselves surrounded by birds. Most of them are seagulls, but the more noticeable ones are humans walking around in chicken mascot costumes, clucking and bobbing their heads. Free wings and water and cookies are handed out from temporary booths. Beneath an inflatable gateway arch that bears the Wing Festival's insignia is a podium, around which reporters and cameramen are gathering.

Sonya and I meet Drew Cerza, who is dressed as his alter ego, the Wing King. The Wing King wears a red velvet cape and a protuberant foam hat that's supposed to be a chicken wing but looks more like a massive orange brain tumor, the likes of which could only be caused by a Chernobyl-caliber atomic disaster. As for the "wing scepter" Drew asked me to bring, unfortunately last year's wing-eating champ, Cookie Jarvis, found it too unwieldy to mail to me.

The press conference begins. The Wing King stands beside a chicken mascot and a tall man with thinning, parted-on-the-side politician hair, who I discover is Mayor Anthony Masiello, a former basketball star who was once drafted by the Pacers. There's another guy, short, buff, stylishly dressed, and with the suspicious remnants of a tattoo peaking out beneath his well-ironed button-down shirt. His skin is an unnatural orange hue that's either the result of chronic buffalo-wing consumption or countless hours at the tanning salon. They all smile for the camera and talk about what the chicken wing means to the city of Buffalo. Orange Guy makes a joke about "having a leg up on the competition." Sonya and I put our luggage in an RV, grab some free wings, and sit on the steps eating.

As we eat and chat, seagulls gurgle and bob toward us, clearly insinuating they'd like to be involved in our meal. Sonya, being the kindhearted sort, tosses a drumstick toward an eager seagull. Without hesitation, the gull swallows the drumstick whole and waddles away. Sonya and I look at each other, eyes wide. "Oh my gosh!" she says.

"Do you think it's okay?" I shake my head and shrug. This feels like an omen, a harbinger of bad things to come, but it somehow strikes me as funny. I bear no ill will toward seagulls, but they lack the ability to tug at my heartstrings. Sonya is distraught though, imagining the impossibility of such a small creature digesting and passing a relatively huge bone. Overwhelmed by guilt, Sonya points out that seagulls and chickens are both birds. It's an exquisitely simple observation that seems to ease her concern somewhat.

After the press conference, we head over to the Anchor Bar and Restaurant, the alleged birthplace of the Buffalo wing. The story goes like this: One late Friday night back in '64, Teressa and Frank Bellissimo, the owners of the Anchor, are cleaning up the restaurant when a pack of their son Dominic's friends walk in. They're all starving. Donnie tells them to wait until midnight and they can have whatever they want. After a round of drinks, Teressa emerges from the kitchen with two huge, steaming, saucy platters. Dominic's friends look quizzically at the plates. Teressa explains that she was about to put the wings in the stockpot for soup, but they looked so scrumptious that she decided it would be a waste. So she cooked them up with some butter and hot sauce, and that was that. "But there's no silverware," one of the kids said. "Keep quiet and use your fingers," said Frank.

As we sit down and order yet another round of buffalo wings, I notice Orange Guy wandering the restaurant. Is he following us? Drew Cerza says a quick hello, and I wonder if this guy's a Bellissimo. The wings arrive and they are truly sensational. I find myself watching Sonya's eating technique to see if I can pick up any pointers. Just as Badlands once showed me way back in our Hooters interview, she strips the bone of meat with one swoop. I begin to feel that I am taking part in American culinary history, sitting with the Wing King and the world's greatest wing eater at the spot in which the buffalo wing was invented. Perhaps something special is afoot.

JUNE 22, 2004
ERIE, PENNSYLVANIA

We've spent the morning doing radio publicity spots, at which Sonya did a two-minute wing-eating exhibition against a deejay. (My job was to keep quiet and take pictures.) Now it's early afternoon. Sonya and I are sitting in Drew's SUV, waiting for Drew and Lon, Drew's brother-in-law, who is here as our resident jack-of-all-trades, to assemble the wing-cooking trailer and the eating-contest tent at each venue. We're sitting here because Sonya claims to be cold, even though it's a temperate seventy-five degrees out. I'm smoldering and ask permission to open the window.

To pass the time, I start asking Sonya questions in an attempt to unearth the enigma behind the appetite. She is generally close-lipped about her personal life, so I'm surprised when she starts to open up. Sonya explains that she was born in Kunsan, South Korea, on July 26, 1967. Her given name is Lee Sonkyong. Her father was a poor carpenter, and she has three siblings—a younger brother, an older brother, and an older sister. From a young age, she was responsible, hardworking, and mature. She always felt compelled to do the right thing. While her siblings were weak, she considered herself strong.

By the age of six, she insisted on walking to school alone. By age nine, she worked a paper route. At age ten, she would walk to the beach and dig clams and oysters to sell for spending money. She competed with adults at digging clams, challenging herself to see how fast she could shuck them from their shells. "I was gooood," she says. "Better than my mom."

She has always been extremely competitive. "In my family, I'm only one who's competitive." Her goal in all things is to be number one. It is an inexplicable drive from within, not just to excel at each chosen task, but to rise above others. "If I'm gonna be in New York City Marathon, I have to win it. That's why I don't do it." Her competitiveness and strong will sometimes caused her problems as a child, such as when she wanted certain types of stylish clothes. Even though her parents couldn't afford the clothes, she begged them ad nauseam, until they relented. "I have to have it. I couldn't sleep."

She explains that traditionally, in South Korea, parents support their kids until they graduate from college, and even into adulthood, but her parents were too poor. In high school, she attended a trade school where she learned accounting, English, and Japanese. In the summers, she got a job at a shoe factory with five of her friends. When her bosses discovered her work ethic, they gave her extra responsibilities. "Even in factory, I'm so good. I work so hard. I don't take it lazy. They give me toughest job and work me so hard."

Sonya always had grand ambitions for herself. As a thirteen-year-old, she wanted to be a basketball player, but they said she was too short. She wanted to be a badminton player, but they told her she didn't have a quick enough reaction time. She wanted to be a TV personality, a news anchor maybe, but was told she wasn't pretty enough. Undeterred, she applied to school for television work, but her parents couldn't afford to send her. "I wanted to be something different than normal people, something extraordinary."

To pay for her college education, Sonya went to night school and worked during the day as a secretary. She found the job boring, but excelled in school, despite some limitations. "My IQ is not high, but I studied so hard. That's me. That's desire!" She earned a degree in hotel management and, in the midnineties, worked at a hotel in Japan.

In 1997, Sonya immigrated to America. She began working for a company that runs Burger Kings on military bases. She started at Fort Hood, in Texas, then transferred to Bolling, then to Andrews, both of which are in Washington, D.C. She was required to take an Army Air Force Exchange test for federal employees and, despite speaking scant English, completed it with the top grade in her class.

It was as a Burger King manager at Andrews Air Force Base that Sonya first stunned coworkers with her eating abilities. Instead of three meals a day, she would eat one extravagant midday feast. A standard meal included twenty chicken nuggets, a Chicken Whopper, three large fries, and a couple large diet Cokes. "I love to eat," she says. Her ideal feast would take place at a Korean buffet, where she would throw down multiple plates of sushi, a few bowls of soup, a smattering of Korean meat and veggie dishes, and some fruit for dessert.

Sonya says if she could sing or act, she would use those skills to the fullest. But she has the skill of eating, so she uses it. In her mind, eating competitions have less to do with eating than competition. "Ten-minute contests are like sprinting, like fighting." Sometimes she gets so caught up in the competition, she loses herself. She wants to win so badly that she finds herself feeling cold and selfish. "I have a heart. I'm a good person. But in competition, sometimes I'm not."

Oddly, despite her world records in chicken wings, chicken nuggets, and hamburgers, Sonya doesn't really like meat. Before age twenty-one, the only meats she'd eaten were eggs and fish. She has always been disgusted by raw meat and still can't bring herself to touch it. She finds pork revolting. In fact, let the record show that when Sonya first tried chicken wings, they disgusted her. The pimply skin gave her the willies, because she could see where feathers had been. The smell of baked chicken and chicken broth nauseates her, she says, because it reminds her of the chicken's demise. In general, Sonya feels a distinct compassion for an animal's suffering in death, which sheds light on how much trauma that whole seagull incident must have caused. Sonya's aversion to meat complicates the fact that, over the next four days, she will eat no less than 350 chicken wings.

The 2004 Erie Regional Buffalo Wing-Eating Championship turns out to be a doozy. It is held near the entrance of Jerry Uht Park before an Erie SeaWolves AA minor league baseball game. A local rock station, Star 104, is playing pop hits and a hundred or so competitive-eating fans have gathered for the spectacle.

"I must say that there's been a lot of doubt in the competitive-eating community about how fast the people of Erie can eat chicken wings," I say. "But today is your chance to prove those doubters wrong." I explain that this is a historic opportunity to upset one of the greatest competitive eaters in the world. "If one of your proud stomachs steps up to the plate and pulls off this upset it will be huge. I'm talking huge like when Ali upset Liston, like when Douglas took down Tyson . . . like when the U.S. Olympic hockey team stole the gold from the Russians!"

I'm feeling it now, as if maybe I'm starting to win over some Sea-Wolves fans. I'm starting to gain confidence in my emceeing skills, learning to channel the Shea brothers, and even becoming a "hot dog" at times on the mic. I introduce the Erie eaters. There's Nate Matusiak, a baby-faced 375-pound car salesman who claims to be the 1998 Duquesne University Greek Week Hot Dog Eating Champ. (Who am I to challenge this claim?) There's Mike "the Destroyer" Dembinski, a 210-pound steelworker who's been eating jalapeños to increase his intestinal fortitude. Nasty Nick McKay is a Big Mac specialist, and Jammin' Jessica Curry is a cute Star 104 morning talk show host.

From left, the author, the Black Widow, the Wing King (in his cape and tumescent orange hat), and rookie eater Nate Matusiak share a naïve smile on the Wing Tour's first stop in Erie, Pennsylvania.

Sonya buries them all. She drops sixty-one, while the runner-up, Matusiak, does thirty-two. It's a classic case of men versus boys, only it's not. After the contest, Sonya wipes the orange from her cheeks, smiles, and waves to the crowd like a princess. The people of Erie adore her.

Afterward, I change out of the carnival barker apparel and into something more comfortable. In need of some *me* time, I amble into the SeaWolves game, grab a cold Bud, and go bask in the rafter sunshine. A voice-mail check includes an ecstatic message from a friend who has just seen "Man Versus Beast," the Fox special in which Kobayashi competes against a Kodiak bear in a hot-dog-eating contest. Just as I'm starting to feel like a fish out of water, I notice a crew of hooligans seated next to the infield, heckling the opposing team's first baseman. Spotting the unmistakable wing helmet/brain tumor, I realize the Wing King himself is affiliated with these guys and walk down to join them.

Turns out the Wing King is hanging with Sonya, Lon, Nate Matusiak, and a pack of Matusiak's friends. Everyone's drinking except Sonya, who explains she can't drink because she hates the smell of alcohol. Matusiak's friends are characters. One of them is unemployed and says he wants my job. Another round of beer arrives.

"Let's get the wave going," somebody says. We start a recruiting mission among people seated near us to stand up when we say so and start the wave. After a few pathetic attempts, although the stadium is at roughly 20 percent capacity, we get it going. It goes around twice and dies. We start it again. It occurs to me that this is the closest I've been to a *Bull Durham* experience. I must be getting drunk.

The problem is, whenever I emcee these eating contests, I lose my appetite. All I've eaten all day is a handful of chicken wings, and the tension of performing in front of people I don't know induces the urge to drink. The Wing King comes up and says we have a problem. We have to drive to Pittsburgh tonight, because we have a radio spot at 7:00 A.M. tomorrow. But we're in no position to drive. Matusiak and his boys overhear and assure us that we're not going anywhere.

When the game ends, they march us over to a nearby hotel and we book rooms.

What happens after that is a blur. We walk to a bar called Fat Boys, where we are treated like royalty. The owner, a good friend of Matusiak and his buddies, introduces Sonya Thomas to the bar as a special guest celebrity. There's a big round of applause. We drink and chat with Matusiak's parents outside on the porch. Jell-O shots happen and we are treated to several varieties of chicken wings, the most memorable being a delightful garlic Parmesan variety. The only evidence of what happens next is a picture on my cell phone of the Wing King crouching near a sign that says FAT BOYS TUESDAY 25 CENT DRAFTS. When the lights finally go out on Erie, Pennsylvania, it is late and I am but a shell of a man.

JUNE 23, 2004
DARK WEDNESDAY

We're driving to Pittsburgh on three hours of sleep. What seemed like a good idea just a few hours ago now reveals itself as a cruel joke. It's inky black out and still nowhere near what I consider to be morning. Sonya, who has made it clear that she doesn't function well without at least eight hours of sleep, is passed out beside me in the backseat. At traffic-light stops, I grab glimpses of the newspaper. Grim news. In Iraq, insurgents have beheaded a Korean translator named Kim Sun-Il.

We roll into the hills and bridges of Pittsburgh right as morning rush hour hits and struggle to find the Infinity Broadcasting building. When we finally arrive, our EMTs are waiting in the parking lot for us. They insist on rolling a stretcher into the radio studio, just in case a bone gets lodged in some poor deejay's throat. Everybody at the radio station is psyched to see our bizarre entourage—the Wing King, a tiny female Asian eating champion, a trough of steaming hot wings, and a medical crew with a stretcher.

We walk into the studio of the B 93.7 morning show. Sonya is forced to answer the same pat questions that she's always asked. "How do you stay so thin? Where does it all go?" It goes forward in the usual fashion, culminating in another two-minute eating exhibition. Toward the end of the minicontest, the deejay named Shelly unleashes a couple of overtly catty comments. First, she says that Sonya "looks like an animal." Then she says with wrinkled nose that she "wouldn't want to eat with her, because it's disgusting." When the competition ends, Shelly asks Sonya directly whether she pukes after contests. Sonya shakes her head adamantly. I'm stunned and feel compelled to defend her, but my role as picture-taker doesn't afford me a microphone, so there's no opportunity.

Afterward, in the SUV, I ask whether anyone else was offended by Shelly's comments. This is a bad call on my part, but my brain is fatigued and I feel the need to convey that someone should have defended Sonya. Drew Cerza and Lon both didn't seem to notice. Maybe I'm being too sensitive. (I'm none too bummed to discover, a few months later, that the B 93.7 morning show has been taken off the air for bad ratings and replaced by Howard Stern.) Sonya, who is generally nonjudgmental, seems not to have been offended, but my recap of Shelly's comments incites something in her, and she suggests that maybe Shelly was jealous. "When I work with a woman, they are always so jealous. Always. But a man, never jealous."

I let the topic drop, but it resurfaces in mutated form when Sonya and I start discussing the headlines in *USA Today*. There's an article about Mary-Kate Olsen having checked into rehab for anorexia. I point out a picture of an emaciated Mary-Kate at a Laker's game, and Sonya reacts with disgust. "Look at her legs," she says, adding that anorexic women are sick in the head. "They eat a little bit, then look in the mirror and see huge fat woman." Though she doesn't say it directly, I understand that she's insisting—as I've read in a few articles about her—that she doesn't suffer from an eating disorder.

I believe her. I have spent quite a bit of time with Sonya, before and after contests, and I have never seen any behavior worthy of suspicion. But that doesn't keep the competitive-eating rumor mills from churning. I have even heard accusations that her teeth are discolored, but my observations don't verify this, and it strikes me as unfair. I believe that her slender physique is due to an abnormally high metabolism combined with an obsessive workout schedule. (One might accuse her of being a workaholic and workout-aholic, but these are relatively healthy habits, especially among competitive eaters.) On any given day, she works ten hours, runs on a treadmill for two hours, and eats only one big meal. It's a matter of calories in minus calories out. If you do the math, it's no wonder she's thin.

Unsurprisingly, though, my badgering has taken its toll on Sonya. Realizing there's no end in sight to her having to eat wings for the amusement of others, Sonya's normally sunny mood darkens. "I'm so disappointed," she says. "It's like prison, you know? Just to the hotel, then eat chicken wings, then to the hotel." When she realizes that, actually, we have no intention of getting hotel rooms today, because we plan to leave for Columbus, Ohio, immediately after the contest, Sonya flips. It's not so much a diva moment as a woman pushed beyond her limit. After a brief negotiation, Drew agrees to put us both up in a hotel for the day.

It turns out to be a wise investment. Sonya goes for a power nap, and I go straight to the bathroom. Seems that my buffalo-wing-only diet is vehemently at odds with my digestive tract. Later, unable to sleep, I go for a jog, buy some baby powder, and eat the most glorious salad of my life at a local eatery.

It's a whole new world. Sonya's in good spirits again, and my Johnson's baby powder works wonders. We take a cab to the competition site, in the parking lot of a mall on the outskirts of Pittsburgh amidst an antique-car show. Sonya's challenger is Big Brian Subich, whom I know from the noodle contest. He's smiley and enthusiastic, and his wife adds a sprinkle of sanity to the whole affair. Subich explains that his eating career began with a bet from a friend over McDonald's double cheeseburgers. The contest is well received, even if the car people seem confused as to why we're here. Sonya wins.

After the contest, Drew allows me to drive Sonya to our next stop, Columbus. Her mood has lifted considerably. She talks freely about various eating injuries she's suffered. At a shrimp-eating contest that was covered by *FHM* magazine, she got a cut in her throat. She was still recovering from the injury at her Bacci Pizza Eating Championship victory, where she cut the roof of her mouth. She talks about her food preferences. She loves watermelon, but hates all things McDonald's except for the shakes. Her favorite food is Burger King french fries with salt and pepper, she says, rolling her eyes up in what looks like a gustatorgasm. We stop for dinner at Burger King, and I must admit the fries are delicious. Feels great to have expanded my diet from deep-fried poultry to deep-fried potatoes.

JUNE 24, 2004
COLUMBUS, OHIO

The scourge returns. Sonya and I have trouble rousing for the morning radio publicity, and Drew is rightfully disappointed. Our spot with the *Wags & Elliot Show* is both funny and tasteful, and I'm not offended that they don't remember my call-in interview from the noodle contest.

That afternoon, Sonya and I are running late for the contest. It's supposed to take place at Nationwide Arena, but I can't find parking. I'm sweating bullets. I'm not used to driving, and I'm stuck on a downtown street that won't allow you to turn right. Will I have to drive straight forever? Frazzled, I park the car and say we'll just have to walk. Sonya's not happy. Drew's pissed. We walk for blocks, and Sonya's going at a snail's pace behind me. When we arrive in front of the arena, the only people there are Brett Barna, the noodle champ, and a few of his buddies.

As I introduce Brett, he makes a request. "If I can eat more than half the amount of wings as Sonya, will she give me a kiss?" Sonya's face reddens, and I'm flummoxed. She accepts the bet. When the competition ends, I announce that Brett has finished with just over half of her total. Sonya looks uncomfortable. After an awkward moment, she concedes a peck on the cheek. After the contest, Sonya, Lon, and I go with Brett's friends to a Chinese buffet. Sonya, who is suddenly effervescent again, astounds everyone by knocking down three stacked plates.

JUNE 24, 2004
CLEVELAND

The Wing Tour rages on. The Marriott Residence Inn is so nice that I'm ready to make it home. I play basketball in the courtyard with a couple of kids. One tiny tadpole of a boy says his family's here because they've lost their home in a fire. I talk to Lon, who gladly offers me a tray of wings to give to the kid's family. Lon and I go out for drinks. Over beer and a plate of Jamaican jerk wings, I conclude that Lon is the only one among us with the slightest shred of sanity left.

JUNE 25

Due to inclement weather, the Wing Tour Cleveland Regional takes place in a vast open area within a crowded mall, the Galleria. The free wings that Lon and the Wing King hand out are snapped up in a matter of minutes. A crowd of a thousand, many of whom are peering over the second and third-floor banisters, gather to watch the showdown between Sonya and Kevin "the Carburetor" Carr, the man who suffered the noodle reversal.

"Good people of Cleveland," I say. "Just a few years ago, an idea was hatched by our good friend the Wing King that each Labor Day, in the city of Buffalo, the world would gather to celebrate the birthplace of the buffalo wing. He took this idea and flew with it, and the

National Buffalo Wing Festival was born. Now, over the past week, the Wing King and I have traveled across this great country in search of talented chicken-eaters, and I assure you that it has been an emotional journey. We have opened up the coops in Buffalo, Erie, Pittsburgh, and Columbus, but as yet no one has proved to be a bigger enemy to chicken-kind than this young lady right here, Sonya Thomas."

The crowd cheers. Sonya smiles and waves.

"But I must say, Cleveland, that I have a bone to pick with you. The Wing King and I spent all day yesterday prowling the streets of this fair city in search of eaters looking to eat their way to the top of the pecking order. And time and time again, the people of Cleveland have chickened out, intimidated by the size of Sonya's formidable gullet. We have heard time and time again, and I quote, that it ain't no thing but a chicken wing."

There are more groans than laughter, but I sense that the crowd is with me.

"I assure you, Cleveland, that it is much, much more than just a chicken wing. Specifically, it is as many chicken wings as you can eat in five minutes. And only one man has stepped up to place the weight of Cleveland's competitive-eating dreams on his weary shoulders. Please welcome a wing-eating champ who very nearly set the world noodle-eating record just weeks ago, Mister . . . Kevin . . . the Carburetor . . . Carrrrrr!"

The crowd cheers for its local contender. That Kevin Carr isn't actually from Cleveland is, for the moment, irrelevant.

"Now, I wouldn't get your hopes up just yet because it's gonna be a cockfight, folks. Our next competitor has records in not only chicken, but in cheesecake, deep-fried asparagus, fruitcake, hamburgers, barbecue sandwiches, oysters, and chicken soft tacos. In perhaps her most stunning feat, which earned her the coveted Cool Hand Luke Award, she ate sixty-five hard-boiled eggs in under seven minutes. Please welcome the little lady with a leg up over *all* the competition . . . she is known as the Black Widow, she is known as the One. She is Sonya Thomassssss!"

The crowd roars. We do the countdown and start the contest. I've pretty much used up all my poultry puns, but I keep pitching anyway. It's a chicken-eat-chicken world! Did I hear somebody cry fowl? Which came first, the chicken leg or the chicken egg? God, am I exhausted. The contest ends and—shocker—Sonya wins again. We say a quick good-bye to Kevin, his wife, and their two little ones. I couldn't exit the Galleria Mall any quicker. It's a long drive back to Buffalo, and I sincerely hope I never see a chicken wing again.

18

THE BIG DADDY
OF THEM ALL:
NATHAN'S FAMOUS ON
THE FOURTH OF JULY

No man can hope to get elected in New York State without being photographed eating hot dogs at Nathan's Famous.

—Nelson Rockefeller, former New York governor

Governor Nelson Rockefeller hands out hot dogs to a horde of hungry and focused New Yorkers at the Nathan's Famous hot dog stand on Coney Island. *(Courtesy of Nathan's Famous, Inc.)*

The day that consumers nationwide have been waiting for has arrived—July 4, 2004, the 228th birthday of the United States of America. As noon approaches, the familiar last-minute preparations have begun. Across the nation, grills are being anointed with that first spurt of starter fluid; ice is being dumped on coolers filled with soda and beer. Grocery stores are flush with revelers stocking up on last-minute supplies—jumbo bottles of mustard and ketchup, buns, giant packs of ground beef, and, let us not forget, hot dogs. Today, according to the National Hot Dog and Sausage Council, Americans will consume 150 million hot dogs.

Twenty of the most committed hot dog eaters have gathered at the entrance of the Holiday Inn Wall Street, nervously awaiting the arrival of the Bus of Champions. The weather is ideal—eighty degrees and sunny with a slight wind, the sky a crystalline blue laced with wispy streaks of clouds. Don Moses Lerman, dressed head to toe in stars and stripes, is pacing back and forth. Oleg Zhornitskiy is sitting on a chair, looking bored. Dale Boone, Allen "Shredder" Goldstein, and Jammin' Joe LaRue are chatting with a reporter, doing their best not to show their nerves.

"You know there's a bet," Dale says.

"What's that?" Goldstein asks.

"The one who comes in last place has gotta take everybody out."

Goldstein says he's not planning on coming in last and hopes to beat his personal best of seventeen and a half. Dale boasts that he already did the deuce, the first year he tried. A reporter asks how he prepares. "I was raised like this," Dale says, patting his belly. "Good old-fashioned Southern stomach."

"He's gonna get the meat sweats," Jammin' Joe says. "That's when the adrenaline enzymes mix with the meat enzymes, and your body loses all control."

Meanwhile, in Coney Island, a crowd is already forming around the stage on the corner of Surf and Stillwell, near the historic site of the Nathan's Famous hot dog stand. Dozens of reporters have gath-

ered in front of the stage and are setting up cameras and micro-
phones. Across from them, on a raised platform, twelve tables are set
up below a ten-foot-long, plastic Nathan's Famous hot dog that hangs
down as if suspended from the heavens. Fans have already taken their
spots outside the barricades. A quick scan of the crowd reveals the
polyglot character of Brooklyn—and of America—a land composed
of immigrants. Among their ranks are tattooed hipsters with digital
cameras, Brighton Beach Ukrainians who have been coming here
each Fourth for years, and gaggles of chirping Japanese girls waiting
for a glimpse of the great Kobayashi.

To the side of the stage, a sign reads ERIC BADLANDS BOOKER FOR
PRESIDENT. A reporter approaches a girl with headphones around her
neck and a sign pinned to her shirt that reads GO KOBAYASHI! She tells
the reporter she's come all the way from Spartanburg, South Car-
olina, to get a glimpse of her favorite gurgitator. And what is it that
she likes about Kobayashi?

"He's the best. Simple as that."

Back on the Bus of Champions, the eaters are exchanging predictions and talking about their role in the most famous eating contest in
the world. Rich LeFevre says that he's gotten fourth place the previous two years, that he wants to eat thirty today but would be happy
with twenty-eight. "It's the most difficult twelve minutes of my life,"
says his wife, Carlene, sitting beside him. "Almost as difficult as the
Great Wall of China, which I did a couple of years ago." Regardless,
Carlene says she'll still be hungry after the competition and will likely
eat ice cream to "fill in the nooks and crannies."

Allen Goldstein says his expectations aren't high. He's only been
eating competitively for six months, and he got the coveted wild-card
slot after getting second place in three qualifiers. "I'm honored to be
on this bus competing with the world's greatest eaters."

In the back of the bus, a group of three men and two women sit
around a table, speaking Japanese. One man is noticeably taller than
the rest, with a disproportionately large head and wire-rimmed

glasses. He is Nobuyuki Shirota, known in Japan as the Giant, and in America as Godzilla. He's the only eater in the world to ever defeat Kobayashi. When a reporter asks if he speaks English, he makes a gesture with thumb and forefinger. "A little bit," Shirota says. According to Dave Baer, who picked up Shirota two days before from Newark Airport, his English is indeed limited. After attempting for a good thirty minutes to explain some urgent thought to Dave on the drive from the airport into the city, Shirota finally dug into his Japanese-English dictionary. "Thirsty," Shirota announced. "I am *very* thirsty."

He is, however, able to answer the reporter's question of how many hot dogs he plans to eat. "Uhhh . . . fifty!" Shirota says with a smile. The reporter turns his attention to a smaller Asian man with a boyish face who is blinking so obsessively you'd think he has Tourette's. The reporter, clueless, asks his name. "Takeru Kobayashi." When asked if he speaks English, Kobayashi shakes his head no and gestures to his interpreter, Robert Ikeda. The reporter asks Kobayashi how many he will eat today, and Ikeda interprets the question. Kobayashi stops blinking and confidently says something in Japanese.

"He says he'll eat fifty-two hot dogs," Ikeda says.

"We gather here under the wall of great men, at the Mount Rushmore of competitive eating, here at the Mount Sinai of Mastication, the sanctum sanctorum of eating, the Coliseum of competitive gurgitators. My friends, we are here where the alpha meets the omega and sends us forth, to go forth, on the Fourth of Julyyyyyyy!"

George Shea is on his soapbox again. He's doing what he does best, standing on a platform, one hand on the microphone, the other pointing into a cheering crowd, setting the stage for an eating contest. I, on the other hand, am terrified. I've spent the morning taping a live pie-eating contest for *The Today Show,* and my nerves haven't recovered. Fortunately, with George Shea running the show, I know I won't have to say much. George extends thank-yous to a slew of people. When he gets around to Mayor Bloomberg, the crowd boos. "They're not actually booing, they're just saying Blooomberg," George says with a smile.

After the singing of the national anthem, the Bus of Champions arrives. As the eaters run from the bus to the tent beside the stage, a.k.a. the bull pen, the crowd goes wild. The musical portion of the show begins. Waving his towel at the crowd, Badlands Booker performs "The Sweet Science of Competitive Eating" with the accompaniment of his son and Hungry Charles's son. The Gowanus Wildcats, a dance troupe featuring eight adorable little girls from Brooklyn, perform a step show that's so endearing that I nearly tear up with emotion. Amos Wengler, the bard of Brooklyn, who cites Lawrence Welk and Liza Minnelli as his inspiration, performs a couple of his folk standards with his guitar. "Hot dogs, hot dogs," he sings. "Watch them eat 'em up. . . ."

I present the three Rookie of the Year candidates as if they were vying for an Oscar. "For excellence in the lunch-meat category, I present bologna-eating champion Allen 'Shredder' Goldstein." George plays the "favorite songs" of each candidate. George and Shredder do a bizarre synchronized arm-pumping dance to "Sister Christian." Buffalo Jim Reeves grooves out to Milli Vanilli. Sonya Thomas's tune, inexplicably, is Dan Folgelberg's "The Leader of the Band." Sensing that he might be losing the crowd, George stops the ceremony to lead a rally cry. "Are . . . we . . . in . . . *Brooklyn?*" he asks.

"Yeahhh!" the crowd answers.

"Are we in the U . . . S . . . AAAAA?"

The crowd goes bananas. Before I can even open the envelope that reveals the Rookie of the Year, fans are already shouting out, "Sonya! Sonya!" Gersh Kuntzman and Mike "the Scholar" DeVito present the trophy to Sonya, and then they make their predictions for the contest. When Gersh says he thinks one of the two Japanese eaters will win with somewhere between forty-five and fifty-five dogs, the crowd boos. George Shea thanks them and takes over, introducing the Nathan's Famous mascot.

"Ladies and gentleman, now I will invite onto the stage the Frankster, that flexible, multicolored, part-protein-based gangster. Last year, the Frankster actually danced with an oversized mustard bottle. And I believe that unnatural act set off a year of nontraditional marriages that embroiled this nation and may play a part in the election this November." The Frankster waddles out and, at George's request, does the "chicken dance."

"Remember, that's not an actual hot dog, folks. That's a person in a hot dog costume. And there's no hip in the hot dog costume, and we all know that rhythm is in the hips. So for this person to be able to do the chicken dance . . . absolutely fantastic! It's a moment of pure joy in our day."

George then introduces Wayne Norbitz of Nathan's Famous, who will present a donation to a nonprofit hunger organization. Norbitz proudly announces that Nathan's sold 360 million hot dogs in 2003, and that they would like to make a gracious donation of ten thousand hot dogs to City Harvest. A female representative thanks him for the "magnificent donation" and shakes his hand. "It will go a long way toward feeding the twenty-three million hungry in America today," she says. I check her facial expression for sarcasm, but it's inscrutable.

Now it's time to introduce the eaters, which means, back to the George Shea show. "Ladies and gentlemen, in the 1770s a man named Daniel Boone roamed the hills of Kentucky and Ohio and Pennsylvania, under an umbrella of a primal forest that stretched for miles. And now his great-grandson nine times over travels the endless strip malls of the Southeast in search of all-you-can-eat buffets and steak challenges."

Dale Boone takes the stage, ringing his cowbell. "You're goin' down Kobayashi," he yells into the crowd. "You're goin' down!" I introduce Crazy Legs Conti, paying particular notice to his daring escape from a popcorn-filled sarcophagus. When George announces the arrival of the contestant from Germany, Markus Steinhof, who he claims is the "bratwurst-eating champion of Lower Saxony," it's my turn to ham it up.

"Er ist der Schweinshaxeweltmeister!" I belt out. "Der groesste Fresser den ganzen Welt!"

"Oh, that's real German," says George.

"Yahh," I say. "And this next eater is the number one hot dog eater in New Zealand. He arrived at South Street Seaport by hovercraft. Please welcome everyone's favorite Kiwi gurgitator, Simon 'the Siphon' Hopewell!"

Jammin' Joe comes up, then Buffalo Reeves. I see that it's my turn to introduce Hungry Charles, and I get psyched. "All I have to say about this next eater is, like George Shea and myself, he represents Brooklynnnn!" I bathe in the crowd's dull roar. Hungry Charles makes a grand entrance to a thumping Biggie Smalls tune, his hair straightened and pulled back in a ponytail like Snoop Dogg back in his "Doggfather" days. "He's the world cabbage-eating champ! The world shrimp-eating champ! They call him the Godfather on the circuit! Please welcome Hungry Charles Hardy!"

George steps up. "Ladies and gentlemen, this next man has continued his journey toward victory despite a persistent neighborhood thief who has stolen all of the topiary shrubs from the front lawn of his Levittown home." Don Lerman doffs his stars-and-stripes baseball hat to the crowd and glances back at George, looking slightly uncomfortable. "He has an extraordinarily intimate relationship with his mouth and alimentary canal, and he has named each of his teeth, men on top, females on bottom . . . it's just good common sense. I give you the butter-eating champion of the world, Don Moses Lerman!" As Don approaches the table, George names off his teeth. "Jimmy, Johnny, Joey, Marky, Mikey, Matty, Timmy, Tommy, Tony, Ted, and Pedro. Mary, Martha, Maggie, Tisha, Taylor . . ."

I introduce Ravenous Ron Koch, as an eater whose obsession with Nathan's Famous dogs has spanned a half century. George describes

Rich LeFevre as part of a rare competitive-eating breed known as the locust, "out in the hinterlands, eating only for themselves at the all-you-can-eat buffets and steak challenges." The crowd begins to stir. In the distance, we can see him—Kobayashi, being carried through the crowd on a palanquin hoisted on the shoulders of four sturdy men. The crowd showers him with carnations. Kobayashi waves to the Coney Island faithful in a way that makes his Japanese nickname, the Prince, seem appropriate. "It is the master, the magician, the alchemist," George says. "The man who has transformed poetry into mathematics, mathematics into science, science into art. It is the Tsunami . . ."

Kobayashi gets as many boos as he does cheers. George introduces Nobuyuki Shirota as the three-time winner of Japan's Food Battle Club, and the only human eater alive to have beaten Kobayashi. Shirota smiles hesitantly and raises a fist. He looks nervous and a little confused. Badlands, on the other hand, looks perfectly comfortable when I announce him. "Put your hands in the air and wave 'em side to side for one of New York's finest!" Booker douses the crowd

Takeru Kobayashi gives love to the Coney Island faithful while being carried in his hot dog–shaped palanquin before the 2004 Nathan's Famous contest. (*Courtesy of Amy Esposito*)

with the contents of his water bottle. He waves his towel and fake-bites at the crowd, and they eat it all up. I notice he's wearing a necklace with a ring on it. In our Carnegie Deli interview, he explained how an eight-year-old girl named Romelie, who knew all about competitive eating, walked up to him at a Brooklyn movie theater and gave him her good-luck ring. It was plastic with green diamonds. In what sounded like a fairy tale, the little girl told him that if he wore the lucky ring, he would defeat Kobayashi and the Giant.

George introduces Cookie Jarvis as "a man who has brought new meaning to the words athlete, champion . . . *neighborhood Realtor.*" Cookie, still the American-record holder with thirty and a half dogs and buns, is wearing his patented stars-and-stripes do-rag. George lists off a handful of Cookie's titles, labeling him a "walking encyclopedia of triumph." Sonya comes last. George introduces her in the most effective way, by listing her staggering records while the crowd looks at how tiny and female she is. Sixty-five hard-boiled eggs in seven minutes! Eleven pounds of cheesecake in nine minutes! Knowing that she's got multiple inexact chicken-wing records, he picks a number between 130 and 150 for the amount she's eaten in twelve minutes.

Mike DeVito swears in the judges and lists the rules. The eaters go through their prematch rituals. Kobayashi, now wearing a floral-print baseball cap, adjusts his water and then stands there, blinking and staring into nowhere. Hungry Charles and Don Lerman lean into the table, narrowing their focus. Lerman keeps adjusting his hat. Crazy Legs plays with his dreadlocks and cracks his neck. Carlene LeFevre and El Wingador both sway from side to side, burning tension. Badlands does breathing exercises. George does the countdown. "We're gonna start in four, three, two, one . . . go!"

And they're off. Specifically, Kobayashi is off. Knowing that George will do most of the talking during the first minute, I walk over and watch Kobayashi intently. He grabs two dogs (without buns) in his right hand and chokes them back in nine bites. Time elapsed: six seconds. Then he grabs two buns in both hands, shoves them in separate cups of water, and crams the soggy, crumbling remnants into his mouth. Seven seconds and it's down. It is a spectacular sight that puts the world's premier sword swallowers to shame. Kobayashi is a shaman, a magician, a wizard, and he seems to be channeling from the same otherworldly source as George Shea.

"Feel the breeze here under the umbrella blue sky of the Almighty, the inverted crucible through which all of His bounty flows. And it looks as if the figure of the Almighty will come down. It will descend to anoint and initiate an eater here today, to transform them from the world of the living into the world of the mystical!"

To Kobayashi's left is Cookie Jarvis, who is eating at a damn respectable clip but still looks like an outdated model in comparison. He takes two dogs in both hands, polishes off half a dog in three rapid-fire chomps, chews for a few bites, swallows, and then does the same with the other half. It is as Kobayashi has said—the Americans chew too much. On Cookie's left, Shirota is rocking a technique I've never heard of before. He breaks both dog and bun into small segments, which he feeds into his mouth and swallows after minimal chewing. Of the twenty eaters, Markus Steinhof appears to be the only one eating dog and bun together in the traditional fashion.

"Ladies and gentlemen, we are involved now in the very essence of human struggle." At two and a half minutes, Kobayashi has seventeen. That's seven dogs and buns a minute. Shirota is right behind him with fourteen. At the four-minute mark, Kobe has twenty-three and Shirota twenty-one. "From the eastern sky, we saw two thunderheads approaching," George Shea announces. "One Nobuyuki Shirota, the other Kobayashi."

Techno music thumps. George keeps the crowd abreast of the American competition, which, at the five-minute mark is a four-way dogfight between Sonya, Badlands, Cookie, and Rich LeFevre, all hovering around fifteen dogs. I keep looking back at the signs held up by the Bun-ettes. The Bun-ettes, dressed in sequined stars-and-stripes

"From the eastern sky, we saw two thunderheads approaching!"
George Shea summons the Gods of Gurgitation while the eaters
scarf down frankfurters. *(Courtesy of Amy Esposito)*

vests and miniskirts, aren't hard to look at. I tell the crowd to watch
for the various styles of dancing—the Kobayashi shake and the Badlands shuffle. "Give it up for Badlands Booker!" I yell, already getting
hoarse.

Sonya sneaks glances at Kobayashi as she eats. She can't match
his pace, but perseveres anyway. "Ladies and gentlemen, I always
thought that Ed Cookie Jarvis, Badlands Booker, and Sonya Thomas
were the three horsemen of the esophagus," says George. "But we are
now witnessing some kind of force from the East here as Nobuyuki
Shirota is pushing Kobayashi. And when the master is pushed, he responds by changing the forces that govern us all. Here is a man in
whom the rules of the universe do not apply. And he is on his way
right now. History, he can see it, like we can see the boardwalk."

At the halfway point, Kobayashi has thirty-three. He does an almost vicious twisting, full-body shake like a dog shaking out its fur after cavorting in a mud puddle. Shirota has twenty-six, Badlands
twenty, Cookie and Sonya have eighteen, Hardy and Lerman fourteen

apiece. I implore the crowd to give them some love to help push the eaters through the wall. Cookie takes time out to blow his nose on his towel. "The hot dog and bun is so difficult," George adds. "It teaches humility to the arrogant, wisdom to the humble."

With under two minutes left, Kobayashi finishes number forty-eight and takes a sip of water. George is so into it his eyes are closed. "You and I see a hot dog and a bun. But he sees proteins and peptides and carbohydrates. He is like Neo in *The Matrix*. He sees the code, he breaks the code." I break the news that Sonya has beaten her own women's world record of twenty-five dogs. As Kobayashi hits his fiftieth, George starts the obvious chant: "Kobayashi! Kobayashi! Kobayashi! Kobayashi!" The Bun-ette recording his tally is Dani Franco, the director of the Crazy Legs documentary, and she's having trouble keeping track. He has changed his method to downing dog and bun together, so she has to adjust. He breaks his record and everyone goes berserk. My voice is gone.

"Ten, nine, eight, seven, six, five . . ."

Kobayashi does one last shake, eats half of his fifty-fourth dog, claps his hands, and pumps his fist. I've never seen Kobayashi this psyched. He puts both hands up and lets out a yell that's muffled by a mouth filled with hot dog detritus. A new world record has been set, the unthinkable topped by the even more unthinkable. Mike DeVito lifts Kobayashi's hand, and George gives his final summation. "Add to looping strings and jumping quarks and bending gravity a new, unexplained phenomenon here, ladies and gentlemen. He is a personal friend of mine, a friend of us all, a citizen of the worrrld! Takeru Kobayashi of Japan!"

After the judges convene, the final tallies are confirmed. Badlands and Rich LeFevre tie for fourth with twenty-seven, Sonya gets third and captures a new American record with thirty-two, Shirota finishes second with thirty-eight. And Takeru Kobayashi finishes with fifty-three and a half hot dogs and buns. In twelve minutes, he has consumed a total of 17,120 calories, almost 750 percent of the

recommended daily allowance. He's ingested 829 grams of fat—
1,100 percent of the daily allowance. His total sodium intake is 24
grams, over 900 percent of the daily allowance. How does he look?
Not unfazed, clearly, bending over at the waist, closing his eyes and
sighing repeatedly—but not bad, considering.

The feat seems all the more absurd when a stack of fifty-three
dogs and buns are placed in front of him. The stack is the size of a
fully developed one-year-old child. In the postmatch interview,
George urges Kobayashi to lift his shirt and show his superhuman
belly to the press. Kobayashi reluctantly agrees. The sight defies all
logic and physics. His six-pack abs have been transformed into a
turgid four-pack, but still one can't see where it's all being stored.
"Ladies and gentleman, look at this man," George Shea says, gesturing at Kobayashi's stomach. "He looks like an anaconda who has just
eaten a goat."

19

LUNCH WITH THE
GREATEST EATER ALIVE

*During competition, as my stomach gets fuller, it gets harder to
breathe. Toward the end, my lungs feel like they're going to collapse. My shoulder muscles tighten up, and my hands start to
shake. A cold, oily sweat washes over me, but I'm excited and full
of energy. I negotiate with my stomach, ask it where I need to put
the next hot dog, and plot the last spurt.*

—Kobayashi, to *GQ* magazine

Dump. "Hai!" Swallow. Stack. Dump. "Hai!" Swallow. Stack.
Dump. "Hai!" Swallow. Stack. Dump. . . .

The repetition is nauseating. Three Japanese men are seated at a
table. To each man's right is a waitress in a robe with a tray of bowls.
In each bowl is a small portion of noodles in soy sauce. Each man is
armed with his own bowl and a pair of chopsticks. The waitress
dumps a bowl of noodles into the eater's bowl, then she stacks her
bowl on the table. The eater grabs the spaghetti-like noodles out of
his bowl with chopsticks, pops them into his mouth, and swallows.
Each dump, swallow, and stack takes about two seconds. Why the
waitresses say "Hai!" after each noodle dump is beyond me.

The young man on the left with the spiked hair looks like an
anime character brought to life. The host has been calling him Takahashi. The guy on the right with the baby face is the only one who's
chewing the noodles, which is why he's about to lose. The kid in the
middle looks as if he could be anywhere between sixteen and twenty,

with doe eyes, frosted hair, and an oval face. That's Kobayashi. All you can see is his upper torso—the rest of his body is behind stacks of bowls. He's eaten 175 bowls of noodles, but is miraculously losing to Takahashi, who's put down 181.

Hold up. Kobayashi's gaining on him. He snaps his head back with each swallow in a way that reminds you of a pelican swallowing a fish. He limits all the variables, keeping his bowl just inches from his mouth. Takahashi raises his chopsticks to tell his waitress he needs a break. Bad Hollywood-epic theme music comes on.

Kobayashi keeps bucking noodles back. Takahashi stops eating entirely—he looks as if he's either going to hurl or die. Kobayashi has the contest in the bag and doesn't need to keep up this pace. But he's Kobayashi. He pounds his chest with his chopsticks, bounces on his chair, shakes, and smiles at a comment made by Yakamuro Yushi, the show's host. When Yushi bangs the drum to end the contest, Kobayashi's bowl count stands at 387. He has just eaten over twenty pounds of noodles in twelve minutes and has beaten Takahashi by 143 bowls.

Welcome to *TV Champion,* a weekly Japanese TV show that focuses on three seemingly unrelated competitions—gardening, tile-laying, and eating. This episode aired on TV Tokyo in the summer of 2001. During the show, twenty-five contestants are eliminated in a series of events that include rice balls, meat buns, sushi, and noodles. Among the contestants who've been eliminated thus far is Nobuyuki Shirota and a bearded man who refuses to answer the host's questions. Kobayashi's prize for winning the tournament is a trip to New York City to compete with Kazutoyo Arai, the show's cohost and the world-record holder in hot dogs, in the 2001 Nathan's Famous Hot Dog Eating Competition. Most of the show's contests are twelve minutes long and thus serve as excellent training for Kobayashi. When the show moves on to Coney Island, the viewer has the satisfaction of knowing what the Americans don't know yet, and what Kazutoyo Arai clearly fears—that this Kobayashi kid is going to kick everybody's ass.

Takeru Kobayashi, flanked by Sonya Thomas and Cookie Jarvis, negotiates with his stomach as he heads into the final sprint at the 2004 Nathan's Famous contest. *(Courtesy of Scott Eels/IFOCE)*

JULY 6, 2004

I am sitting at a table with Kobayashi, his interpreter, Robert Ikeda, and both of their girlfriends at Sea, a Thai restaurant in New York's East Village. Kobayashi and his crew are all hip dressers—they look more East Village than I do. Wearing a stocking cap and a muscle T-shirt, Kobayashi looks like a hipster with a workout fetish. He's in incredible shape, with jacked biceps, thick shoulders, and a bulging chest. I've been concerned about footing the bill for Kobayashi's lunch, but he says his jaw is still sore from the contest and seems more focused on talking about the Japanese circuit than eating. I suppose seventeen thousand calories will tide you over for a few days.

Kobayashi explains that he's the leader of the FFA, or Food Fighter Association. It is a group of the most elite competitive eaters in Japan, the best of which are Kobayashi and Shirota. He has lost to Shirota thrice, but each time it was in longer contests, anywhere from a half hour to an hour long. Most of the contests are televised events with prizes ranging between $50,000 and $100,000.

Competitive eating, or *ohgui,* as it's called in Japan, is Kobayashi's occupation. In his first two years on the Japanese circuit, he made around $400,000. Kobayashi lives far away from his hometown of Nagano, in Nagoya, and I gather that this is due in part to the hassle of fans, stalkers, and paparazzi. Kobayashi isn't overly forthcoming with intimate information, which I ascribe equally to Japanese decorum and to his being a legitimate celebrity. He requests that I don't take pictures, as he is protective of his girlfriend's identity. He would like to distance her from the potential wrath of thousands of rabidly jealous teenybopper fans.

That said, the Japanese eating circuit has fewer competitions these days, ever since "the accident." His interpreter, Ikeda, explains that on April 24, 2002, a fourteen-year-old Japanese kid choked on a piece of bread while challenging two classmates to a speed-eating competition. The kid spent three months in a coma before he died. (Five years prior to that, a contestant died in a Japanese sushi-eating competition.)

Soon thereafter, television networks began to shy away from the contests due to liability concerns. In July of 2002, after TV Tokyo declined to cover the Nathan's contest, the network's New York bureau chief claimed it was due to fears of a potential Independence Day terrorist incident in Manhattan, which would cause their production crews to be stranded in Brooklyn. It sounded like a dubious excuse. Since then, though Kobayashi seems reluctant to confirm this, one source who recently visited Japan tells me the food-fighting circuit there had ground to a halt, but has begun to pick up of late.

I change the subject and try to find out how he got started as a food fighter. Kobayashi says he's always been athletic and extremely competitive. He played baseball from elementary school through high school and dreamed of being a baseball star. In his first eating competition, Kobayashi remembers being annoyed by the derisive tone of the contest's hosts. "They were displaying it like they were these fat freaks going out there. I was interested in it, but I thought they could make it more."

In college, while pursuing a business degree, Kobayashi decided to attempt a twenty-minute-long restaurant challenge that involved eating curry rice. On his first attempt, Kobayashi broke the all-time Japanese curry-rice record. He ate seventeen bowls, or a total of about thirteen pounds of food. After graduating from college, Kobayashi was faced with an uncommon career dilemma: Should he become an accountant or a food fighter? The latter sounded more exciting.

When I mention the rumors about Kobayashi—that he is taking muscle relaxants, has undergone stomach and/or esophagus expansion surgery, or is blessed with a second set of teeth—he just laughs. "I do things that people can't understand or believe. That's why they say things." He adds that he doesn't mean that in an arrogant way, and in fact he's flattered by the rumors. "It's wild that people would say that, when actually I'm just eating and there's no trick to it."

So how *does* he do it then? Kobayashi gives a one-word answer: discipline. He trains. Two months before a contest, Kobayashi starts religiously building up his stomach capacity. For any given contest, he gives himself a capacity goal and keeps training until he reaches it. For the Nathan's contest, he trains with healthier foods until the end of the cycle, when he starts focusing on how to attack the particular competitive foodstuff.

Over the first half of the training period, Kobayashi gains a tremendous amount of weight. To illustrate this, he pulls out his cell phone to show me a picture of himself from two months before. At that point, around the beginning of June, he weighed over 180 pounds. He doesn't look fat exactly, but he's chunky with pudgy cheeks. Over the next month, he lost all the weight he'd gained—around forty pounds—with vigorous weight training and exercise. In keeping with the Belt of Fat Theory, he believes that if some of the heavier American eaters lost weight, their capacity and speed would increase and they'd be "pretty invincible."

The most difficult and important part of training involves getting the swallowing technique down. The concept is not much different from what a sword swallower does—he teaches his esophagus to relax and not close up while swallowing unchewed food. "Anyone in the world can stretch their stomach to what I stretch mine to," he says. It takes extensive training, however, and a certain reckless bravery to relax one's esophagus and condition the brain to ignore the gag reflex.

Being a champion food fighter, he explains, is as much mental as it is physical. "If your mental game is weak, you'll stop at your mental limit and you won't go to your physical capacity," and vice versa, Kobayashi says. As an example, he says that in 2003 he was physically prepared, in terms of stomach capacity and swallowing speed, but the excessive humidity threw off his mental toughness, which is why he finished with a disappointing forty-four and a half hot dogs and buns.

Despite reports to the contrary, Kobayashi says he doesn't meditate as part of his training. He is a secular Buddhist, but it doesn't play much of a role in his training. His mental training for eating contests involves focusing and getting pumped, much as he does when he works out. Ikeda, his interpreter, assures me that Kobayashi is extremely strong. "I took him to my gym once, and all the big guys were trippin' on how much he can lift." I tell Ikeda that I've heard Kobayashi talks to his stomach before competitions. Is it true? After a protracted discussion with Kobayashi in Japanese, Ikeda turns to me. "He says he doesn't really talk to his stomach, but he does feel that his stomach has its own *soul*."

Whoa. My eyes widen, and I start scribbling in my notebook. This is as close as I've come to confirming that Japanese dominance in competitive eating has a spiritual component to it. This possibility, which I believe has some basis in truth, would shatter all notions of eating competitions as mere exercises in gluttony.

Kobayashi says that the contests are more difficult in Japan than in America. Usually, they are longer, which really tests stomach capacity. One contest is called Weight Crash, where eaters are weighed before and after eating Japanese buffet food for forty-five minutes. The most weight he has ever gained in Weight Crash is twenty-six and a half pounds—*twenty-six and a half pounds!* Imagine the food coma! Imagine the aftereffects! George Shea's analogy of an anaconda ingesting a goat seems not at all hyperbolic for such a feat.

Kobayashi explains that he has suffered the only defeats of his career in these longer contests—three times, all to Shirota. Some Japanese contests are the opposite—two-minute sprints. The Nathan's Famous contest, he explains, is a sort of middle-distance competition where he is not quite sprinting but also cannot reach his full capacity.

Once Kobayashi seems warmed up—he is laughing and says he enjoys the food—I decide to ask some slightly more invasive questions. I'm worried that I'll ask something that won't translate well or will offend some Japanese sense of propriety I don't understand. What does he think of drug testing? He's all for it, he says, though he can't imagine what they would test for. Oddly, right after he answers the question, he pulls out a couple pills from his girlfriend's purse and takes them with water. "What's that?" I ask. Kobayashi laughs. Vitamins, he answers. He takes lots of vitamins.

So what happens after the contests? In other words, how does he, uh . . . get rid of the . . . you know . . . Before I can finish, Ikeda's phone rings. It's the producers from the reality TV show *Average Joe*. They want people on the show who can do crazy feats to impress the women. Once Ikeda hangs up, he doesn't force me to keep stammering awkwardly and gets straight to the point. "Are you asking if he throws it up or shits it out?" Ikeda says. Uh, more or less, I say.

Ikeda says it's a normal question and discusses it with Kobayashi. Kobayashi says he just drinks lots of water to flush it out. The resulting bowel movements are, just as you would suspect, voluminous and frequent, he says without elaborating. As for vomiting, that is against the code of the Food Fighter Association. I imagine a band of ninja eaters who, when they discover a traitor going to the bathroom to purge after a contest, force him to commit hara-kiri. "It's about pushing yourself to the limit and holding on," Ikeda says. "So after a match, if you throw up, you're not holding on. . . . The guys who don't puke are the strong ones." Kobayashi interrupts Ikeda with a stream of Japanese, and Ikeda turns to me again. "He said, 'The day I throw up is the day I retire.'"

The only time I strike a sensitive cord is when, after Ikeda says Kobayashi would not participate in a TV show where they make fun of the sport, I ask about their participation in the Fox show *Man vs. Beast*. Without parlaying the question to Kobayashi, Ikeda says in a defensive tone, "I mean, they weren't making fun of the sport." I explain that I didn't mean to insinuate that the show was demeaning. Ikeda says that Kobayashi met Carl Lewis on the set before the contest, so it felt like a real sporting event. He felt honored to compete among fellow physically gifted masters of their respective disciplines.

Man vs. Beast is a show in which humans test their mettle against animals. It's among the most entertaining reality TV shows I've ever seen. A sumo wrestler competes in tug-of-war against an orangutan, a chimpanzee faces a Navy SEAL on an obstacle course, a sprinter runs the hundred-meter dash against a giraffe and a zebra, and an 8,800-pound elephant competes against forty-four little people in pulling a DC-10 aircraft. Highlights include the orangutan's victory smile, the photo finish between the elephant and the little people, and the Navy SEAL's contempt for his opponent, the chimpanzee, "I've sized up the enemy . . . it's just a wannabe human."

The show's first segment is called "Mean Scene of Cuisine." It's a bunless hot-dog-eating competition between Kobayashi and a Kodiak bear. The contest is emceed by Michael Buffer, the "Let's get ready to rrrumble!" guy. The venue is a darkened, foggy soundstage with two raised stages surrounded by chain-link fences. In between the bear's stage and Kobayashi's are electrically charged wires that "hopefully will prevent the beast from bolting out of his ring and attacking Kobayashi." If the bear is able to charge through the wires, the host explains, two game wardens are on hand with tranquilizer guns.

When Alaskan Cruncher, who weighs 1,089 pounds, is released from his cage, he stands up on his hind legs and growls, baring his formidable incisors. Kobayashi, wearing a gray muscle shirt and a rising-sun bandanna, looks smaller than ever. Behind his stage is a Japanese flag, and though Alaskan Cruncher doesn't appear to be in this for patriotic reasons, the Stars and Stripes hangs behind him. We are told that the competition begins when the bear starts eating. Alaskan Cruncher waddles up the ramp to the table, sniffs the food, and deftly pulls a single hot dog toward him with his giant claws.

It's on. Kobayashi starts feeding dogs into his mouth two at a time, watching the bear's progress out of the corner of his eye. After the first dog, Alaskan Cruncher switches to an infinitely more efficient no-hands technique. Soon thereafter he gets distracted and stops eating. "See, he looks away and he takes a break," Michael Buffer explains. "Because he doesn't know it's a competition."

Alaskan Cruncher gets back into it and, after the first minute, starts pulling ahead. It's a clear advantage that he doesn't need to drink water. Between the first and second minute, it is truly a thrilling contest, but at the two-minute-fifteen-second mark the bear only has seven dogs left. He stops and looks over at Kobayashi with a certain tenderness, then finishes the last seven dogs in sixteen seconds flat. Krazy Kevin Lipsitz's dream of a cross-species competition has finally been realized, though probably not in the way he'd hoped.

When Kobayashi realizes he has lost, he leans against the table, despondent and sad. It's unbelievable. That he has eaten thirty-one and a half hot dogs in two and a half minutes is no consolation—he lost. I've never seen Kobayashi look so bummed, and I find myself wanting to pat him on the back. "Give yourself a break, man," I want to say, "you just lost to a Kodiak bear! Besides, pound for pound, you're clearly the better mammal."

For Kobayashi, however, losing just doesn't cut it. Listening to him talk makes me feel like a slacker. As our interview draws to a close, he says that he believes he can do anything he sets his mind to, and the moment he feels as if he's stopped improving, he'll quit. His sole motivation for returning to Coney Island is to beat his own record. His favorite accomplishment, he says, is the hot dog record he set two days before, because he outdid even his own expectations.

Once he thinks he's maxed out his abilities, he'll retire, which won't be long from now, he claims. When he does retire, he'd like to work on the media side of the sport, as an emcee, a producer, or a consultant. In the end it's not about the money, it's about advancing the sport of competitive eating. For now, he's just happy to see that the sport is progressing in America, and that ESPN is starting to cover the Nathan's contest and other events. In fact, if the sport keeps booming in the States, Kobayashi would strongly consider moving stateside, but there is still a ways to go before his dreams for the sport are realized. "I would be proud if it were an event in the Olympics," he says. "I want the Mustard Yellow Belt to turn into a gold medal."

20

SOARING ON THE WINGS
OF A BUFFALO

Ain't no man can avoid being born average, but there ain't no man got to be common.

—Satchel Paige

SEPTEMBER 3, 2004

The sight of Badlands and Hungry Charles in the front seat of a rented Toyota sedan is a study in proportions. It's as if we're driving a Tonka toy, and I feel like a twelve-year-old in the backseat. *Are we there yet?* We are. We pull into the VIP parking lot at Dunn Tire Park, the site of the National Buffalo Wing Festival. Charles, a.k.a. the Godfather, tells the parking attendant that we're here for the eating contest. Access granted. The man would have to be a fool to deny the Godfather access.

Dunn Tire Park, home to the Buffalo Bisons, a triple-A minor league affiliate of the Cleveland Indians, is lined with stands dispensing wings from restaurants representing every region of the country. The pervading scent is exactly what you'd expect—hot sauce and chicken grease. It has a Pavlovian effect, my mouth already juiced up with saliva. A few thousand people are milling about, gnawing at wings from paper plates, their fingers and faces stained orange.

It doesn't take long to spot the IFOCE crew. Our honing devices direct us to the circle of oversized humans standing near the news cameras. It's Cookie, Don Lerman, Crazy Legs, the whole crew. Hungry Charles tells Buffalo Jim Reeves he just met one of Reeves's friends at Central Booking in New York. He hands Reeves a note from his buddy, who was picked up by NYPD for protesting the Republican National Convention.

Someone taps me on the shoulder. It's Jammin' Joe LaRue with the Footy's Wing Ding Championship belt slung over his shoulder. The belt is from a competition in Miami that I co-emceed with Dan Marino, the former Dolphins quarterback, whom I recall being unnaturally tan and uncomfortable doing play-by-play for a wing-eating contest. Lerman hands me a refrigerator magnet for his Web site that shows a picture of him as Moses and a slogan underneath, A COMPETITIVE EATER'S PARADISE. Crazy Legs tells me he's exasperated, having been here since 4:00 A.M. for a media event that never materialized.

Cookie Jarvis pulls me away from the other eaters to tell me a semisecret: Some guy who owns a chain of wing restaurants wants him to be a spokesman and pay him untold thousands. Not sure how this involves me, but I say it sounds like a good deal. I notice that Cookie has a constellation of moles on the left side of his neck and wonder what would appear if you connected the dots. In general, the body of Cookie Jarvis is a source of endless wonder, the belly in particular. It hangs almost aggressively over his belt line in a way that illustrates the strength of gravity, stretching T-shirts to the breaking point. Cookie tells me that he'd like to make the leap from competitive eating to the entertainment world the way the Rock did from pro wrestling. I see some flaws in the analogy, but decide not to get into it.

Drew Cerza announces that the .5K Running of the Chickens is about to start. The Running of the Chickens is the festival's token nod to fitness beyond the world of gobbling poultry. It's the shortest road race sanctioned by the USA Track & Field association, equivalent in length to twenty-two driveways, four city blocks, or fifty-one Winnebagos parked end to end. Up on the JumboTron, I see a half dozen people in chicken mascot costumes leaning forward and ready to run. There's a guy in a wheelchair dressed as a baby being pushed by a nurse with an exaggerated ass. The official shoots his gun, and the whole tribe of misfits takes off.

It's a truly exhilarating race. After a few hundred yards, I recognize the runner in second place—Crazy Legs. Not far behind him is Buffalo Jim Reeves, being chased by a chicken. The first place guy is clearly the only *real* runner, and I'm assuming his imminent victory is some clever ploy to help establish his place in the USA Track & Field rankings. After the race, Crazy Legs, who finishes an impressive fourth, is absolutely spent, gasping for air as if he's got emphysema. It makes me question the physical fitness of one of our most in-shape gurgitators, not that I—sitting on my ass drinking beer and eating deep-fried wings—am in any position to talk.

That evening, after getting situated in the hotel, I go out with a group of gurgitators to what is known on the circuit as a "cultural outing," or in Dale Boone's terminology, "the Canadian ballet." These are code words for hitting up the strip clubs—specifically, the gentlemen's establishments situated right over the Canadian border. It's a relatively common form of group bonding between eaters while visiting random cities. Since I've heard that the Buffalo Wing Festival is widely considered one of the wildest stops on the circuit—one that has been known to feature competitive-eating groupies—it seems my duty as a responsible journalist to go along . . . strictly in an observational capacity, of course. Though nothing out of the ordinary occurs, let the record show that pre- and postcontest camaraderie among America's top gurgitators is in stark contrast to their cutthroat competitiveness at the table.

The next morning, we assemble in the hotel lobby for a bleary-eyed brunch. When I step out of the elevator, I see Hardy and Booker talking to a wiry guy with a Mohawk haircut and a salt-and-pepper goatee. He's bouncing around with this crazy energy like some manic cartoon kangaroo. This has to be Coondog O'Karma, the renegade secessionist eater from Ohio. I introduce myself and mention that I once e-mailed him. He apologizes for his rather aggressive reply e-mail, in which he accused me of being a scoundrel in cahoots with the Shea brothers. Then he hands me an article he wrote for *Cleveland Magazine,* entitled "Dog eat dog . . . after dog, after dog, after dog."

Outside, in the hotel parking lot, we run into Don Lerman and Cookie. Lerman seems vaguely ill at ease, and I soon find out why. "Am I hostile?" Coondog suddenly says, to no one in particular. He turns to face Lerman. "Don, am I anti-Semitic?"

I have no idea what this is in reference to, but am stunned by Coondog's candor. Hungry Charles later explains that there's been an ongoing soap opera involving Coondog, Lerman, and Beautiful Brian Seiken. Seems that Beautiful Brian sent an instant message out to several eaters implying that Coondog had made an anti-Semitic remark. In response, Coondog generously offered to kick Beautiful Brian's ass. When Beautiful Brian responded that he owned a gun, Hungry Charles decided to step in. "I had to get involved. I said, 'What's wrong with you guys? You're acting like fucking kids.'" For the time being, the situation dissolves smoothly with a handshake between Coondog and Don Lerman.

On the walk to breakfast, the ever-present topic of Kobayashi comes up. "The way I see Kobayashi," Coondog says, "it's like my eighteen-inch-dick theory." *What?* He explains that you always hear of some guy who's got an eighteen-inch member, and this guy exists, but he is one in a billion. Kobayashi's ability to speed-eat is like that,

Coondog reasons. Sure, he trains, but he's got something innate that the rest of us don't, perhaps an abnormally large esophagus combined with some sort of Jedi-like mental power. It's a decent theory, actually, one that almost lives up to its name.

Coondog explains that he, too, is genetically predisposed to be a competitive eater. In all of his early childhood photos, he says, his tongue was hanging out of his mouth. During a standard checkup, his family doctor told O'Karma his tonsils were the biggest he'd ever seen and should immediately be removed. Coondog, who calls himself "the Satchel Paige of eating" because he won his first competition at age fifteen and then came out of retirement at age forty, extrapolates that the organs in his throat/pharynx/esophagus region are all generally oversized, which explains his ability from a young age to swallow large chunks of food.

"Guess what?" Coondog says. "I've got a plan to sneak into the qualifier this afternoon." He turns to me. "You've got to promise you won't tell George."

"I don't think I can do that," I say. "Just tell me."

"All right. See, I made this chicken costume . . ."

He explains that he plans to use a Buffalo resident named Pat Maloney as a decoy. Pat will sign up for the local qualifier in the chicken costume, and then, right before the contest, Coondog will slip into the costume. He has even fashioned a hole in the mouth area of the chicken's beak that will allow him to eat. It's an elaborate ploy to gain admission to an eating contest, but you have to admire the man's persistence. "I know it will work!" Coondog's getting all animated again, arms flying everywhere. "You guys didn't recognize me yesterday, did you?"

Coondog says he was wearing the chicken costume the day before and even ran in the .5K run. In fact, Pat the Buffalo Chicken, as his creation is called, won the prize for best costume. The only one who had recognized him was Cookie Jarvis, who spotted the trademark Coondog duck-footed bounce.

"Coondog," I say, "I think you're really naïve to believe George Shea won't look behind the mask. He has already warned me to watch out for you signing up under fake names at three separate contests."

It's common knowledge that Coondog is a man of many aliases. At various contests, he has gone by Evad "the Inhaler" Amrako (his name backward), Forkless Dave (a reference to Shoeless Joe Jackson), and TEFKAC, an acronym for The Eater Formerly Known As Coondog. He has attempted, more than once, to sign up for IFOCE contests using fake e-mail addresses. With all this evidence stacked against him, I try to convince Coondog to apologize to George, who I sense has a bit of a soft spot for Coondog, but Coondog says he's not too good at apologies. He'd rather pull the chicken costume bait and switch.

We eat breakfast at the Towne Restaurant, a Greek joint renowned for its rice pudding. Coondog's decoy buddy, Pat Maloney, joins us for a protracted discussion about the most famous restaurant challenge on the circuit, the eleven-pound 96er Burger at Denny's Beer Barrel Pub in Clearfield, Pennsylvania. (It's the same challenge that earned Kate Stelnick, a 115-pound college student, national overnight semicelebrity, several talk show appearances, and a Web site dedicated to her, katestelnick.com.) The 96 part of the burger refers to the ounces of ground beef, exactly six pounds' worth, but it's the five pounds of fixin's, I'm told, that really gets you. Badlands says he went at it bun first and found the toughest part to be the mayo. Coondog mentions a restaurant challenge he witnessed where Jammin' Joe LaRue exceeded his capacity and started filling up multiple clear glasses with vomit. He adds, rather poetically, that it looked like a milk shake being made.

SEPTEMBER 5, 2004

The crowd gathered for the eating contest is the biggest I've ever seen outside of Wing Bowl. Well over a thousand are huddled around the stage, with at least three thousand in the stadium beyond. George Shea has been on the mic for countless hours over the past two days, announcing such events as the Miss Buffalo Wing Contest and Bobbing for Wings, in which local contestants wade through a kiddie pool filled with blue cheese to dig out chicken wings with their teeth. I sense that George is getting a little punchy, but it's hard to tell. Over the years, he has developed the attitude while emceeing of *You're at my mercy, because I'm the one with the microphone*. He feels in no way restrained to making his verbal flights of fancy relevant. After introducing me to the crowd as his cohost, he says, "Ryan, do you know what the wave of the future is?"

"What's that, George?"

"Tagless comfort. For decades we have been irritated by tags—on the back of our T-shirts, our trousers, our undergarments. And not until now, at the dawn of a new millennium, are we finally beginning to break free of this brutal dermal discomfort."

I look into the crowd and see hundreds of blank stares. "And how is it, George, that this relates to today's wing-eating competition?"

George makes a surprisingly seamless transition into today's big event. We start the introductions, Crazy Legs first, who gets big love from a group of young drunkards from Los Angeles known as the Wingy Dingys. Their official capacity at the festival remains unclear to me, but as far as the contest goes, their role is to heckle George and I with apparently good-natured cheers along the lines of "George sucks!" I introduce "Big" Brian Subich, only to have George immediately change his nickname.

"He is known as Yellowcake, ladies and gentlemen, not only because he is a champion corn bread eater, but because he does work with treated uranium, known as yellowcake in the industry. This man is a terrorist threat. He has high top-level security clearance. If you're looking for yellowcake, this is your man."

"George sucks! George sucks!" The Wingy Dingy crew is gathered at the front of the stage as if they're at a *Phish* concert. They've taken to calling me "Mini-George," which I interpret as a term of endearment. George introduces Tim Janus, his face painted with a superhero-like mask, as the future of our sport, a day trader who wants to be a house dad. I introduce Nate Matusiak, the guy I found in Erie, Pennsylvania, on the Wing Tour. When George brings up Oleg Zhornitskiy, I inform the crowd that he once ate eight pounds of mayonnaise in eight minutes, which elicits the standard huge gasp from the crowd.

When Hungry Charles approaches the table, it's clear that he's fully in the Zone, not smiling, and even looking a bit angry. It reminds me of what Badlands said in our interview about him. "If you notice, before every contest, he stops the socializin', the hand-shakin', the autographs, the talkin' to the guys, the talkin' to the other competitors. . . . You can't disturb the man at that point."

Badlands Booker takes the stage wearing a Frank's Red Hot Sauce bib signed by all the eaters. He gives the crowd love, then does a rehearsal where he pretends to be bringing wings up to his mouth at a breakneck pace. George decides it's an ideal time to try out his own rapping abilities. "He is Badlands from New York, one of the best with a spoon and a fork. . . . He's got the eye of the tiger, the gangster walk. And when it's time to chew, there is no time to talk, my friends."

Sonya enters wearing white, baggy (how could they not be?) nylon shorts, and a red tank top. The crowd explodes and she responds with a big smile and her patented double-handed wave. Her entrance song is "Hells Bells," by AC/DC, which strikes me as a somewhat morbid anthem. "You're only young, but you're gonna die!"

I look down at the Wingy Dingy crew, recognizable by their powder blue baseball jerseys. They are a sight to see. The leader of their crew has a video camera in his right hand, a beer in the other, and goggles pressed against his forehead. He's yelling incomprehensibly up at the stage. Behind him is a skinny blonde in a bikini, looking sexy but sloshed beyond belief. "Crazy Legs!" she blurts out, apropos of nothing.

Cookie Jarvis, the defending champ, makes a grand entrance, carrying the Chicken Scepter through the crowd. George tells the crowd that the Chicken Scepter was created by the descendants of a Mayan prince. The last introduction is Jammin' Joe, the Florida hot-dog- and wing-eating champ, because he's been cooking the competition wings, and he's clearly been meticulous about keeping them piping hot. So hot, in fact, that we have to delay the competition for a good five minutes for them to cool down.

The contest itself doesn't merit a fleshed-out description. I've emceed so many contests at this point that it feels like déjà vu. That said, it's always fun to hear the George Show, which blends pure absurdity with the standard play-by-play. "In every compression of the jaw, in every drop of saliva, in every twitch of the epiglottis, I see the human struggle, Ryan," George says. Badlands Booker, he claims, has created a sort of Powell Doctrine for competitive eating, using overwhelming force against chicken wings. He describes Sonya as an alien who hovers above the stage as if on the wings of the very chicken wings she is eating. After each comment, the Wingy Dingys belt out another "George sucks!" until he is finally forced to respond. "The Wingy Dingys follow these eaters on the road," he says, "as if they were a revival of Bachman-Turner Overdrive, going to venues across the nation."

Shocking no one, Sonya wins by eating nearly five pounds of wing meat. I congratulate her afterward and ask if this makes all that training on the Wing Tour seem worthwhile. She just giggles and nods. A big group of eaters gather around the front of the stage afterward to chat and plan our meeting later at a rock concert nearby. Though the Nathan's Famous contest is clearly the mother of all competitions, the Buffalo Wing Festival contest is where the American eaters go to get together and have a good time. Looking around at the smiling faces of Badlands, Hungry Charles, Don Lerman, Jammin' Joe, Crazy Legs, Cookie, Buffalo Reeves, Brian Subich, and Tim Janus, I can't help but feel a pang of sentimentality for the sincere camaraderie fostered by the competitive-eating circuit.

Hungry Charles Hardy (seated, left) and Crazy Legs Conti (standing, in the EAT THE WORLD T-shirt) are spurred on by the crowd at the 2004 Buffalo Wing–Eating Championship. The two fans standing in the front row between Hardy and Crazy Legs are members of the notorious Wingy Dingy clan, a band of rabid competitive eating groupies. *(Courtesy of Joe Casio)*

But my momentary reverie is broken by the frowning face of an older woman who I recognize from the Wing Tour as Nate Matusiak's mother. "Why was Nate pushed off to the side like that so no one could see him?" she asks. I explain that it's customary for veteran eaters to receive the prime real estate. While Nate rolls his eyes and tells his mother to shut up, she presses me further, clearly pissed. Exhausted and delirious, I quote a lyric from one of Badlands' songs about eating your way to the middle of the table, but that, too, falls on deaf ears. "If you want respect on the circuit," I finally say, looking over at Hungry Charles, "You've gotta pay your dues first."

21

THE GODFATHER

And if by chance an honest man like yourself should make ene-mies, then they would become my enemies. And then they would fear you.

—Don Corleone, a.k.a. the Godfather

Hungry Charles Hardy exhibits his superhuman hand-eye-mouth coordination while Cookie Jarvis sneaks a glance at his progress. *(Courtesy of Matt Roberts/IFOCE)*

SEPTEMBER 10, 2004

A week after the Buffalo competition, I met up with the IFOCE's most esteemed veteran, Hungry Charles Hardy, at an Austrian restaurant in Park Slope, Brooklyn. He pulled out a scrapbook filled with newspaper articles and pictures that chronicled his six years on the circuit. Over a lunch of bratwurst and Wiener schnitzel served by a Teutonic transvestite waiter/waitress, he told me his story. It was the fascinating story of a man—a police officer, a father, and a gurgitator—whose experiences captured the essence of competitive eating, in both America and Japan, and how that sport has evolved over the last half decade.

Before he was the Godfather he was Hungry Charles.

Hungry Charles came into being on June 25, 1998, on the observation deck of the World Trade Center. He didn't even want to be there; his union president, Norman Seabrook of the Correction Officers Benevolent Association, had cajoled him into signing up. Seabrook knew that Hardy had worked for ten years in a Rikers Island mess hall as a cook, and that his appetite was champion status, but Hardy was worried about getting laughed at by the guys in the crowd. He was thinking about just not showing up, and he told his wife so. "Just go down there and have some fun with it," she advised.

So he showed up for the Nathan's Civil Service qualifier. He checked out the trophy and liked the looks of it, then watched amazed as Ed Krachie did a hot-dog-eating exhibition—sixteen in six minutes. Afterward a man with a sly grin in a straw hat walked up to Charles.

"How are you doin', sir?"

"Hey. What's happenin'?" Charles said.

"I'm George Shea. What's your name?"

"Charles Hardy."

"Are you hungry?"

"Yeah, I'm real hungry."

"Okay then. You're Hungry Charles."

And he really was. He ate sixteen and a half that day, beating out two sanitation workers, two court officers, two policemen, and a fireman. His dog dominance wasn't entirely by choice—President Seabrook was literally shoving frankfurters into Charles's mouth, repeatedly chanting, "Where my dogs at?" Hungry Charles was a natural, and the press took notice. He woke up the next morning and found his name "in every damn newspaper in the city. They were calling me America's next hopeful." The buzz around the competitive-eating campfire was that Hungry Charles had the best natural game since Peter Washburn's record-setting performance back in '59. A few weeks later, Hungry Charles stunned the Coney Island faithful with seventeen and a half HDBs. He took second place, finishing behind Hirofumi Nakajima.

Going into the 1999 contest, Hungry Charles could fairly smell victory. At the Civil Service qualifier on July 1 in the lobby of the World Trade Center, he did the deuce. Though he would still have to take Nakajima and a Floridian upstart named Andrew Becker, who had eaten twenty-two in his qualifier, Hardy knew this was his chance. Even Mayor Giuliani went on record as a Hardy supporter. "I'm with the guy from Brooklyn," Giuliani told the New York *Daily News*. "If he doesn't win, we'll have an inquiry."

Giuliani had no idea how portentous those words would be. The 1999 Fourth of July finals were dubbed "The Great Nathan's Hot Dog Eating Scandal" by New York City newspapers. The official victory went to Steve Keiner, a 325-pound electrical inspector from Atlantic City, who downed twenty and a quarter. Hardy tied fellow Brooklynite Bartoszek Tadeusz with twenty even, but several observers claimed that Keiner started eating a few seconds before the opening countdown finished. Hardy complained, and a local news station aired a replay that seemed to confirm his position. In a July 5 article entitled "Nathan's Champ Called Cheat," the *Daily News* printed a video still that clearly showed an illegal head start.

Though George Shea conceded after the contest that footage showed Keiner jumping the gun by "half a dog," the contest rules did not allow replays. Mike DeVito defended Keiner, claiming that one of his dogs wasn't even counted. Hardy demanded a rematch and doled out more accusations. He claimed that Nakajima stashed a hot dog in his towel. "Nakajima did some sleight-of-hand shit. It was like a three-card Molly."

Though Hardy's best shot at a title was cruelly stripped from him, he got some good publicity out of it. Jay Leno invited Hardy and Keiner out to Los Angeles, but Keiner declined unless he was paid several thousand dollars. So Hungry Charles went alone. At first, the idea was to bring him out in a pair of skimpy Speedo swim trunks. "I was like, 'I'm not fuckin' going out onstage in no damn Speedos,'" Hardy says. Instead, Leno sat him down and they had a civilized chat about the mental strain of speed-eating. "Your body is saying, 'No, I can't take no more,'" Hardy told Leno. "But you're saying, 'Yes, you are,' and you just keep ramming them in there." Later, Leno challenged Hardy to a contest. While Hardy ate, Leno threw dog after dog over his shoulder. Afterward, the tally was seven to two in Leno's favor. "Charles," Leno said, "you got screwed again."

In February of 2000, Harry Solomon, who was working as a stateside producer for TV Tokyo, called Hungry Charles. "You like sushi?" Solomon asked. When he heard the word *sushi*, Hardy immediately suspected that this implied a potential trip to Japan. "Yeah, I love sushi," he answered, even though he had never tried it. Hardy went to see Solomon the next morning. "You think you can eat a thirty-foot sushi roll in thirty minutes?" Solomon asked. "Hell, yeah," Hungry Charles said. "No problem."

Solomon suggested that they go eat some sushi. Hungry Charles said he had just eaten and wasn't hungry. "No, I wanna watch you eat sushi," Solomon snapped. He then sent out a courier, who came back with two enormous platters of sushi. Hardy stared at it, panic-stricken. "So which one is your favorite?" Solomon asked. Hardy said he liked them all. After Hardy popped a few pieces of sushi into his mouth with his fingers like popcorn, Solomon asked, "Don't you like wasabi?" Hardy said he loved wasabi. "I didn't know what wasabi was," Hardy admits. "I didn't know how to mix it with the soy sauce or none of that." But whatever suspicions Solomon might have had dissolved when Hardy finished off two heaping platters of sushi in less than an hour. The next day, Hardy went to pick up a passport. He was told he'd earn $12,500 for his participation.

On March 6, 2000, Hardy flew with his mother to Japan to compete in the sushi challenge. "As soon as I got off the plane, you would've thought Michael Jackson had landed." Japanese fans had made signs and had Hungry Charles pictures for him to sign. A TV Tokyo producer explained that a commercial featuring him had been playing there for over a month.

Charles stayed at the Century Hyatt Tokyo. He recalls looking out his window at hordes of Japanese commuters swarming like preprogrammed bees around Shinjuku train station, the world's busiest. His mother suggested they go out for something to eat. "I'm not going out there," Charles said. "I'm waiting for the fuckin' interpreter."

Not wanting to insult his hosts, Charles decided to refuse nothing offered. Strange drinks and foods kept coming in waves. Some of it tasted good; some of it didn't. The most memorable dish was the platter of chicken breastbones. "And I'm sittin' there crunchin' and crunchin'. It wasn't good. Eatin' cartilage. That's all it was, was cartilage."

When Hungry Charles saw the sushi chef making the thirty-foot sushi roll, he knew he was in trouble. *I know I can't eat this damn thing,* he thought. Though he wasn't competing against anyone, Hungry Charles's goal was to beat the record recently set by a Japanese rock star, who had eaten twelve and a half feet. Hardy had been studying footage of the feat for a month.

From the mock contests that Hardy had shot in New York for the commercial, the TV producers knew his weaknesses—salmon roe and sea urchin. The thirty-foot roll was double-wrapped with seaweed, so Hungry Charles couldn't see what he was eating. It was the "little egg bursts" of the salmon roe popping that really got to him. "Those eggs were just spurtin' in my mouth. I almost heaved it up." There were several close calls in which Mount St. Hardy seemed poised to erupt. "They were screaming and shit, because they thought I was going to let it all out. I thought, *I'll be damned if I'm gonna come this far to embarrass myself like that.*"

By this point, Hungry Charles had actually taken a liking to sushi, but thirty feet in thirty minutes seemed absurd. As he completed each section, Hardy won a prize, as did select members of the audience. In the end, he ate fifteen feet of sushi to set the new world record. It was a particularly satisfying feat because of the nausea Hungry Charles endured and because the Japanese rock star had been cocky beforehand. "In the commercial, he talks a lot of shit about how I'm going to fail."

Soaring on the wings of a world title, Hardy returned home to New York with inflated confidence. He e-mailed the organizer of the Ben's Deli Matzo Ball Eating Contest. "I'm gonna be your next matzo-ball-eating champ," he wrote. At the contest, he showed up in ghetto-fabulous attire—a Puff Daddy T-shirt and a shiny gold necklace. He didn't much look the part of a Jewish matzo-ball *fresser,* so the Ben's Deli mainstays scoffed at his bravado. "You know, I was the only black guy there," Hardy remembers. "And when it was my turn to qualify, they were in awe. They were like, 'Oy vey! Look at him go!'"

In the finals, using a ravaging no-utensils technique, Hardy ate thirteen matzo balls in five minutes, twenty-five seconds. When the tallies came back, he was tied with an up-and-comer named Ed Jarvis. Contest host Curtis Sliwa said they'd have to do a one-minute-and-twenty-five-second eat-off. Hardy looked over at Jarvis and saw matzo meal coming out his nose. "I'm cool with that," Hardy said. "All I need is five minutes to smoke me a cigarette." The contest officials sent Gersh Kuntzman outside with Hardy to make sure he didn't throw up. "Went out there for a couple minutes, came back in, got that burp out, and it was *on,*" Hungry Charles remembers. He ate two and a half more in the overtime period to become the first non-Jewish

Ben's Deli matzo-ball-eating champ. The prize was a trophy and a $2,500 gift certificate.

Though he was making a name for himself on the circuit, Charles wasn't exactly making allies. Don Lerman, who considered matzo balls his specialty discipline as a New York Jew, wasn't pleased. "Don was pissed," Hardy remembers. "He hated the fuckin' ground I walked on. He even made a T-shirt that said BEAT HARDY." Ed Jarvis wasn't a big fan either, taking particular exception to Hungry Charles's swagger and his comment to a reporter that he was the "Michael Jordan of competitive eating."

Competitive eating, however has a way of punishing its practitioners for such hubris. Hungry Charles received his comeuppance back in the land of the rising bun. His sushi challenge had been a big hit with Japanese audiences, so TV Tokyo invited him back for a stunt called the Superman Dash in January of 2001. He first flew to Tokyo for a quick sushi exhibition, then was flown to a Japanese town so rural it "was like being in Siberia," Hardy remembers. The production crew drove Hungry Charles and Kazutoyo Arai to a warehouse in a remote area, where an elaborate conveyor belt was set up. "What the hell's going on here?" Hardy asked. The conveyor belt, they said, was there to transport nearly two hundred bento boxes from all over Japan toward the gaping maws of Hardy and Arai.

A bento box is, in essence, a single-portion take-out meal that is popular among commuters, travelers, and schoolchildren in Japan. Its origins date back to the late twelfth century, and one could make a case for bento being the first societally sanctioned fast food. The proportions of a bento meal tend to be as follows—four parts rice, three parts meat or fish, two parts vegetables, and one part pickled veggies or dessert. Bento boxes come in many different varieties—from aluminum trays to elaborately decorated wooden, lacquered boxes. After World War I, there was a movement to abolish bento in schools because the boxes were such overt indicators of a child's social status.

Outside of Ed Krachie's experience several years before, the Superman Dash was among the most grueling competitive-eating situations an American had ever faced. Hungry Charles and Kazutoyo Arai were supposed to eat bento boxes nonstop for *twelve straight hours.* They ate for forty minutes each hour, and then were granted a twenty-minute break. After four or five hours, the impossibility of the task overwhelmed Hardy. Arai, on the other hand, seemed neither stuffed nor dyspeptic. Where was he putting all that food? As the challenge dragged on, Hardy noticed that Arai made hourly trips to the Porta Pottie, from which he returned spry and unencumbered. Hardy soon realized that Arai was only storing his food temporarily. "It made Arai look like a fuckin' superhero. And it looks like this American guy can't hang with him."

Finally, Hardy decided that he'd had enough. He is diabetic and is always careful about maintaining his glucose levels before, during, and after competitions. But during an extreme stunt like the Superman Dash, maintenance is near impossible. His glucose levels surged to the 300s. "These people are killing me," Charles remembers thinking. "I can't do this no more." At the apex of his misery, Hungry Charles lay on the stage and passed out.

After that, Arai took Hardy to the Porta Pottie to show him a technique he called purging (though some might call it puking). Arai took a liter of water and drank it all at once. Without putting a finger down his throat, he simply leaned over the toilet and bento came out in a variegated stream. "He was so quiet, you could hear a pin drop," Hardy explains. "He wiped his face, wiped away the tears, wiped his mouth off, and went back out." Realizing that purging would be instrumental in continuing—and surviving—this diabolical stunt, Hardy decided to follow suit.

When the stunt finally ended, Hardy and Arai had downed 180 bento boxes, or the equivalent of ninety lunches apiece. Even by the standards of Japanese sadomasochism, it was an unnecessary amount of consumption. Or in the words of Badlands Booker, who watched a videotape of the show on Hardy's plasma TV, "That Superman Dash was *gangster.*"

Jokes aside, it was a traumatic and eye-opening event for Hungry Charles, and he earned every cent of his $7,000 appearance fee. But on a positive note, he became friends with Kazutoyo Arai. (He considers Arai a wise man, but suspects that he may have been anorexic.) Arai showed Hardy around Tokyo, and Hardy became familiar with the labyrinthine Japanese subway system. He even befriended a group of young ladies whom he calls "extreme tanners." The women were young, attractive, extravagantly dressed, and had darker skin than Hardy. They recognized him, and one of them addressed him in English. "How do y'all get the money to buy all this shit?" Hungry Charles asked the girl. "We have—how do you Americans say?—sugar daddies," the girl answered.

Hungry Charles nodded. Pimping, like competitive eating, was a concept that bridged cultural barriers.

Before he was Hungry Charles, he was Charles Hardy, Brooklyn born and raised. Grew up in Crown Heights, raised by his grandmother. They didn't have much, but they made ends meet. Grandma made no more than $20,000 a year, but Charles and his three siblings always had food on the table. Grandma got his sneakers under the table and his jeans from a man at her job who sold them on payday.

It was a happy childhood. Charles had lots of friends. Partied his ass off in high school, deejayed on the weekends. Charles was into old-school rap and started collecting thick stacks of vinyl. He met legends like Grand Master Flash while playing clubs in the city. While deejaying a sweet sixteen party in January of 1982, Charles—or Crazy C as he was known in his deejay group, the Master Blasters—found his eyes wandering to the birthday girl's cousin. Her name was Valerie, but everyone called her Z, an abbreviation of her middle name, Zena. Two years later, on June 9, 1984, Charles and Z got married.

The first year of their marriage, Charles was broke. He hustled as much as he could, but it wasn't enough to support a family. One day, not long after Charles's graduation, Z's uncle, Xavier Hospler, whom

Hardy called Uncle Brother, walked up and told him his destiny straight-up, "You're gonna be a CO." Charles didn't know what a CO was, but he needed a job, so he filled out the paperwork and took the test. Uncle Brother made sure he got the job, and Charles Hardy has been a corrections officer ever since.

He started working the mess hall at Brooklyn Detention Center. Worked there for ten years, improving the cooking skills he'd learned from his dad, who had been a cook in Vietnam. When they closed the mess hall in 1995, Charles was transferred to the women's house on Rikers Island. His job was to provide the three C's—care, custody, and control—for the inmates. It wasn't an entirely pleasant experience. Being a male officer amongst female inmates, Hardy says, is like being a female officer in a male prison. Naked women would make disgusting overtures and flick bodily fluids on him. "Though it's sad for me to say it," Hardy says, "I went from 'Excuse me, miss' to 'Hey, bitch.'" He found that they were the only words the women would respond to.

Charles spent much of his time at Rikers with the baby killers. He would escort them from one place to the next, making sure the other inmates didn't assault them. His job offered many revelations, few of them uplifting. Foremost on the list was that "the women in the system, they get the shaft." In his view, women did more time than men did for the same crimes. "It's nothing for a man to go to jail. He can bounce back. But once you're a woman in jail, you're fucked for life. And I kind of feel for them with that."

One day in August of 1996, Charles Hardy, his wife, and their three kids had returned from a Florida vacation and went out grocery shopping. On the way home, at an intersection in Brownsville, Brooklyn, a car slammed into his minivan head-on. There was a second impact, which Hardy later discovered was a cop car hitting him. The driver of the first car was a woman fleeing the police in a stolen car. In a desperate, last-ditch effort to escape, she backed up and slammed into Hardy's minivan again.

Hardy heard his ten-year-old son, Edmund, in the backseat saying that he couldn't feel his legs. Pinned behind the steering wheel, Charles, fueled by rage, managed to squeeze out of his car, suffering several cuts. While the perp lay facedown in the street, handcuffed, Charles walked up, pointed his gun at the woman, and said, "When I come back to work, bitch, I'm going to kill you."

Hardy was immediately transferred off Rikers Island. Two officers escorted him to his locker after hours and allowed him to clean it out. Due to the sensitive nature of the incident, Hardy says, NYPD brass agreed to brush the whole episode under the rug, but he was so upset with the way the officers had handled the police chase that he filed charges against the city. To rationalize why they were driving over the speed limit, the sergeant at the scene allegedly told Hardy it was a "hostage situation." Hardy was sure it wasn't. He felt he'd been lied to, and that the cop had no real concern for his family. When the case finally closed in 2004, Hardy says he got a negligible settlement. "I got pennies out of it, but it's the principle of the matter."

Since the incident, Charles has worked the night shift at Central Booking in Manhattan, which he calls a "retirement home for correction officers." His job is to put perps in their cells, keep the system updated as to each perp's whereabouts, then let them out when the paperwork comes through. He's met dozens of famous people, including several hip-hop stars—Tupac Shakur, Busta Rhymes, Fabolous, and Cam'ron, a Harlem-bred rapper for whom Hardy has served as a bodyguard. He's stayed up all night drinking coffee with Mike Wallace. He remembers the night that kid from the "Dude, you got a Dell?" commercials got busted buying pot on the Lower East Side. Hardy greeted him at the station with a smile and said, "Dude, what happened?" Hardy remembers having in-depth discussions with hundreds of protesters during the 2004 Republican Convention. "No offense," he says, "but I've never seen so many white people locked up in my life." Officer Hardy has enough stories in him to write a juicy memoir, and he's already thought of a title: *You Just Can't Make This Shit Up.*

It hasn't been all celeb run-ins and protesters. Charles vividly remembers the morning of September 11, 2001. He had just got out off his shift and was sleeping with the TV on. He woke up right after the first plane hit. "I said, 'Damn those are some real good special effects. What movie is this?' " It took him a good ten minutes to realize it was real.

He went to work that night. When the shift was over, he and some of his Central Booking buddies decided to help out at the rubble pile. They knew dozens of officers who'd died, men who had brought their prisoners to Central Booking. The least they could do was go help out. Hardy's first look at the area surrounding the site is etched indelibly in his brain. "The most eerie thing was to come down Broadway, right by City Hall, and there were just thousands and thousands of shoes on the street. People literally ran out of their shoes. There was so much soot on the ground, it was like walking through fine snow. And you'd see hands and limbs lying around. The stuff was untouched. It was like walking onto a movie set."

For the first week, he drove people back and forth from the site to a rest area on Canal Street. In the weeks after that, he started working on the rubble pile itself. They gave him a mask, but he only wore it for about five minutes until the filter clogged. It was too hard to breathe through, so he took it off. Hardy's most difficult memories were from the time he spent working at the morgue. "We didn't get no whole bodies. We'd get a lot of torsos or half bodies, gloves, arms, whatever body parts. And I'd have to go through their pockets and try to find their ID. Remove jewelry off their fingers. Lots of fingers." Hardy started having disturbing nightmares, including a recurring one about walking down a haunted, empty Broadway. After two weeks at the morgue, he told them he couldn't work there any longer.

Each day it was the same numbing routine. Hardy worked his shift from eleven at night until seven in the morning, went down to work at the pile, then went home for a nap and started all over again. He was so stressed and fatigued that he went into autopilot mode.

He'd like to put that time behind him now, and he has, except for one thing. His voice box got singed so badly by the smoldering chemicals and carcinogens at the pile that it changed his voice. He now speaks in a baritone so raspy, low, and quiet, it reminds you of a certain character played by Marlon Brando. Even after Hardy retires, it will serve as a permanent reminder of the years he spent serving his city.

Now he's the Godfather.

Coondog O'Karma, a close friend of Hardy's, gave him the name. In the instant messages they sent back and forth to each other, Coondog often found himself in a confessional mode, asking for advice. He would say, "Godfather, I'm having a problem. What should I do?" And Hardy would IM back his sage response. When Coondog went to qualify for Wing Bowl XII, he alluded several times to "the Godfather" while talking to the *WIP Morning Show* hosts. They picked up on it, and now, at Wing Bowl, the name Hungry Charles Hardy is meaningless. He's known simply as the Godfather.

It's appropriate that the name stems not only from his deep, gravelly voice but also his abilities as a paternal dispenser of advice, because the Godfather has become the unofficial captain of the American eaters. Three weeks after September 11, while Hardy was still occasionally coughing up blood from his experiences at the rubble pile, he went to compete at the Glutton Bowl. There, he mended his relationship with Don Moses Lerman.

Hardy had stripped Lerman of the matzo-ball-eating title just seven months before, and Lerman was still sore about it. During Lerman's butter-eating qualifier, Hardy walked out from behind the stage and started cheering Lerman on. "Come on, Don!" Hardy yelled. "Eat that fuckin' butter!" After the competition, Hardy congratulated Lerman on his victory and showed sincere concern for Lerman's well-being during the grueling postbutter recovery stage. Lerman recognized that he'd judged the Godfather too harshly and apologized. "You know, Charles," Hardy remembers Lerman saying, "I've been acting like a real ass. You really do have my back." The Godfather told Lerman not to worry about it, and they've been tight ever since.

The Godfather again showed his team spirit during the taping of *GutBusters in Alaska,* a documentary for the Discovery Channel. The show tracks Hardy, Dale Boone, and Crazy Legs Conti in their attempts to qualify for the Hibernation Cup. After Hardy won his first-round qualifier by downing four and a half pounds of Alaskan spotted shrimp, he became a full-time cheerleader and adviser to his fellow eaters. After Crazy Legs lost to Boone at the reindeer-sausage qualifier, the Godfather critiqued Crazy Legs in a concerned, fatherly way, then helped him prepare for his last chance to qualify, at the lumberjack-breakfast competition.

"I was just eating steadily, and obviously eating too slowly," Crazy Legs said after the contest.

"You were nibblin'," the Godfather said.

"I was nibbling."

"You were nibblin' like a damn squirrel sittin' there with a fuckin' nut. That's not what I expected of you."

"Yeah," said Crazy Legs.

"Now, you figure with pancakes, if they're the same size as the ones we had this morning, you should get one down in thirty seconds if you dip it. Okay. So you do that for like the first three minutes. After that, you just take your time."

"I'll make you proud tomorrow," Crazy Legs said. "I appreciate it."

"I'm proud of you now," the Godfather replied.

But it was at Wing Bowl XII that the Godfather became the true captain of the IFOCE. In his storied career as a gurgitator, it's the competition he's most proud of, because it wasn't just about individual accomplishment. The Godfather won the first round, and when Sonya stripped El Wingador of his title, the IFOCE squad danced around her and lifted her in the air to show that the victory was communal. The team win was particularly sweet for the Godfather because he had lost to El Wingador in the Glutton Bowl (taped right after 9/11) after suffering an unfortunate reversal during the sushi round. "At Wing Bowl, we were all there as a team effort, to fuckin' wipe Philly off the face of the map," Hardy explains. "And we did it."

In keeping with this ethos, the Godfather firmly believes that the future of the IFOCE lies in developing a broad swath of eaters with strongly developed characters that fans can relate to. If the circuit starts focusing on a limited number of eaters—Cookie, Sonya, and Kobayashi, say—then media saturation and fan boredom will quickly set in. "You take the WWF. These guys put on a good show. They've all got character. You can actually individualize each one."

The analogy that the Godfather likes to use for his vision of a united squad of IFOCE eaters is the *Super Friends* cartoon. The IFOCE office is the official Hall of Justice where the squad gathers. From there, they shoot off to contests, where each member's skills are unique and useful in battle. "You've got Wonder Woman, who's good at one thing. You've got Superman, who can see through fuckin' brick walls. Everybody has to have something to be known by." As an example, he cites the rookie eater Tim Janus, a.k.a. Eater X, who shows up at every competition wearing a face-paint mask that's specific to that competition. "And you know, it's like, what is Tim Janus gonna look like today? You never know until he shows up." In keeping with this analogy, the Godfather sees secessionists like Gentleman Joe and Chowhound Chapman as the enemy, the Legion of Doom.

If the IFOCE squad can stick together and become a recognizable band of close-knit gurgitators, the Godfather thinks the sky is the limit. He's the link from the old-school eaters—guys like DeVito and Krachie—to the new-school crew of characters like Eater X, Crazy Legs, and the Black Widow. He's seen the media attention and the prize money on the American circuit steadily increase over the years. "Whether people think it's a freak show or a sport or just a spectacle, people are gonna pay," he says. When asked about his plans for his competitive-eating career, the Godfather has developed a go-to response. "I'm gonna eat my way to Beverly Hills." The IFOCE has been such a big part of his life that he got a new tattoo at the 2005 World Grilled Cheese Eating Championship in Venice Beach—the letters *IFOCE* in a tribal-style font—to add to the two he already has on his right arm.

After almost a decade of gurgitating glory on the circuit, the Godfather announced his retirement in the summer of 2005. Having recently retired from the Department of Correction as well, he's focussing on his health and spending more time with his family. And, of course, planning his send-off party. Knowing the Godfather, who, according to Badlands, "likes to do things in a big way," it will be a *party*. Think hot tubs, Veuve Clicquot dribbling down champagne flutes, Cuban cigars, bikinis, and endless platters of food.

Though he's officially retired, the Godfather says he won't stray too far from the table. The IFOCE recently named him commissioner, replacing Mike DeVito. Now that he's got some idle time on his hands, he plans to implement some big ideas for his beloved sport. "I want to do some of the decision-making and try to take this thing to a higher level, where everybody can profit from it, where everyone can live like a rap star. You know what I'm saying?"

22

TRAINING FOR
GURGITORY GREATNESS

*Statistics show that of those who contract the habit of eating, very
few survive.*

—Wallace Irwin

I try eating competitively for the first time in Maui. The foodstuff is
Maui onions, four of which sit on a paper plate before me. I know
all about them, because Dave Baer and I have been talking about
them for the last six hours. We've been doing our best Food Network
shtick, introducing chefs who prepare dishes like the Maui Onion
Stuffed Veal Loin with Leek Fondue and Wasabi Garlic Mash and
Purple Sweet Potato Mash. We've been lobbing trivia questions to the
crowd, giving out T-shirts, bibs, and restaurant gift certificates as
prizes. Maui onions are grown on the upper slopes of what Hawaiian
volcano? Haleakala, that's correct, sir. What are the three factors behind the sweetness of Maui onions? Sunshine, altitude, and volcanic
soil. We've started referring to the elderly couple in the second row as
the Trivia Mafia, because they've got a steadily rising stack of gift certificates but keep greedily raising their hands.

"Ryan has told me he plans to beat the world record right here,
before your very eyes," Dave says. "He claims he ate one pound of
onions in a minute during training."

Damn him. Dave has been eating with me for a decade and knows how unbearably slow I am. How many times has he eaten me under the table in late-night, besotted Chinese take-out chowfests? Now the crowd's looking at me as if I've got skills and they're about to witness history. I just smile and act serious, do a few mock jaw exercises. What do they know?

Dave gives me the three-two-one, and I start. I take a big chunk out of the peeled Maui onion. Onion juice dribbles down my mouth and onto my tie. I chew and chew and try to swallow, take another bite. My bite-to-swallow duration is pathetic. I'm hyperconscious of how slow I am, how openly untalented I am as a gurgitator. Though I've been told that eating slow is a good thing, I've always considered it a plague. At family dinners as a child, I would keep eating while plates were cleared and everyone else fled to the living room, my food going from lukewarm to cold. I take another bite and flash a stuffed smile at the crowd.

"Come on, Ryan, don't play to the crowd. Just eat."

It's Badlands Booker. Great. Even he's disappointed, and it's rare you see Badlands bummed out about anything. So not only do I suck at this, but I've upset one of my heroes in the sport. Other than that, though, I'm kind of digging this. I like eating competitively, even if I am bad at it. Maybe it's because nothing could be negative here in sunny Maui, standing in the shade of this banyan tree, but I think it's more than that—something more fundamental. It's fun trying to eat as fast as you can with people cheering you on, and Maui onions are delightful—healthy and sweet, with the consistency of an apple and without the eye-watering aftereffect. I take another bite and revel in my juicy lips and clogged mouth. Eat lots fast! That's my new motto. So what if I'm not a natural.

I finish my one-minute sprint and the crowd gives me a big round of applause. "Let's go to the scales and see if Ryan broke the world record." Dave comes back and announces that I've eaten .41 pounds of Maui onion, which doesn't approach the record and would have earned me a depressing fourth place in the junior competition we have just judged. Whatever. Besides, the winner looked well over fifteen years old to me, and I wasn't shy about discussing what smelled like fraud with the crowd. (In the process, I said the word puberty three times, until Dave finally whispered into my ear, "If you say puberty one more time, I'm gonna turn off your microphone.")

So the unsurprising conclusion to my first eating contest is that I lack skills. Big deal—failure never slowed me down before. I make the obvious leap of logic under such circumstances: It's time to train.

OCTOBER 5, 2004

On this, my first night of training, I decide to work on capacity instead of speed. The vice-presidential debates are on TV, so I reason that tonight's exercise will be to spend the entire debate consuming. I purchase thirty bucks' worth of cheap Mexican food, a gallon jug of water, and a six-pack of Budweiser tall boys. By the time John Edwards makes the snarky comment about Dick Cheney's lesbian daughter, I've killed three tall boys, a roasted chicken, a beef burrito, and a salad. I'm completely stuffed.

The phone rings. It's my girlfriend's father, a doctor, who gave me a physical the day before. The plan is to get a physical before and after training, so as to gauge the effect competitive eating has on health. Because I lack health insurance, Dr. Girlfriend's Dad is the obvious choice. That said, the prostate exam was a level of intimacy we hadn't previously shared.

He's got below-average news. My cholesterol is a little high. I turn down the tube. I'm at 232, and I should be about 190 to 200 for my age. (I'm thirty.) On the bright side, my triglycerides are normal at 127, and my HDL cholesterol, which is the good kind, is pretty solid at 56. So I've got that going for me.

Unfortunately, my LDL cholesterol—the bad kind—is also high.

He starts asking questions. Does heart disease run in my family?
Does high cholesterol? I don't know. Does thyroid disease? Diabetes?
No clue. Because I might need medication like Lipitor if I can't get my
LDL down. Great. The whole death thing hangs out there. I pace past
the TV. Edwards and Cheney seem to be mocking me. To compensate
for my panic, I thank Dr. Girlfriend's Dad profusely. "I've always been
concerned about my cholesterol level," I lie. "It's just great to finally
know."

He gives me the standard spiel. Avoid fatty meats, fried foods,
and all things tasty. Get consistent, if not daily, exercise. Alcohol's not
great for cholesterol. Eat fiber, grains, oatmeal. Maintain ideal body
weight. He asks what foodstuff I plan to compete in. Krystal
burgers—they're the Southern version of White Castles. That certainly won't help anything, he says.

I thank him and say good-bye. I decide to mellow out on the Mexican food and spend the last twenty-five minutes of the debate putting
down a gallon of water. At a quarter gallon, I feel my belly and am
proud of its turgidity. At a half gallon, I'm hurting. Toward the end of
the debate, as Cheney and Edwards are issuing their canned final
summations, I pound down the final gulp.

I've exceeded my limit. Beads of sweat form on my brow, and that
sickly taste of warm saliva rises into the back of my throat. It's the
feeling of knowing it won't stay down, but with a new twist of no va-
cancy. Involuntary moaning. I need to relieve this pressure somehow.
I go to the bathroom and pull the trigger. A few spurts of water and
debris come up. I try again, with a little more success this time. Soon
thereafter, a plague of endless hiccups sets in.

The next day, I call a diet hotline posted in the *Daily News*. A
nurse is befuddled by my questions and passes the buck to a general
surgeon from NYU Medical Center named Christine Ren. Dr. Ren is
informative. She says the main physiological strain of eating
competitively—with, say, hot dogs—is absorbed by the liver. The
abundance of salt can cause hypertension, or high blood pressure.

There's also pancreatic stress, because all the sugar pushes the insulin into overdrive. Anatomically or functionally, she doesn't know if there are any negative results of the stomach, intestines, or the colon being overstretched. She doesn't think any academic studies have been conducted on this sort of thing. Overall, she says that it all depends on caloric intake. If one only eats a huge number of calories sporadically—say, once a month—but eats healthfully and exercises regularly throughout the rest of the month, the body would likely be able to compensate.

Through my girlfriend, who is attending medical school, I then interview an M.D. and a Ph.D., both of whom specialize in gastroenterology. I quiz them on the short- and long-term physiological effects of competitive eating. Immediately after a training session or eating competition, I'm told that the main impact would be on insulin maintenance and electrolyte maintenance. If one eats twenty-five hot dogs and buns in twelve minutes, for example, there's a spike in insulin and the sodium levels soar. (Insulin is a hormone that regulates the metabolism of carbohydrates and fats.) The insulin spike occurs because the body is gearing up the system to store as much nutrients as possible. In the short term, the body can compensate for this in the same way it compensates for the digestion of a large meal. But in the long term, the results can be, well, bad.

I ask about the worst possible scenario—competitive eating over a decade, training frequently, and with a generally unhealthy lifestyle outside of competitions. Dr. Paul Black, a Senior Scientist and Professor at the Ordway Research Institute Center for Medical Science, says that the primary problems would come in the areas of electrolyte balance, fat metabolism, and glucose metabolism. If one engaged in dozens of contests over several years with foods high in trans fats and cholesterol, there would likely be an inflammatory response that could lead to conditions such as diabetes, coronary disease, and kidney disease.

Another potential side effect could be lipotoxicity. What occurs, he explains (and I am paraphrasing here), is that even though one's insulin levels are high, your body can no longer respond to it appropriately. Over time, the body starts storing lipids where it shouldn't—the pancreas, the heart, even the skeletal muscle. "And it starts to impact negatively on metabolism in those cells," Dr. Black says. He also adds that big weight fluctuations as part of training, especially for people with low body-mass indexes, aren't generally a good idea. All this, he explains, is simply conjecture, and the fact remains that the body is resilient. If one is careful to maintain a healthy lifestyle outside of this aberrant behavior, the negative impact could be minimal.

Regardless, considering my recent diagnosis, I am a little spooked. I decide to train with healthy foods. On my second day of training, I do water training—a gallon of water as fast as I can. (Keeping in mind warnings from Badlands and Dr. Black about hyponatremia, or water intoxication, I do some research to make sure this is relatively safe.) I throw on some hip-hop music and try to establish a rhythm as I gulp it down, but it's too damn cold. I get serious brain freeze, then full-body freeze. At five minutes, I've got just over a half gallon. I try to establish a better rhythm and drink bigger gulps at once. It's my first glimpse of what the Zone feels like—lug, lug, lug—but at eight minutes, I've still got only five-eighths of a gallon down. How pathetic am I? Cookie Jarvis polishes off a gallon in a minute. At ten minutes, when I finally finish, I feel that nauseous warning saliva in the back of my throat. I take a picture of my bloated belly and sink into the couch. A half hour later, I feel kind of good. Don Lerman said the first few times would feel like a cleansing—a reverse enema, as he called it—and that's oddly appropriate.

Day three, October 7, is grape training. I put down three pounds of grapes in ten minutes. Not terrible, but very mediocre by professional gurgitating standards. In competition, I'd be close to last place. Afterward, I'm a little stuffed, but decide that a beer will help my capacity. After polishing off a tall boy, I get this icky feeling. It's a pressure that starts in the stomach and blossoms into the lower esophagus. There's also a spine-ache rising into my neck, a weird pressure that suffuses my entire abdominal region.

On the fourth day, I do the Orange Challenge. The plan is to peel and eat a dozen oranges in a half hour. Sure, it's not that ambitious, but I'm thinking baby steps. While watching the Laci Peterson murder special on A&E, I start peeling and eating. The peeling takes time and the oranges have seeds, which slows me down considerably. At eight oranges, I show signs of fatigue, but it's mainly just boredom with the same redundant flavor. By the time Scott Peterson is spying on the Coast Guard while they troll San Francisco Bay, I'm done. Mission accomplished. A dozen peeled Valencia oranges in twenty-three minutes—definitely a personal record, and I'd venture to guess it's a neighborhood record to boot. I decide that, despite my meager talents, the great thing about competitive eating is that each time I step up to the plate, I will achieve an all-time personal best.

Within moments of finishing, I see an ad for *Crazy Legs Conti:*

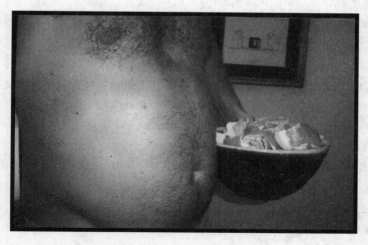

The author shows off his distended belly and discarded peels after completing the Orange Challenge.

Zen and the Art of Competitive Eating. Uncanny timing. The Gods of Gurgitation shine down upon me. In the hour after the Orange Record, I use the toilet—in a sitting position—three times. In the next hour and half, I make five more visits. Talk about reverse enema. The last five would all qualify as "loose stools" and take on a dull brownish orange hue.

The fecal fun continues the next day. While watching Crazy Legs' publicity stunt for the A&E premiere of his documentary, I start to get the rumbles. After Crazy Legs downs a dozen doughnuts while washing a downtown Manhattan window in a flame-print Speedo, I immediately scuttle to the subway. When I finally get home to Brooklyn, I drop the coolest poop of my life. There's no actual poo substance; it's just this big blob of orange skin, membrane, and pulp, and its shape looks like the Shmoo (a lovable blob of a cartoon character from the seventies). I take pictures but my camera doesn't really capture the details.

The next day, I talk to my literary agent about my feat, and he expresses disappointment that I didn't tear the oranges open with my teeth and devour them, peels and all, like some craven varmint. I consider the possibility of becoming a poop artist. Surely I'm not the first to have this artistic breakthrough, but an Internet search results in surprisingly few poop artists. There's one exhibition of bird-poop art, which consists of framed poop on paper with the corresponding bird pictured above. For the record, peregrine falcon dootie looks like amoeba. That said, the artist claims it was traveling at 45 mph at the time of poop, so maybe the splat was distorted.

On October 13, 2004, I eat four pounds of seedless white grapes in fourteen minutes. Not terrible. For the first time, I experience the competitive-eating sensation of "catching a burp." It occurs at the eleven-minute mark and opens up crucial space for the final stretch. On October 14, I eat thirteen bananas in thirteen minutes, which may or may not be a record for thirty-year-olds. I learn firsthand that you can drink too much water. Once over that hurdle, I get a technique going—two bites, sip, and swallow. Two bites, sip, and swallow. I stand the whole time, adding gravity to the down-the-pipe force and do my own snaky version of the Kobayashi shake. Overall, I consume 5,200 grams of potassium, which should hold me for a day or so. Aftereffects: one respectable poop and a symphony of belches.

Departing briefly from my healthy training, I devote three days to Orange Training. And by orange I don't mean the fruit; I mean the color. On day one, I put down a large bag of Doritos, a carton of Tropicana orange juice, and four peaches in a half hour. (I don't recommend this combo.) On day two, I knock down two boxes of Kraft macaroni and cheese in twelve minutes. Volume-wise, this may be my best feat yet. On day three, I do a Carrot Challenge to work on jaw strength. It takes me thirty-seven minutes to put down two pounds, and afterward my jaw is sore. The use of veggie dip violates the all-orange-foods rule, but makes the process infinitely more enjoyable.

On October 19, I have no intention of training because my Mexican Food Slam (MFS) from the day before is still whistling. The MFS included lots of beans, and as George Shea often points out, "Beans are a musical fruit." Then, at 3:20 in the morning, I suddenly come to the disappointing conclusion that I haven't been hard-core enough. I decide to rollerblade through the pouring rain to the nearest White Castle. At Crazy Legs' stunt, I chatted with Tim Janus and he told me he downed a Crave Case—thirty burgers—in eight minutes. The late-night clientele at White Castle includes a chatty homeless guy who says he used to be a ringer with chitlins and wishes me luck with my training.

Once home, I decide not to dunk the burgers. I do ten in eight minutes (amateur) and thirteen in eleven (sad), but, hey, at least I'm out there on the circuit, doin' my thing. Later, I fall into a delirium not unlike the kind Krazy Kevin once described. I drink water and beer to capacity, then take pictures of my distended belly. Trying to sleep proves painful; I'm forced to sleep on my side. At 5:00 A.M., I awaken to a searing Dutch oven, the odor of which is a delicate blend of White Castles and raw sewage. (For those unaware of the Dutch oven, it's what happens when flatulence becomes trapped beneath the covers, forming a temporary and malodorous prison cell.) The smell is potent enough to wake me up and keep me up for a good half hour. The next day, everything I am reeks of White Castles. Pee. Poop. Gas. Sweat. Breath.

Though my competitive-eating issues are manifold, the most significant problem is swallowing. The thing is, I can't swallow unchewed food. I just can't. I do research on swallowing. The Internet has a single-minded approach to the subject that focuses on oral sex. Turns out that the skill I'm looking for is not unlike the "suppressible gag reflex" employed by Linda Lovelace in *Deep Throat.*

I learn that swallowing is a series of actions, several of which involve the brain. Seeing, smelling, or thinking about food causes the body to prepare for eating. The mouth coats with saliva. Waves of contractions called peristalsis begin to flow from the base of the throat, down the esophagus, and through the stomach. The stomach enlarges. The first three processes are voluntary—introduction of food, chewing, and swallowing. The first checkpoint is the pharynx, wherein lies the gag reflex. The gag reflex can be suppressed but not controlled. It's not a simple skill to learn. It took a sword swallower named Roderick Russell a full year to learn how to suspend his gag reflex. If it takes such intensive gag-reflex training to develop my gurgitating skills, forget it.

The esophagus has another sphincter known as the lower esophageal sphincter (LES). The antiquated term for this is the "cardiac sphincter," which Don Lerman once told me was extremely important to competitive-eating training. (Of the three medical authorities I interviewed, only one had heard of the cardiac sphincter.) The LES is located at the bottom of the esophagus, where it joins the top of the stomach. It prevents food and stomach acid from backing up into the esophagus and into the trachea, or windpipe. For gurgitators to avoid a reversal during a contest, he or she must learn to control both esophageal sphincters.

Realizing that my lack of courage and control in swallowing is my greatest flaw as a gurgitator, I do more research on the subject. The most fearless swallower of all time, it turns out, is a Frenchman named Michel Lotito. He is known as Monsieur Mangetout, or Mr. Eat Everything. At age seven, while drinking a glass of water, Lotito's glass broke. He'd heard of eating glass before, so naturally he ate it. When he told his friends, they didn't believe him. The next time he tried it, he cut himself, so he decided to focus on getting the technique down.

Before long, Monsieur Mangetout was putting down beer bottles, and then champagne bottles. At a county fair, he ate a bicycle. Using a pair of snips, he cut the bicycle into bite-sized chunks and ingested it. It was smooth sailing until he got to the chain. "Fortunately, the doctor was able to extract the chain from my rectum," Lotito explained afterward. He's eaten eighteen bicycles and as many TV sets, supermarket trolleys, razor blades, and a coffin. The feat that got him into the *Guinness Book of World Records* was his ingestion, over a two-year period, of a Cessna airplane. Besides an extrathick stomach lining and some serious dental issues, doctors say Lotito is totally normal.

I'll never be as hard-core as Lotito, but I'm willing to take the Milk Challenge. There's an urban myth that says it's impossible to down a gallon of milk without booting, but Badlands tells me this isn't true. Online, I discover entire chat rooms devoted to this topic, one in particular on cyberdorks.com. Most of the testimonials result in failure, and about 75 percent end with a stream of ivory-colored vomit. I ask Dr. Girlfriend's Dad about it, and he says that milk is a powerful base and that lactose (the sugar in milk) is an irritant. My research shows that, though lactose intolerance is particularly bad with those who have inadequate amounts of the enzyme lactase, most humans have some degree of lactose intolerance. In many areas of the world where drinking milk after infancy is uncommon, lactase deficiency among adults is widespread.

On October 20, 2004, I try the Milk Challenge with a gallon of skim while watching game five of the Yankees–Red Sox AL Championship. Forty minutes in, the pain starts, and I'm freezing. Fifty minutes in, I feel pain everywhere—shoulders, head, stomach, bowels. At an hour, I'm almost there, just a couple cups of milk left, but it doesn't feel right. I go to the bathroom and retch. I decide to throw in the towel, not so much out of a fear of puking as the fact that my body really *really* doesn't want any more milk. Later, I ward off intense stomach pain and finally fall asleep. When I awaken, I'm beset by the most penetrating gas I've ever experienced.

On Monday, October 18, I had called up Dave Baer at IFOCE HQ and challenged him to a White Castle competition that Friday. He agreed and immediately started showering my cell phone with smack-talking text messages. "Prepare to be dominated," one message said. On October 22, I buy forty White Castles in Brooklyn and smuggle them onto the subway in my backpack. On the long ride to the Upper East Side, I notice fellow passengers sniffing and looking around suspiciously.

At Dave's Upper East Side apartment, we're all business. Dave's wearing a Rangers jersey, and I've got on a Reggie Miller Pacers jersey with Pacers tear-away sweatpants, a hat with BAD ASS embroidered on it, and two wristbands. In preparation for the big show, we both down a glass of red wine. Dave hands me an IFOCE waiver. We both complete them and sign at the bottom. Under "type of employment," Dave writes, "Poorly chosen."

"I know you're a better eater," I say, "but this no-dunking policy could prove to be your downfall."

"We'll see."

The EMT arrives. He's a young black guy named Rudolph. Nice guy. When he sees that we're both dressed in sporting gear and listening to "Eye of the Tiger," he asks what's going on here. We say we're about to have a one-on-one eating contest, and he's here to make sure it's safe. Rudolph shrugs. "Okay," he says, his brow wrinkled in confusion. I tell him we don't have any accidents planned and ask if he wouldn't mind taking photos with my digital camera. "Okay." I try to imagine what Rudolph is thinking and can only come up with *White people are crazy*.

We give the White Castles a minute-long zap in the microwave, then stack them up in two twenty-burger pyramids on the pool table. I line up two glasses of water and stare down the burgers for a moment. Dave hands the iPod to Rudolph and tells him to press play when he says to. We shuffle back into Dave's bedroom.

"How freaked-out must this guy be?" Dave asks.

"He seems fine, actually."

"All right, Rudolph," Dave yells out. "Now!"

Rudolph presses play and the *Rocky* theme comes on. Dave makes his entrance, jogging out to the pool table with both fists raised. I follow behind him, making fake jabs and waving to a pretend crowd. Rudolph doesn't even crack a smile.

We square off at the pool table. Dave counts down from ten, and we're off. Right out of the gate, you can see he's got a speed advantage. The *Rocky* theme keeps us both on top of our game. "Gonna fly now! . . . Flying high now!" I can't tell if my dunking technique is helping or hurting, but I still can't force myself to swallow until my cud is fully chewed. At the three-minute mark, Dave's up seven to five. Rudolph keeps taking snapshot after snapshot from the same angle. He seems less concerned with artistry than just getting this over with.

When the *Rocky* theme finishes, the next song in queue is "Rocky Mountain High," by John Denver. I start cracking up and a snot wad flies out of my nose onto the pool table. Dave is laughing, too. Finally, he goes over and changes the song. This is an act of supreme confidence that, were I a lesser man, I would take advantage of. But I slow my eating chivalrously. Dave picks out a mellow Dave Matthews tune that's not much of a competitive eating anthem. We're at the halfway mark. I've got to pick it up.

I stop dunking. White Castles aren't my favorite, and when sop-

The author (in the Indiana Pacers jersey and BAD ASS hat) and
Dave Baer compete in an unsanctioned White Castles eat-off.
(Courtesy of Rudolph the EMT)

ping wet, they're awful. Rudolph keeps taking snapshots. Just another
Friday night in New York. I'd continue to describe our battle, but to
be honest, there's not much to it. Dave wins, seventeen to twelve. The
sad thing is, this is an improvement for me.

"I'm disappointed in you, Dave," I say afterward.

"Why's that?"

"You could've done the deuce."

We pay Rudolph and he wastes no time getting out of dodge. Before he leaves, Dave tells him we have contests like this all the time,
so we might be calling him again soon. We spend the rest of the night
imagining our next phone call to Rudolph.

"Hey, Rudi, this is Dave. I'm at the Royal Buffet on Seventy-fifth
and First. Can you be here in fifteen minutes?"

"But it's three o'clock in the morning!"

"I know what time it is, but it's about to *go down!* Are you in or
are you out?"

Next call. "Rudi, Ryan here. Meet me at Chow Fun Delight

Restaurant in Spanish Harlem in thirty minutes, all right? Oh, and bring a stopwatch and some needle-nosed pliers."

Follow-up call. "Yo, Rudi! Ryan here. Where the hell were you? My opponent here at Chow Fun just choked on a sparerib and went into a coma. I hope you've got insurance, because my lawyer will be contacting you within the week."

We never get around to calling him. The day after the contest, I hang out with my girlfriend. She's got a keen sense of smell and keeps mentioning that I "don't smell like Ryan." Note to self: Schedule two days of alone time after each contest. I have every intention of going for a second checkup with Dr. Girlfriend's Dad, but out of laziness and fear of a follow-up prostate exam, I never get around to that either.

23

DOWNING SLIDERS ON
THE KRYSTAL CIRCUIT

*I want to keep fighting because it is the only thing that keeps me
out of the hamburger joints. If I don't fight, I'll eat this planet.*

—George Foreman

The Krystal Square Off Burger Eating Championship circuit, on
which I intend to make my debut as a competitive eater, is a series of eleven qualifying competitions that culminates in a championship contest in Chattanooga, Tennessee. The winner of each
qualifier gains a spot in the championship, which offers a total of
$17,500 in prize money. I am scheduled to emcee four contests and
compete in two. In my second-ever contest, in Jacksonville, Florida, I
will compete against Takeru Kobayashi, whom many consider to be
the best athlete alive.

SEPTEMBER 19, 2004

The Krystal circuit gets off to an auspicious start when Sonya Thomas
eats forty-two burgers in eight minutes in Chattanooga. My start is
less promising. The journey to the third qualifier in Knoxville, Ten-

nessee, is plagued by travel snafus. My cab ride to La Guardia is beset by pond-sized puddles, the remnants of Hurricane Ivan. At the airport, I discover that my flight has been canceled because the Atlanta hub I'm supposed to transfer through is a mess of posthurricane missed flights. After umpteen phone calls, I'm able to transfer instead through Chicago, where I'll have a six-hour layover.

It gets better. The contest is scheduled at the worst time imaginable. Sunday, September 19, 12:30 P.M., at the Tennessee Valley Fair. What better time for an eating contest than midday on Sunday in the middle of the Bible Belt? To make matters worse, the gates open only a half hour before the competition, so the place is empty. I do my best to build a crowd, shamelessly appealing to local sensibilities by comparing the contest to the Tennessee Volunteers' home upset last night over the University of Florida. I take off my carnival barker's hat and put on an orange Tennessee hat brought specifically for this purpose.

I make a long, rambling speech about James Wilhoit, the Tennessee kicker who went from goat to hero in the previous night's home game against Florida. We find ourselves in a similar position in today's burger-eating contest, I say. We have athletes coming from outside of Knoxville, trying to humiliate you on your own turf. Specifically, we have Bill "El Wingador" Simmons, fourtime Wing Bowl champion, who has made the twelve-hour drive from New Jersey to win this qualifier. "And I know you proud Tennesseans don't want to lose to no damn Yankee," I add, sensing by the resulting silence that the word *damn* doesn't sit well on Sunday at noon in Knoxville, especially when spoken by a Yankee.

My long diatribe about an unlikely hero turns out to be an appropriate analogy. El Wingador, who tells me before the contest that he plans to eat only enough to secure a victory, is matched burger for burger by a local named Jeff Hicks. They're tied with five two minutes in, then at eleven four minutes in. To beat the thirteenth-ranked eater in the world, Jeff Hicks needs Knoxville's support, I say. I try to start up a cheer of "Wilhoit! Wilhoit!" but it comes out garbled and the crowd doesn't understand. At the eight-minute final buzzer, it's too close and I have to consult with my judges. After a few recounts, I announce that second place goes to El Wingador with twenty-one delicious Krystal burgers. The crowd starts buzzing. "Ladies and gentlemen, it looks like the Volunteers have done it again! In first place, with twenty-two burgers, your new Krystal-burger-eating champion, Knoxville resident Jeff Hicks!"

SEPTEMBER 28, 2004

The travel nightmare continues. Ten minutes into my cab ride to the airport for my flight to Memphis, I realize I've left my ticket at home and we have to turn around. I arrive an hour late at La Guardia, only to discover my plane is delayed two hours. This time the culprit is Hurricane Jeanne. In the Atlanta airport, I guide the busty Israeli girl seated next to me to the smoking lounge, which is among the most depressing, overtly cancer-ridden environments I've ever laid eyes on. An announcement over the PA system says that my connection flight is delayed until 2:00 A.M., another six hours, because Hurricane Jeanne is presently having its way with Memphis.

I sit at an airport bar until it closes, reading *The Doughnut Dropout,* a children's book about competitive eating. Judging from the scornful looks I receive from barstool football-watchers, it's not exactly a testament to my masculinity. By 1:00 A.M., I'm tipsy and exhausted but have just enough time before my flight that I can't take a nap. I conclude that there is a special section in hell fashioned after an airport terminal, in which planes neither arrive nor depart. Within this special section is a punishment area for the worst sinners—the smoking lounge.

The PA system keeps making the same announcement over and over: "Maintain control of your carry-on luggage at all times . . ." *Maintain control? MAINTAIN CONTROL?* I imagine myself strangling the woman behind the robotic voice. *Are you telling me to maintain control?* When we finally touch down in Memphis, the entire cabin breaks into relieved applause. It's 4:00 A.M. A sign says WELCOME TO MEMPHIS, THE DISTRIBUTION CAPITAL, but it's unable to distribute me to my hotel room, because the rental car centers are all closed.

The next morning, I decide to shave off my goatee but leave the mustache. I imagine that this will give me a sort of game-show-host look, but I look more like a cop or a gay porn star from the seventies. The competition takes place at the Mid-South Fairgrounds, where a good-sized crowd gathers around the main stage. Don Lerman is already there when I arrive. In keeping with my game-show-host theme, I ask trivia questions and give out prizes. What female country singer took her name from her love of the Krystal burger? That's right, folks, Crystal Gayle. To egg on the crowd, I claim that eaters from up North have been claiming that Southerners are "a bunch of gastronomic wussies," and if a local is going to take Lerman, the eighth-ranked eater in the world and a champion burger eater, the crowd's support will be the deciding factor.

The goading comes in handy. For the first two minutes of the contest, Don is neck and neck with a local named Sam Vise. Then Vise starts to pull away, and Memphis gets behind him. The competition ends in a stunning upset: Vise eats thirty-four to Don's twenty-one. Another example of the many lone wolves out there just waiting to be discovered.

OCTOBER 13, 2004

I keep waiting for someone to perform an intervention. Honestly. I'm fully prepared to come home and find my closest friends assembled in the living room. "Ryan, this competitive-eating thing has gone too far," one of them will say. And how could I argue? I've lost contact with friends and family. I spend random Tuesday nights timing myself eating White Castles. I have a stopwatch on my key chain in case a spontaneous competitive-eating situation arises, and I check multiple competitive-eating Web sites daily. While eating dinner with friends, I've started noticing who takes big bites, chews fast, and cleans their plates first.

I think about stuff you probably shouldn't think about, such as competitive-defecation events as follow-ups to contests, stomach-enlargement surgery, and how competitive eaters would make great drug-smuggling mules. I have had a half dozen conversations about the word on the bottom of the broken cup at the end of the movie *The Usual Suspects:* Kobayashi. I know that, in the beginning of *Star Trek II: The Wrath of Khan,* Captain Saavik, a Vulcan lieutenant in Starfleet, loses to the Kobayashi Maru simulator's preprogrammed no-win situation and have wondered if *Kobayashi Maru* also describes the feeling eaters have when facing Kobayashi. This is my mind-life. Am I in too deep? No time to ponder that, because the circuit keeps moving forward, and I with it.

Next stop, Montgomery. The competition takes place on October 13, during the third and final presidential debate. I feel punchy and start rambling to the crowd about how we'll be conducting our own debate, not about domestic policy, but about ingestive prowess. Competitive eating has gotten so popular, I claim, that the National Hockey League has canceled its season out of pure fear of the IFOCE overshadowing them. Taking a cue from George's playbook, I toss in some irrelevant material. "Did you know that Engelbert Humperdinck wasn't even his real name?" The crowd at the Alabama National Fair stares at me, bewildered. "True story. He stole it from a nineteenth-century German composer. Just a little trivia for you."

The eaters include a soldier who has just returned from Iraq, a pawnbroker who does a somersault when I introduce him, and a man who sells jerky for a living. They will face Carlene LeFevre, whose husband, Rich, is sitting in the front row. "We say sexism is a thing of the past, but clearly this is not the case. Even now, in the twenty-first century, we underestimate women. Why, for example, do they call Ivan a hurricane and Jeanne a tropical storm? It's sad."

OCTOBER 31, 2004

This may not be the best spot for a man on the verge of losing his mind.

It's Halloween night, and Dave and I are at Sloss Fright Furnace in Birmingham, Alabama. Sloss Fright Furnace is an abandoned factory certified by the National Association of Psychics as one of the most haunted locations in the world. Its history has been covered by the Fox TV show *Scariest Places,* and the history is pretty grim. From 1882 to 1971, Sloss Furnace transformed coal and ore into the hard steel that became the building blocks of the industrial revolution. More than sixty-seven workers died at Sloss. In 1921, Brad Hainsworth was crushed by a giant gear that kept spinning, revealing less and less of Hainsworth's body with each revolution. A few years later, Noah Tyson was killed by an inexplicable blast of molten ore.

The eeriest legend is that of James Wormwood, a hard-driving graveyard-shift foreman unaffectionately known by his underlings as Slag. To impress his bosses, Slag Wormwood forced his men to speed up production, which involved taking dangerous risks. In his four-year tenure, forty-seven of his workers lost their lives—ten times the mortality rate of any other shift in Sloss Furnace history. On October 16, 1907, Slag lost his footing at the top of the highest blast furnace and plummeted into a pool of molten iron ore. His body was instantly incinerated. That Slag had never before set foot on top of the furnace led to speculation that his fed-up workers murdered him, but nobody was ever brought to trial.

So why would we come to this godforsaken place? Because I'm about to eat in my first contest here, and in keeping with the tradition of Sloss Furnace, I am transforming myself into a beast. A wolf, to be specific. I pull the mascot costume out of the huge hockey bag I've been carrying it in. The furry body suit goes on first, then I step my feet into the paws. I slide my hands into my two other paws and pull the wolf head over my head, tightening the chinstrap. I can hear Dave Baer warming up the crowd. "Today's contest will feature eleven humans and one nonhuman. The winner will compete on November 13 in Chattanooga for the grand prize of $10,000."

I put on my dead-serious game face like Hungry Charles and visualize putting down burgers the way Badlands might. The plan is to act like a villain before the competition and a rabid animal during it. *You are a wolf.* As part of my method acting, I have decided that I despise Birmingham and all its residents, using as fuel the fact that we were grossly (and I'm convinced deliberately) overcharged for drinks last night at the bar.

Time to make my entrance. I look through the wolf's mouth but can't see much. As I clomp toward the stage, my snout bounces off spectators. I hear gasps and laughter, see vague forms pointing. It's moments like this when the mascot costume seems worth the investment. "Whoa!" Dave cries. "And here he comes now. Ladies and gentlemen, I welcome to the stage the eater known as the Wolf. He is combative and unpredictable, so please be careful."

I rush toward him in a crouched, slinky way that I hope appears wolfish. I bounce my snout into Dave and pretend to claw at him. "Settle down now, Wolf," Dave says. "Now you've told the press you'll eat forty burgers and a human hand in tonight's contest. Is that true?" Dave points the microphone at my snout. I say nothing. Wolves don't talk, and neither do mascots. I'm staying in character.

"I'm sure many of you don't speak wolf," Dave says, "so let me interpret. He says that, before the night is over, Birmingham will bow before the Wolf."

I lunge at the crowd, convinced that they'll cower in fear, but they just laugh. The kids in particular find the Wolf amusing, and not in a menacing way. A group of kids gather around me and start opening up the Wolf's mouth, trying to get a glimpse at the man behind the mask. "What are you doing in there?" one of them yells. Valid question. I stare at him and resist the urge to smile. Wolves don't talk, I tell myself, but the kid won't stop tugging at the Wolf's tongue.

"Hey," I say. "Quit that."

I grab the tongue with my paw. But the boldness of one kid escalates into a full-fledged kiddie mob. I feel hands on my fur and tugging on my wolf tongue. They pry the mouth open and I find myself staring at a half dozen smiling kids.

"The Wolf seems to have met his match," Dave says.

They try to pull off my wolf head. Thank God for the chinstrap. But I think my villain role is ruined at the hands of these meddling children. As Dave starts introducing my fellow eaters, I clomp backstage for some precontest alone time. Sweating profusely, I pull off my wolf head and secure it in the Krystal wagon. I try to get hungry and focused. *Eat lots fast,* I tell myself.

If ever a chance for competitive-eating dominance presented itself, today is the day. I think about Tim Janus, who called before the contest to give a few pointers and express his confidence in my ability to win this thing. No ranked eaters are in attendance—Badlands backed out at the last moment. That said, Bill "the Bottomless Pit" Pendleton is here, and he ate twenty-three in Montgomery. Pendleton's entourage, the Pit Crew, who are quickly emerging as the circuit's answer to Jimmy Buffett's Parrot Heads, have predicted an outright victory. I do a couple breathing exercises and envision myself dunking and eating, dunking and eating.

"This next eater came by foot from Brooklyn, New York. He got his start on the circuit devouring live game over a period of thirty years. Please welcome, the Wolf!"

I run out and give my liveliest entrance, high-fiving all my fellow eaters. When I get to my spot at the table, I stare at my pack of kid admirers and growl. Interestingly, they seem much more terrified by a bearded man in a fuzzy suit growling than by the Wolf.

The eater known as "the Wolf" takes his place at the table next to circuit veteran Stu Birdy. Note the intimidating stare-down and salivating tongue. *(Courtesy of Kevin Caldwell/Krystal)*

"Research has shown that when clowns and Mickey Mouse mascots reveal their true identity, the resulting trauma can scar children for life," Dave says. "I apologize in advance if the Wolf has inflicted any psychological damage on the children of Birmingham."

Dave explains the rules and does the countdown. I start dunking and eating at a reasonable clip. I've only eaten a bagel in the last twelve hours so I'm pretty hungry, but when I look over at the Bottomless Pit, he's going twice as fast. It is a strange, helpless feeling, like a flat-footed runner trying his hand at the hundred-meter dash. Effort has little to do with it—I'm chewing and swallowing as fast as I can. I'm just not good. This comes as no shock, so I compensate by enjoying it anyway. I do a little Kobayashi shake and let out a little belch. The kids who were just attacking the Wolf are now staring at me. They appear genuinely confused at how slowly I'm eating, after all that hype. I don't care. I can see that the Bottomless Pit's got this one, but the Wolf is doing his thing. At the six-minute mark, I roll my head back and howl at the moon.

I finish with thirteen burgers, another personal best. Later, Dave and I pay the ten bucks for a tour of the Sloss Fright Furnace. As we walk in groups through the maze of tunnels and staircases, goblins pop out of nowhere and ghoulish men with open head wounds grind chain saws against metal, shooting off sparks. I'm not as full as expected, but my stomach is angry and the pain shoots up from there into my chest. My head buzzes and my thoughts come through fuzzy, as if transmitted by a cheap transistor radio. I don't want to keep walking, but sitting down doesn't sound much better. When a pale-faced specter suddenly screams into my ear, it is as close as I will ever come to literally having the shit scared out of me.

November 7, 2004

I make the seven-hour drive from Fort Myers Beach to Jacksonville, Florida, on no sleep, fueled by coffee, Red Bull, and carrots. At one point, I narrowly avert a snooze-and-drift accident when an urgent honk awakens me at the wheel. Upon my arrival, I put on my lucky Allen Iverson jersey and my lucky BAD ASS hat. While waiting in line to get into the Greater Jacksonville Agricultural Fair, my neck crisping in the hot sun, I see an IFOCE hat. It's Badlands with Dave Baer, Kobayashi, his girlfriend, and Robert Ikeda. I flag them down. Badlands gives me a hug. I'm flattered when Kobayashi recognizes me, stroking his chin to acknowledge the goatee I've grown since last we met.

We walk in and say hello to the Krystal people—Kitty and Keith, Kevin Caldwell, and Brad Wahl. Brad makes a joke about the Wolf's unspectacular performance in Birmingham. We check out the stage, which is big, situated next to a 4-H barn, a fried-Twinkies stand, and a giant Ferris wheel. Badlands says he and Kobayashi ate some Krystals the night before and adds that, in training, he put down a Crave Case in six minutes. I say that I could train for a year and I'd never eat more than twenty sliders in eight minutes. Badlands doesn't buy it. I notice that Kobayashi keeps taking spoonfuls from a bag labeled WHEY PEPTIDES and, thinking that maybe this is his secret training powder, ask him what it's for. He gestures at his biceps—it's for building muscle.

Dave Baer and Brad Wahl start warming up the crowd. Brad asks the crowd when Krystal was founded, and after a long pause, I shout it out: "Nineteen thirty-two!" He wads up a T-shirt and throws a long ball into the crowd. Dave tells the crowd that the number one and number four eaters in the world are here, as well as an unknown rookie known as the Wolf. He calls me up onstage.

"I understand that you've been training very hard, and you have your sights set on taking down the great Kobayashi. How many delicious Krystal burgers do you predict you'll eat today?"

The truth is unspectacular, so I go with a lie. "My goal is to eat fifty-two."

"Wow. That would be something. Now, I know you competed last week in Birmingham. How many did you eat there?"

"Well, I ate thirteen there, but I had a debilitating calf injury at the time."

"So how is it that you expect to up your numbers?"

"I've been doing a lot of training, and the calf injury's feeling much better. I ate fifty-two Krystals this week in training."

"But that was over the course of a week. You do realize that this is an eight-minute contest?"

"I do."

"Ladies and gentlemen, the Wolf has vowed that, if he loses to Kobayashi today, he will hang his undies on the flagpole and drive back to Birmingham in the nude."

The crowd cheers and I step off the stage. Brad Wahl gathers all the eaters to the side of the stage and gives us a pep talk. He tells us to make big entrances to hype up the crowd. A local guy confides that he thinks Kobayashi is beatable. I just nod. He says maybe the intense heat will be a chink in Kobayashi's armor. I tell him his only shot is if Kobayashi suffers a reversal. "What's a reversal?" he asks. Dave starts calling out the eaters. When my name is called, I run up the stairs, jump up in the air, and do a fake karate move. When Badlands is called, he gives me a monster belly-bump and looks me in the eye. "Come on, Ryan, let's do this Brooklyn style."

Dave does the countdown and we start putting them down. When I finish my third, Kobayashi's on fifteen. When Kobayashi hits thirty-six, I'm on six. But it doesn't bother me a bit. I'm living every amateur gurgitator's dream—eating alongside Kobayashi. It's like playing one-on-one with Jordan or eighteen holes with Tiger. I'm just basking in the sun, wearing my BAD ASS hat, eating my free lunch as fast as I can. This is my shining moment, and it's worth all the training. I let out a wolf howl, smile at the crowd through stuffed cheeks, and keep chewing. I will never forget this day.

At the six-minute mark, Kobayashi reaches fifty and stops eating. I look at him and am shocked to see that he looks a bit dyspeptic. Is it possible? Will the great Kobayashi blow? Of course not. He shakes it off and holds it down. As Dave does the countdown, I stuff one last Krystal in and it stretches my cheeks to their limit. I finish with fourteen, my season high. If I keep improving at this rate, I'll be up to twenty-two by the year 2012. When the competition ends, I stick around onstage, not wanting to let the moment go. I get some pictures with Kobayashi and listen to reporters ask Ikeda questions. "Why do you think the fans like competitive eating?" a journalist from Philadelphia asks. "Why don't you ask them?" he answers without bothering to translate the question to Kobayashi.

A kid walks up to me, a teenager with tattooed arms and a T-shirt that says DRUG-FREE ALL-STARS. He holds out one of the red trays that just held a stack of competition burgers in one hand, and a Sharpie marker in the other. "Will you sign this?"

My first competitive-eating autograph! This is huge. I don't even attempt to hide my excitement. I hand my camera to Dave Baer and tell him to get a snapshot of this, my one shining moment. After a quick identity crisis, I sign "the Wolf" in my best signature script. Underneath it, I write my new motto: EAT LOTS FAST.

As he walks away, I think about this and realize it's not really my motto. I can't eat lots fast. That's not really where my eating strength lies. Maybe I'm like a super-long-distance man, and I don't mean minutes, or hours, more like days. I may not be fast, but I'm persistent. Give me twenty pounds of steak and a month, and I'll show you some destruction. I could be like the good little girl from that Shel Silverstein poem "Melinda Mae," who ate small, well-chewed bites, exactly like she should, so even though it took her eighty-nine years to eat a whale, she did it—"because she said she would!"

EPILOGUE
WING BOWL XIII:
THE END OF THE LINE

You can put wings on a pig, but you don't make it an eagle.

—William Jefferson Clinton

FEBRUARY 4, 2005

It's 2:30 A.M., and already the Wachovia Center parking lot is packed. A soft blanket of fat snowflakes is drifting down, and it's actually quite beautiful out. Trunks are open, U-Hauls are packed with kegs, and kids are gathered in circles around bonfires. The crowd is even younger than I thought—there are as many high school sophomores as college freshman. One factor remains constant, though: They're all *wasted*. But then I shouldn't talk shit, because I'm not exactly sober myself.

Nine of us, four eaters and five civilians, have driven here from New York in a rented Econoline van. Crazy Legs has qualified by eating twenty-five Twinkies in five minutes, and I've been invited as part of his entourage. The drive was a highly entertaining testosteronefest. We drank whiskey out of bottles that Crazy Legs brought from his new job at the Penthouse Executive Club and watched plot-driven soft porn from the eighties with titles like "Sorority Babes in the Slimeball Bowl-o-Rama" on "Wet" Levi Nayman's portable DVD player. While talking to Tim "Eater X" Janus in the way back seat, I picked up random tidbits of lewd conversation from the front of the van. "May I take your temperature rectally with my meat thermometer?" someone asked. Good times, but now that the weigh-in at a local bar has ended and the buzz has faded, the frigid weather and fatigue is wearing us down. I'm beginning to wonder if this is another case of the journey being better than the destination.

The problem is, we're in foreign territory. Because the Philadelphia Eagles will be playing in the Super Bowl in two days, the parking lot is a sea of green jerseys. Nobody in our crew is wearing Eagles jerseys, so we are regarded with suspicion. I naively expect to hear shouts of "Wing Bowl!" or see signs, anything related to the upcoming competition. But this party has nothing to do with Wing Bowl and everything to do with the Eagles and getting plastered. We hear the Eagles fight song no less than a dozen times in a half-hour. "Fly Eagles fly, on the road to victory . . . Fight, Eagles fight, score a touchdown one, two, three . . ."

The enthusiasm is appreciated, but there is an undercurrent of blind patriotism that's a bit scary. At one point, Wet Levi and I, feeling indignant that no one is here for the right reason, start our own cheer, "W-I-N-G-S, wings wings wings! W-I-N-G-S, wings wings wings!" But within seconds, we are drowned out by a crooning band of Eagles fans. "Fly, Eagles, fly . . ."

We spot a teenage kid sitting on the bed of a truck, staring down with bloodshot eyes at the puddle of puke in front of him. Another pubescent girl walks up to us. When she finds out that Crazy Legs is competing today, she gives him a kiss on the cheek. It's almost touching, in a somewhat creepy way, the first sign that someone actually cares about Wing Bowl. A truck full of girls drives by, and a mob surrounds them and starts shoving it until it rocks back and forth. "Tip it over!" someone yells. "Tip it over!" An explosion rings out some-

Crazy Legs and his merry band of Smurfs mentally prepare themselves for the onslaught while waiting backstage in the bowels of the Wachovia Center.

where in a distant section of the parking lot, and people cheer and run toward it like a herd of lobotomized mules.

Crazy Legs's roommate, Johnny C, is videotaping the festivities. He walks up to a girl who looks no older than fifteen and asks her a reporterly question, "What does Wing Bowl mean to you?"

"Wing Bowl is like the biggest event . . ." She thinks for a second. ". . . *ever.*"

A guy walks up behind her, lifts up his shirt and shows off his nipple. "Show us your tits!" he yells. A kid with a doughy face wearing a Super Bowl T-shirt pushes past them both, in search of some camera time. "I've been to five Wing Bowls," he says proudly to the camera. "Since my freshman year in high school, I've missed one year. One fucking year! Wing Bowl means everything to me. It's all about the girls, titties, and drinking."

"Oh yeah?" says Crazy Legs. "You see a lot of titties out here, in weather like this?"

The kid, who looks like he may someday compete in Wing Bowl

himself, thinks about this. "I've seen titties here, but not as many as you'd think," he says thoughtfully. "All I'm sayin' is that we should see more titties." On cue, another kid with glazed-over eyes walks up and knocks over the kid's beer. "You just knocked over my fucking beer, Chris!" the pudgy kid says, pushing the intruder away. "I'm on fuckin' camera! You can't be doin' that shit on camera!"

Once inside the Wachovia Center, we wait an interminable two hours in the bowels of the arena before our grand entrance into the stadium. We are all wearing blue fuzzy hats and T-shirts designed by Crazy Legs that say BIG NATE APPAREL: NON-ACTIVE WEAR FOR THE NON-ACTIVE. Crazy Legs is wearing a powder blue jacket with matching shorts. We look like an exhausted tribe of Smurfs.

A parade of eaters walk by, flanked by curvy female flesh. I snap pictures. Obi Wing Kenobi, a Villanova physics student who qualified by eating eight live Madagascar roaches, comes by with his crew of Jedis. Hank the Tank rolls by in his tank, and another guy is thrashing about in a wire cage like an animal. I'm disappointed to see that Wingo Starr, a wing-eating version of the Beatles drummer, isn't competing this year. Just before our turn comes around, Crazy Legs is appointed two near-naked Wingettes in cowboy hats as arm candy. Before we exit the tunnel into the arena, we do a final hands-in. "Eat all you can on three," Crazy Legs says. "One two three . . . EAT ALL YOU CAN!"

When Crazy Legs is introduced, the crowd goes silent. They look rapaciously at the Wingettes and then contemptuously at us. Then the downpour begins. Some of the thrown drinks come from high enough up that you can spot them in time to bat them away. I watch helplessly as the Wingette directly in front of me gets pelted in the head with what looks like a Slurpee. As we turn the corner, I exchange the middle finger with a couple of seething fans in Donovan McNabb jerseys. Just as we are about to finish up, Crazy Legs's buddy Mike Sandwich leaves our delegation, runs over, and hurls himself at the Plexiglas.

On the other side of the glass, a bald, bearded man in a black leather trenchcoat takes this as a personal affront. People around him are laughing, but not this guy. He pounds his fist against the glass, his veins visible on a reddened forehead, then he flips Sandwich the double bird. As security pulls Sandwich away, the guy pulls up his pants and tries to compose himself, only to start bugging out again like a rabid dog.

Still yet, our reception is mild in comparison to Sonya Thomas's. The defending champ rides out on a float with a black spider web, waving an Eagles flag. The crowd starts chanting, "U-S-A! U-S-A!" and you can see it coming a mile away. They pelt her so mercilessly with drinks that it knocks her off the float. Security steps in to pull her away, but they keep hurling drinks and racial slurs. The guy behind me grabs my blue fuzzy hat and throws it behind him, laughing diabolically. The mood has shifted gears toward outright aggression and I can't help but think to myself: *Is this fun?*

Waiting patiently for the results of the second round and still angry that Badlands has been disqualified for a controversial upchuck, I feel like an old codger who won't stop talking about how the sport was better in the good old days. Out of twenty thousand people in this arena, I sense that I am one of a few hundred who is actually into the eating contest. Why is that? Have I lost all perspective, or is this actually a sport worth watching? It occurs to me that, though I've got a decent capacity for ogling tits and ass, I've actually seen enough for one morning. So then, who's crazier—me, or all these drunk high school kids leering at the strippers onstage?

The moment of silence for Rufino "Chili Dog" Cachola, a perennial Wing Bowl contestant who passed away a month before the competition at the age of thirty-six, does little to improve my darkening mood. Angelo Cataldi brings Chili Dog's family up on stage and the moment is all the more somber in contrast to the party atmosphere.

And then, just as I'm convinced things can only get better, they don't. The final one-on-one two-minute battle is between El Wingador and Sonya Thomas. Wingador wins by one wing, despite the fact that Sonya appears to be eating much faster. I'm pissed. The Wing Bowl method of counting consumption, which is not sanctioned by the IFOCE, involves arbitrary rulings of whether or not the wing has been "completely cleaned of meat." I feel there's a solid chance the competition is rigged, and I'm doubly pissed that it's rigged in a way that reinforces the dominance of both white men and the city of Philadelphia. Sickened, and in need of a hot shower, I forego an afternoon of more boozing at a local strip club and catch a ride back to Brooklyn.

When I first got involved with the circuit, I thought that Wing Bowl was the end-all, be-all of competitive eating. Sure, the Nathan's contest was more visible, but it wasn't held in a stadium, with over twenty thousand fans watching, and with a car offered as the prize. Wing Bowl seemed to me a modern American version of ancient Rome—flesh and gluttony and gladiators in a huge coliseum, all for the entertainment of the commonfolk. I was right, actually, but not necessarily in a good way.

But now a year has passed since that sobering ride home from Philly, and the disillusionment with the competitive eating circuit that I felt on that day has disappeared. I now understand that Wing Bowl is not competitive eating; Wing Bowl is just Wing Bowl. It's a promotional event started by a couple of radio deejays that took on a life of its own and turned into an annual large-scale carnival act. Even Angelo Cataldi, one of Wing Bowl's founders, admitted to me that "it has outgrown us." To his credit, certain eaters have reviewed the tape and determined that perhaps Wingador's win was legit.

And on the topic of Rufino "Chili Dog" Cachola, the man who died in between qualifying for and competing in Wing Bowl, Cataldi said that the warning signs were there. At Chili Dog's qualifying stunt, Cachola was sweating so profusely that Cataldi mentioned on the air that he should get checked out by a doctor. Though the sport's detractors might suggest that Chili Dog's death was linked to competitive eating, this theory holds little weight because he only competed twice a year (qualifier and Wing Bowl). This doesn't detract from the tragedy of his death, and serves only as a reminder of the fact that certain gurgitators (especially the overweight ones) should pay close attention to their health, both at and away from the competitive eating table.

But what I find most interesting about the Chili Dog tragedy, and Wing Bowl in general, is not about the addiction to food, but to media attention. If in fact Chili Dog did his qualifying stunt despite health concerns merely because he had become, in Cataldi's words, "a cult sports hero in Philly," then that's kind of scary. Regardless, the power of the spotlight could not have been more evident than at Wing Bowl. When I reviewed the tape from the Wachovia Center parking lot, it was stunning to see how quickly that pudgy kid went from elated to violent when his buddy stepped between him and the camera. In fact, many would claim that the only reason that George Shea (who's not exactly shy when it comes to media) would allow his eaters into a non-IFOCE contest that's judged so subjectively, is that the magnetic draw of the spectacle was too strong to resist.

But it is this same force—media attention—that has, for better or for worse, fueled competitive eating from the get-go. And in my opinion, it's been mostly for better. When I think of competitive eating, it's all smiles. I think of the eaters, many of whom were "regular guys" before the circuit, but have transformed themselves into larger-than-life characters to entertain both fans and media.

I think of Tim Janus in a Philadelphia hotel room, applying makeup for his newest Eater X face. I think of Dale Boone, with his cowbell and coonskin cap, just out there being Dale Boone. I think about the Memphis Krystal contest, where an anonymous observer claimed that Don Moses Lerman blew a wad of snot on a soaked burger late in the contest, looked at it with some trepidation, then took it down for the team. (Now *that's* commitment.) I think of Cookie's coat, Badlands' lyrical flow, the Godfather's command of all situations. I think of Sonya Thomas knocking down whatever food-stuff you give to her with an almost terrifying ferocity. And I think of Takeru Kobayashi, at once the Harry Houdini and Michael Jordan of the competitive eating world, dunking buns and swallowing chunks of hot dog in the same breath, making this bizarre sport something you can't take your eyes away from.

And, of course, I think of the Shea brothers, the sport's founding fathers, and how they have created a cultural phenomenon that deli-cately balances real competition with a dramatic form of satire that reflects the absurdity of modern life. When George Shea says, "In every compression of the jaw, in every drop of saliva, in every twitch of the epiglottis, I see the human struggle," he is being both sarcastic and a little bit serious. Because competitive eating really is a meta-phor for the Darwinist consumerism that has taken over American— and even global—culture. Eat or be eaten; dominate or be dominated; consume or be consumed. The battle at the table is a microcosm of the battle at large. In the end, whoever gobbles up the most stuff the quickest, wins. Yet, when George Shea pleads with ESPN producers to use his patented ChewTrak system of counting bites per minute, it's difficult to tell whether he thinks it's a great gag or if he's just *in too deep.*

But then why not get in too deep and become absorbed by com-petitive eating? It seems no less arbitrary than getting into competi-tive table tennis or bowling or poker or even major sports like boxing, auto racing, and football. The thing is, the influence of money and media on our everyday lives has become such a juggernaut that it's difficult to determine what's valuable. Is a pro athlete really worth the twenty million dollars he makes in a year? Is *American Idol* such a significant event that more people watch it than a presidential de-bate? Is eating as much as you can in a timed interval a worthwhile endeavor?

I don't have the answers. All I can say is that, for better or for worse, my stint as a competitive eating emcee is the best job I've ever had. I get paid to travel to places I've never been before, where I provide a half-hour of entertainment that is, at the very least, memorable. I love the competitions for their simplicity and their shock value. When life is otherwise filled with bills and endless complications, I can always rely on them for a simple twelve minutes of thrills and fun.

What is the future of competitive eating? I don't know, but having interviewed the world's best gurgitators and watched them perform, having trained and attempted (pathetically) to compete myself, I have come to the conclusion that it is a legitimate pursuit and not just a carnival act. I believe that new eaters will arise to the forefront of the world's most egalitarian sport, and they will increasingly look like "real" athletes. (Already, only three eaters in the top ten could be considered overweight, in keeping with the Belt of Fat Theory.) Joey Chestnut, a fresh-faced athletic-looking college student now ranked third in the world, took Kobayashi to the wire in the 2005 Krystal Championships. And Sonya Thomas, whose dominance of the 2004 season threatened to make the American circuit tedious, recently took third place behind Chestnut in a corned beef eating contest. The winner was Pat Bertoletti, now ranked tenth, who made his debut at that chaotic Bacci pizza-eating contest I emceed in Chicago.

I believe that, as the Godfather said, whether the world believes that it's a spectacle or a sport, they will pay to watch eating competitions. The amount and variety of contests will continue to increase, as will the cash prizes and media coverage. While the draw of the sport remains that it is, at times, hilarious, I will not be shocked when competitive eating is accepted as an exhibition sport at the 2012 Summer Olympic Games in London.

But *why?* Why would people line up, and even buy tickets, to watch an eating contest? Why would it ever be accepted as an Olympic sport? Just ask the fans. After the 2005 Fourth of July Nathan's Famous Hot Dog Eating Contest, while I was onstage, a friend of mine interviewed fan after fan who said that they loved the contest. Not a single interviewee expressed disappointment. Howard from Coney Island said he loved to hear George Shea talk. Greg Packer from Huntington, New York, said he liked to watch the eaters go head-to-head and was rooting for Badlands Booker, his hometown favorite. Edwin Nichols from Flushing, Queens, who was watching the contest for the sixth straight year, said that his favorite part was watching "the little ones that eat all that food . . . especially Sonya, she's just awesome." And Barbara from Pennsylvania said, "It's just amazing that in America, we have this crazy event that happens every Fourth of July, that celebrates eating and competition in such an entertaining way. I stood on my tippy toes the whole time, laughing and biting my nails. I feel so lucky to have seen it, and I'll definitely come back next year."

APPENDIX
IFOCE COMPETITIVE
EATING RECORDS

Check out updated records at **www.ifoce.com**.

Armour Vienna Sausage
8.31 pounds Armour Vienna Sausage
10 minutes
Sonya Thomas

Asparagus
5.75 pounds tempura deep fried asparagus spears
10 minutes
Sonya Thomas

Baked Beans, Sprint
Six pounds baked beans
1 minute, 48 seconds
Donald Lerman

Baked Beans, Long Course
8.4 pounds baked beans
2 minutes, 47 seconds
Sonya Thomas

Beef Tongue
3 pound 3 ounces pickled beef tongue whole
12 minutes
Dominic Cardo

Birthday Cake
5 pounds
11 minutes, 26 seconds
Richard LeFevre

Bologna
2.41 pounds pork and chicken bologna
6 minutes
Allen Goldstein

Bratwurst
35 Johnsonville Brats
10 minutes
Sonya Thomas

Buffet
5½ pounds of buffet food
12 minutes
Crazy Legs Conti

Burritos
15 Burritoville burritos
8 minutes
Eric Booker

Butter
7 quarter-pound sticks, salted butter
5 minutes
Donald Lerman

Cabbage
6 pounds, 9 ounces, giant cabbage

9 minutes
Charles Hardy

Candy Bars
2 pounds chocolate candy bars
6 minutes
Eric Booker

Cannoli
21 cannoli
6 minutes
Cookie Jarvis

Cheesecake
11 pounds Downtown Atlantic Cheesecake
9 minutes
Sonya Thomas

Chicken Fingers
2 pounds, 2.5 ounces, Hooter's chicken fingers
5 minutes
Cookie Jarvis

Chicken Nuggets
80 Chicken Nuggets
5 minutes
Sonya Thomas

Chicken Wings, Wing Bowl
167 chicken wings
32 minutes
Sonya Thomas

Chicken Wings, National Buffalo Wing Festival
161 chicken wings, 5.09 pounds
12 minutes
Sonya Thomas

Chicken-Fried Steak
11-ounce Lone Star Café chicken fried steak with country gravy
12 minutes
Cookie Jarvis

Chili
1½ gallons Stagg Chili
10 minutes
Richard LeFevre

Conch Fritters
45 conch fritters
6 minutes
Joe Menchetti

Corn Dogs
12 Fletcher's Corny Dogs
10 minutes
Richard LeFevre

Corned Beef and Cabbage
5 pounds Freirich Corned Beef and Cabbage
10 minutes
Cookie Jarvis

Corned Beef Hash
4 pounds of hash
1 minute, 58 seconds
Eric Booker

Cow Brains
57 cow brains (17.7 pounds)
15 minutes
Takeru Kobayashi

Crab Cakes
40 crab cakes

12 minutes
Sonya Thomas

Crawfish
331 crawfish
12 minutes
Chris Hendrix

Doughnuts
49 glazed doughnuts
8 minutes
Eric Booker

Dumplings
91 Chinese dumplings
8 minutes
Cookie Jarvis

Eggs
65 hard-boiled eggs
6 minutes, 40 seconds
Sonya Thomas

French Fries
4.46 pounds Nathan's Famous Crinkle Cut Fries
6 minutes
Cookie Jarvis

Fruitcake
4 pounds, 14¼ ounces, Wegmans Fruitcake
10 minutes
Sonya Thomas

Gelatin Dessert
7 16-ounce portions gelatin
3 minutes
Steve Lakind

Grapes
8 pounds, 15 ounces, grapes
10 minutes
Cookie Jarvis

Green Beans, French Cut
2.71 pounds green beans
6 minutes
Crazy Legs Conti

Grilled Cheese Sandwiches
32.5 Goldenpalace.com grilled cheese sandwiches
10 minutes
Joey Chesnut

Ham and Potatoes
6 pounds of Easter Feaster meal
12 minutes
Cookie Jarvis

Hamburger: Giant Barrick Burger
9-pound cheeseburger
48 minutes, 10 seconds
Sonya Thomas

Hamburgers
11¼ Burgers (¼ pound) "Cloud Burgers"
10 minutes
Donald Lerman

Hamburgers
7 Burgers (¾ pound) Hardee's "Thickburgers"
10 minutes
Sonya Thomas

Hamburgers
69 Krystal Square Burgers

8 minutes
Takeru Kobayashi

Hamentaschen
50 traditional Purim cookies
6 minutes
Eric Booker

Hot Dogs
53½ Nathan's Famous hot dogs and buns
12 minutes
Takeru Kobayashi

Hutspot (potato-based "hotchpotch," or stew)
13 bowls
10 minutes
Henry Hatau

Ice Cream
1 gallon, 9 ounces of vanilla ice cream
12 minutes
Cookie Jarvis

Jambalaya
9 pounds crawfish jambalaya
10 minutes
Sonya Thomas

Maine Lobster
44 Maine lobsters (11.3 pounds of meat) from the shell
12 minutes
Sonya Thomas

Matzo Balls
21 baseball-sized matzo balls
5 minutes, 25 seconds
Eric Booker

Mayonnaise
4 32-ounce bowls (8 pounds) mayonnaise
8 minutes
Oleg Zhornitskiy

Meat Pies
16 6-ounce meat pies
10 minutes
Boyd Bulot

Meatballs
6 pounds Carmine's Meatballs
12 minutes
Sonya Thomas

Onions
8.5 ounces Maui Onions (three peeled, raw onions)
1 minute
Eric Booker

Oysters
46 dozen Acme Oysters
10 minutes
Sonya Thomas

Pancakes
3½ pounds pancakes and bacon
12 minutes
Crazy Legs Conti

Pasta
6⅔ pounds linguini (no. 115)
10 minutes
Cookie Jarvis

Peas
9.5 pounds peas

12 minutes
Eric Booker

Pelmeni
274 Russian dumplings
6 minutes
Dale Boone

Pickles, Vinegar
2.7 pounds kosher dills
6 minutes
Brian Seiken

Pizza
7½ extra large Bacci Pizza slices
15 minutes
Richard LeFevre

Pommes Frites
2 pounds, 9 ounces, Pommes Frites
8 minutes
Cookie Jarvis

Pork and Beans (84 Lumber)
84 ounces of baked beans
1 minute, 52 seconds
Dale Boone

Pork Ribs
5.5 pounds pork rib meat
12 minutes
Joey Chestnut

Pork, Smoked
7 pounds, 1 ounce, smoked pork
10 minutes
Richard LeFevre

Posole
109.75 ounces posole
12 minutes
Carlene LeFevre

Pulled Pork
23 pulled pork sandwiches
10 minutes
Sonya Thomas

Pumpkin Pies
4⅜ Entenmann's Pumpkin Pies
12 minutes
Eric Booker

Quesadilla
31.5 4-inch cheese quesadilla
5 minutes
Sonya Thomas

Reindeer Sausage
28 Glacier Brewhouse Reindeer Sausage
10 minutes
Dale Boone

Rice Balls
20 pounds rice balls
30 minutes
Takeru Kobayashi

Shoo-Fly Pie
6 pounds Shoo-Fly Pie
8 minutes
Timothy Janus

Shrimp
4 pounds, 9 ounces, spot shrimp

12 minutes
Charles Hardy

SPAM
6 pounds of SPAM from the can
12 minutes
Richard LeFevre

Steeplechase/Ultimate Eating Tournament
Shrimp, bread sticks, hot dogs, chicken wings, frozen custard
10 minutes
Dale Boone

Sweet Corn
33½ ears sweet corn
12 minutes
Cookie Jarvis

Sweet Potato Casserole
8.62 pounds potato casserole
11 minutes
Sonya Thomas

Tacos
48 Zocalo chicken soft tacos
11 minutes
Sonya Thomas

Tamales
36 Tamales
12 minutes, 30 seconds
Levi Oliver

Tex Mex Rolls
30 Tex Mex Rolls
12 minutes
Richard LeFevre

Toasted Ravioli
4 pounds Charlie Gitto's toasted ravioli
12 minutes
Sonya Thomas

Turducken
7¾ pounds Turducken.com Thanksgiving Dinner
12 minutes
Sonya Thomas

Waffles
18.5 8-ounce Waffle House Waffles
10 minutes
Joey Chestnut

Watermelon
13 pounds rind-less, seedless watermelon
15 minutes
Jim Reeves